AUTOMATIC

AUTOMATIC

Changing the Way America Saves

WILLIAM G. GALE

J. MARK IWRY

DAVID C. JOHN

LINA WALKER

editors

BROOKINGS INSTITUTION PRESS
Washington, D.C.

Copyright © 2009
THE BROOKINGS INSTITUTION
1775 Massachusetts Avenue, N.W., Washington, D.C. 20036
www.brookings.edu

Library of Congress Cataloging-in-Publication data

Automatic : changing the way America saves / William G. Gale ... [et al.], editors.
     p.   cm.
Includes bibliographical references and index.
Summary: "Argues for a fresh approach to saving, simplified retirement planning,
and managing risks associated with today's IRA environment. Calls for transformation
of 401(k)s, incorporating features of defined benefit plans as automatic arrangements.
Considers experiences of countries with automatic saving structures and presents
proposals to implement similar features in this country"—Provided by publisher.
     ISBN 978-0-8157-0278-8 (pbk. : alk. paper)
     1. Individual retirement accounts—United States. 2. Saving and investment—
United States. I. Gale, William G. II. Title.
     HG1666.A87 2009
     339.4'30973—dc22   2009023363

9 8 7 6 5 4 3 2 1

Printed on acid-free paper

Typeset in Adobe Garamond

Composition by Cynthia Stock
Silver Spring, Maryland

Printed by R. R. Donnelley
Harrisonburg, Virginia

Contents

Part II. Taking the Money Out

Part III. Retirement Saving for Vulnerable Groups

Preface

This volume is based on work undertaken through the Retirement Security Project (RSP), a joint venture of Georgetown University's Public Policy Institute and the Brookings Institution, that is supported by the Pew Charitable Trusts and the Rockefeller Foundation. The Retirement Security Project is dedicated to promoting commonsense solutions to improve the retirement income prospects of millions of American workers.

This book explores methods of making the nation's system of 401(k)-type plans and Individual Retirement Accounts more effective. It does not address any issues related to Social Security reform. Indeed, although the authors have strongly held views regarding the potential introduction of individual accounts into Social Security, the proposals contained in this book are intended to have no implications, one way or the other, for that type of change to the Social Security system. Also outside the scope of the book are changes to our employer-sponsored defined benefit pension system.

The Pew Charitable Trusts has provided both initial and ongoing support for the Retirement Security Project and the policy work on which this book is based.

The staff of the Retirement Security Project and the Brookings Institution labored patiently to make this book a reality. Spencer Walters, Catherine Lee, and Ruth Levine provided outstanding research assistance. The staff of the Retirement Security Project and the staff at the Brookings Institution Press were key to getting the book through the editorial stage and to press.

RSP is grateful to a very large number of individuals, in the United States and around the world, whose feedback and input have helped shape the analysis and policy recommendations in this volume.

The views expressed in each chapter are those of the authors of that chapter alone and should not be attributed to authors of the other chapters or to the Brookings Institution, Georgetown University's Public Policy Institute, the Pew Charitable Trusts, the Rockefeller Foundation, AARP, the Heritage Foundation, or the National Council of La Raza.

1

Introduction

WILLIAM G. GALE, BENJAMIN H. HARRIS,
J. MARK IWRY, AND DAVID C. JOHN

This book is the second of two volumes put together by the Retirement Security Project (RSP). A partnership between Georgetown University's Public Policy Institute and the Brookings Institution, supported by the Pew Charitable Trusts and the Rockefeller Foundation, RSP was founded in 2005 to develop and help enact commonsense reforms that attract bipartisan support and make saving for retirement easier and more rewarding for lower- and moderate-income households. While everyone recognizes that retirement policy entails a host of sweeping and interrelated concerns—from reforming Medicare and long-term care, to making Social Security fiscally sustainable, to shoring up and reforming the private defined benefit pension system, to improving day-to-day living for the elderly—the Retirement Security Project has chosen to focus its mission on making significant and tangible progress in one particularly important area.

The first RSP volume, *Aging Gracefully,* identified several key shortcomings in the retirement income system facing lower- and moderate-income workers. The continuing trend away from traditional pension plans and toward defined contribution plans, such as 401(k)s and individual retirement accounts (IRAs), has placed more responsibility on the individual worker to save for his or her own retirement. Fully half the working population is left out of the retirement system. Among those who do participate, contribution rates are often too low,

investments are often poorly allocated, and participants often cash in their benefits before retirement. In addition, the tax benefits of participation are small for
moderate- and lower-income households, and the overall distribution of tax-
favored retirement and tax benefits has been skewed toward the most affluent.

To address these challenges, the papers in the first volume described and
motivated a policy agenda with four key components. First, expand 401(k) participation by automating plans to reduce the decisionmaking burden on workers and improve 401(k) outcomes while still preserving workers' freedom of
choice. Second, move the system toward universal coverage by extending the
power of automatic enrollment—through the creation of Automatic IRAs—to
those who have no workplace plan. Third, expand and revamp the Saver's
Credit, which is intended to encourage lower-income households to save, so
that it provides a more effective and transparent matching incentive for retirement contributions. Fourth, reduce the steep and confusing implicit taxes on
retirement saving often imposed through means-tested government programs
such as Medicaid, Supplemental Security Income, food stamps, and Temporary
Assistance for Needy Families. Taken together, these proposals would expand
access to saving, remove procedural obstacles and negative incentives for saving,
and increase the transparency of and rewards to putting money away.

Since that volume was completed in 2006, much has been accomplished.
The acceptance and take-up of automatic enrollment and other automatic features has increased dramatically in the 401(k) market—both before and after
the Pension Protection Act of 2006 encouraged this movement by eliminating a
number of key obstacles. Surveys suggest that the percentage of larger 401(k)
plans using automatic enrollment rose from about 19 percent in 2005 to about
51 percent in 2009.[1] The Department of Labor further encouraged the spread
of automatic 401(k) features by publishing regulations making it easier to
include diversified equities (such as balanced or target-date funds or managed
accounts) in 401(k) investments. Investment patterns in the 401(k) system
appear to have moved toward greater diversification, including at least somewhat diminished concentration in employer stock. As a further measure of
progress, the board of the three-million-member federal employee Thrift Savings Plan decided to switch to automatic enrollment (subject to congressional
approval) even though the participation rate (about 87 percent) in that plan was
already considered quite successful.

The Automatic IRA proposal was introduced as legislation on a bipartisan
basis in both the House and Senate. The proposal was the subject of several congressional hearings and was endorsed in the 2008 presidential campaign by then-
Senator Barack Obama as well as by his Republican opponent, Senator John
McCain. In a related development, the Internal Revenue Service was persuaded
to facilitate saving outside of the workplace by allowing taxpayers entitled to

income tax refunds to instruct the IRS to directly deposit a portion of the refund in an IRA while depositing the remainder in the taxpayer's checking account.

The Saver's Credit, previously scheduled to expire after five years, was made permanent and indexed for inflation by the Pension Protection Act of 2006, thereby increasing saving incentives for moderate- and lower-income households. In addition, Congress in 2008 stipulated that savings in tax-preferred retirement accounts would no longer be counted in the asset test determining eligibility for the food stamp program. Most recently, as this book goes to press, President Obama's 2009 budget contains proposals for an Automatic IRA, a revamped Saver's Credit, and additional asset test reforms.

At the same time, however, the massive decline in financial markets since late 2007 has shaken confidence in many of the most commonly used diversified 401(k) financial investments. This, in turn, has led some to question the validity of the basic 401(k) and wealth accumulation model, even though the 401(k) is a saving vehicle that can accommodate a wide range of investment strategies. Moreover, even before equity markets toppled, many feasible and well-designed improvements to the retirement system had not been implemented, proposals to encourage effective payout of 401(k) benefits had received little attention, and several key populations remained outside the retirement system and vulnerable to economic shortfalls in old age.

The chapters in this volume pick up where previous research and development stopped and are divided into three sets. The first set provides new analysis of the automatic 401(k) and Automatic IRA. The second set extends the analysis of automatic saving structures from the "accumulation" to the "decumulation," or payout, phase to encourage the provision of lifetime income. The third set of essays looks at the circumstances and saving behavior of vulnerable groups—Latinos, women, and African-Americans—and proposes specific policies to help them achieve retirement security. These papers provide an integrated set of findings that can help policymakers make retirement security a feasible and accessible outcome for millions of American households.

Improving the Automatic 401(k) and Creating the Automatic IRA

As William Gale, Mark Iwry, and Spencer Walters explain in chapter 2, the Pension Protection Act of 2006 made significant improvements to 401(k) plans, but much additional work remains to be done. For employers who offer automatic 401(k)s, these improvements include a measure of protection from fiduciary liability for automatic (default) investment choices, preemption of state regulation to protect employers from being treated as violating state law by instituting automatic enrollment, and flexibility for 401(k) plans to undo automatic enrollment (without risk of penalty) for employees who so request within ninety days. As noted, the Pension Protection Act also made the Saver's Credit permanent and indexed its eligibility thresholds to inflation.

Further reform, however, could improve households' incentives to save and help Americans better prepare for retirement. First-generation automatic 401(k) plans were adopted mainly by large firms and featured automatic enrollment for new employees only, low default contribution rates that do not escalate over time, and money market or stable-value default investments. The goal now is to develop second-generation automatic 401(k)s adopted by as many 401(k) sponsors as possible, of all sizes, automatically enroll all nonparticipating employees (not just new hires), significantly escalate default contribution rates over time, and offer default investments (and other options) that appropriately reflect the best thinking in the expert financial and policy communities.

In chapter 3, Christopher Geissler and Benjamin Harris examine the revenue and distributional effects of automatic enrollment in 401(k) plans. The authors find that if automatic enrollment were adopted by all 401(k) plans—which would reduce federal revenue by increasing tax-free contributions to retirement plans—it would cost the federal government between $35 billion and $69 billion over ten years (about 2 percent of the total amount of federal tax expenditures devoted to retirement saving). This benefit would be particularly valuable to those in the bottom 80 percent of the income distribution, helping to equalize the gains from retirement tax benefits that traditionally have most benefited those with the highest incomes.

The fourth chapter describes a proposal—the Automatic IRA—to extend the benefits of automatic saving structures to the 50 percent of the labor force that does not have access to any work-based pension or 401(k) plan. As David John and Iwry explain, Automatic IRAs would build on the success of automatic 401(k)s, extending easy access to tax-favored, workplace-based retirement savings to tens of millions of American workers. The chapter fleshes out many of the operational and logistical aspects of the automatic IRA. Under the proposal, most firms that do not sponsor any kind of retirement plan would be required to automatically enroll workers in IRAs that provide a standard, low-cost default investment. Workers would be free to opt out. Contributions would be made by direct deposit to accounts managed by a financial institution, using existing electronic payroll systems to facilitate the transfer whenever possible. Private-sector financial institutions would continue to compete for the right to act as IRA trustee or custodian, but arrangements would be made to guarantee availability of low-cost accounts to all, including nonemployees. Businesses would receive small temporary tax credits for instituting the Automatic IRA, in recognition of the modest administrative effort required.

As David John and Ruth Levine point out in the fifth chapter, the United States is not the only country to experiment with retirement saving policy. The authors explain the key features of Chile's privatized pension system with individual accounts; Australia's hybrid system of mandatory contributions with a guaranteed means-tested benefit; New Zealand's KiwiSaver program, a voluntary government-sponsored pension plan incorporating automatic enrollment; and the United Kingdom's complex, multipillar system incorporating both public and private accounts. Based on this review, John and Levine reach several conclusions: high saving rates can be achieved through automatic enrollment without the political cost of a mandatory system; having a limited set of investment options is both necessary and sufficient; simple investment platforms—with default investment funds and a high proportion of index-type funds—can hold down administrative costs; sufficient income guarantees are crucial to the health of a retirement scheme; and retirement systems can and should encourage, but not mandate, some degree of annuitization of retiree assets.

Taking the Money Out

The chapters in the first section of the book, like most of the analysis and discussion in the retirement saving world, focus on getting money into retirement accounts and managing those funds. Hence, the focus on automatic enrollment, escalation of contributions, and investment allocation. Less attention has been devoted to the distribution, or payout, stage. How the money comes out of the plan, however, is critically important. Indeed, a flawed withdrawal strategy can negate the benefits of decades of intelligent accumulation strategies. As the 401(k) system reaches maturity and as the number of retirees and near-retirees grows, with the baby boomers entering retirement years, these issues will become even more critical. Thus, the next frontier in automatic saving structures involves developing better ways to manage and pay out the accumulated savings.

Lifetime income products, however, present a quandary. On one hand, it seems clear that many households could realize significant improvements in their well-being and retirement security were they to convert some of their existing asset balances into annuities or into related financial products that provide income flows over time. This would reduce their asset risk and reduce the chance that they outlive their resources. On the other hand, very few households tend to make such choices. The suggested reasons for this vary from consumers' unfamiliarity with lifetime income products, to certain consumer biases, to the fact that some people may not want to purchase more annuities since they already have Social Security and Medicare benefits, to unattractive pricing of annuities, to fear of the loss of control resulting from permanently giving up liquid assets. At the same time, the private market is experimenting with a wide variety of alternative ideas and hybrid instruments to attract more consumers to lifetime income products. The challenge, then, for designing an effective structure for lifetime income payments is to respect the diversity of people's situations and the evolving market, while helping to overcome consumer unfamiliarity and biases and make pricing more attractive. A related challenge stems from the fact that defaulting a worker into a particular 401(k) contribution rate might generate a less than fully optimal saving level that could be changed by increasing contributions. In contrast, defaulting someone into an annuity that is inappropriate for his or her circumstances carries greater risks and is more difficult to undo. How, then, can the benefits of automatic saving structures be extended to the payout phase? The chapters in the second section of the book focus on this issue.

In chapter 6 Gale, Iwry, John, and Lina Walker propose defaulting retirees into a "test drive" of an annuity by automatically enrolling recent 401(k) retirees in a two-year monthly payment plan. After the two-year trial, the regular monthly income would continue for life unless the individual opted out in favor of an alternative distribution option. The proposal would help expose retirees to the benefits of annuities or other guaranteed income without forcing them to buy fully into the arrangement at the time of retirement. In addition, it would likely reduce the price of an annuity by taking advantage of the plan's bargaining power while exposing a broader group to annuities and hence reducing the adverse selection that affects annuity markets. The automatic nature of the proposal takes advantage of inertia and makes it easier for participants to sample the benefits of guaranteed lifetime income. The opt-out provision allows individuals to tailor the program to their own specific needs, and forgo participation if it is not the best choice for their circumstances.

In a companion chapter (7), Iwry and John Turner propose strategies to encourage the accumulation of lifetime income in 401(k) plans on a partial, continual basis throughout an individual's working years. Workers who do not opt out would be defaulted into accumulating units of annuity income in their 401(k) accounts over many years. This would "dollar cost average" the risk of purchasing lifetime income when interest rates are low and avoid the resistance many individuals have to annuitizing when confronted with a one-time all-or-nothing choice between an annuity and a lump sum at retirement. The annuity purchases could be funded by employer matching contributions (which have often been invested in employer stock) or could be embedded in a target-date fund or other qualified default investment alternative as the gradually increasing fixed-income portion of that fund. The proposal would also allow savers a period in which to grow comfortable with the concept of lifetime income. Partial annuitization would help workers tailor their portfolio to include their preferred level of risk and lifetime income. Moreover, the gradual accumulation of lifetime income would frame a portion of the plan benefit as a "pension pay-check" income stream rather than a lump sum.

Vulnerable Populations

While the first two sections of the book address proposals to reform the retirement system, the last section focuses directly on vulnerable populations. In particular, the goals are to understand the saving and economic experience of Latinos, women, and African-Americans, and to design public policies that can effectively address each group's distinctive situations and needs.

Peter Orszag and Eric Rodriguez show in chapter 8 that, relative to other groups, Hispanics tend to participate less frequently in retirement saving accounts, with fewer than half of Hispanic adults nearing retirement age having any assets in a 401(k) or IRA. Hispanics also have, on average, lower incomes than other households, meaning that saving incentives may be insufficient to induce many households to contribute to a retirement account. In response to these circumstances, Orszag and Rodriguez propose promoting financial literacy programs tailored to the particular problems faced by Latinos and automatically enrolling workers in IRAs to increase participation rates in retirement saving accounts.

In chapter 9 Leslie Papke, Walker, and Michael Dworsky explain how the challenge to save for retirement differs for men and women, focusing in particular on the challenges faced by women in low-income households. The authors note that differences in longevity can heighten the necessity for women to secure retirement assets with guaranteed income distributions and that different labor force patterns increase the need for flexible policies regarding the accumulation of retirement assets. Papke, Walker, and Dworsky offer proposals that would support the ability of women to adequately prepare for retirement, including allowing unpaid caregivers to contribute to IRAs and providing Social Security credit for periods of unpaid caregiving.

Ngina Chiteji and Walker note in chapter 10 that much of the saving challenge for African Americans derives from the group's income and labor force characteristics, but the authors also find that differences in saving behavior between whites and African Americans persist even after controlling for income disparities and dissimilar labor market experiences. The authors find that these differences are explained in part by differing financial literacy, attitudes toward saving, and family structures. The authors conclude with recommendations for several policies that would address these issues, including the introduction of financial mentoring programs in public schools and removing the implicit tax on saving in asset tests that can make families ineligible for program benefits because of accumulated retirement assets.

Moving Forward

The papers in this volume present a set of proposals that is simultaneously ambitious and feasible. Policymakers will face many challenges posed by an aging American population in the years to come. Making retirement saving easier, simpler, fairer, and more rewarding for lower- and moderate-income households generally attracts bipartisan support and would be good place to start.

Note

1. Calculations are based on Hewitt Associates annual survey of mid- to large-size companies.

PART I

Automatic Saving Structures

2

Retirement Saving for Middle- and Lower-Income Households: The Pension Protection Act of 2006 and the Unfinished Agenda

WILLIAM G. GALE, J. MARK IWRY, AND SPENCER WALTERS

The proposition that public policies can and should be used to encourage retirement saving among middle- and lower-income households commands broad, bipartisan support. Perhaps the most promising recent development in this area has been the rise of the automatic 401(k). Plan sponsors and policymakers are increasingly interested in using automatic, or "opt-out," 401(k)s to promote retirement security among rank-and-file employees. Because these workers also need meaningful financial incentives to save, the Saver's Credit, which interacts constructively with automatic 401(k) features, is specifically targeted to help them.

The Pension Protection Act of 2006 (PPA) took significant steps to encourage the use of automatic 401(k)s and the Saver's Credit. However, much remains to be done. This chapter describes the automatic 401(k) and the Saver's Credit, assesses the effects of the recent legislation, and outlines the next steps needed to promote retirement saving for middle- and lower-income workers, focusing on four initiatives:

—Fulfilling the potential and expanding the implementation of the automatic 401(k)

—Creating automatic individual retirement accounts (IRAs) for the 78 million workers who have no employer retirement plan

—Expanding the Saver's Credit, making it refundable, and converting the credit to a flat-rate match

—Changing current rules that penalize saving by limiting eligibility for government programs based on 401(k) or IRA savings

The Automatic 401(k)

Over the past twenty-five years private pension plans in the United States have tended toward a do-it-yourself approach in which eligible workers are required to take the initiative to save, bear much of the investment risk, and make their own decisions about their retirement saving. Some workers have thrived under this more individualized approach, but for many, the 401(k) revolution has fallen short of its potential. Work, family, and other more immediate demands often distract workers from the need to save and invest for the future. Those who do take the time to consider their choices may find the decisions complex: financial planning is seldom a simple task. For many the result is poor decision-making at each stage of the retirement savings process, putting both the level and the security of their retirement income at risk. Even worse, many people simply procrastinate when faced with difficult choices and avoid dealing with the issues altogether, thereby dramatically increasing their risk of being financially unprepared for retirement.

The automatic 401(k) is designed to improve retirement security for millions of workers without requiring them to become financial experts. In a nutshell, the automatic 401(k) harnesses the power of inertia by setting the default option at each phase of the 401(k) saving cycle to make sound saving and investment decisions the norm, even when the employee never gets around to making an explicit choice.[1]

By contrast, traditional 401(k) plans do not cover workers unless they actively sign up. Employees can participate only if they take the initiative to complete an enrollment form that requires them to decide whether to participate, how much to contribute, and how to invest. The result: about one in four eligible employees "leaves money on the table" and fails to participate even when offered valuable employer matching contributions and tax advantages for contributing.

Under automatic enrollment, eligible employees participate unless they actively choose not to. The automatic 401(k) uses this same default approach to help employees increase their contribution level gradually over time, invest prudently, and preserve benefits for retirement through rollovers when jobs change—all without putting the onus on individuals to take the initiative for any of these steps. At the same time, workers remain free to override the default options by choosing whether and how much to contribute and by controlling

---

Box 2-1. *Automatic Enrollment: An Example*

A newly hired employee is automatically enrolled in her employer's 401(k) plan at a contribution rate of 4 percent of pay. Contributions are automatically invested in a sensibly priced, professionally managed account or life-cycle fund. The 4 percent contribution level automatically escalates to 5 percent of pay in the following year and continues to escalate at 1 percent a year up to 12 percent. The employee may depart from any of these automatic or default arrangements at any time, opting out of the plan or into a different contribution level or different investment options. When the employee leaves her job, the account balance is automatically rolled over to an IRA owned by the employee or automatically retained in the former employer's plan, unless the employee chooses otherwise.

---

how their savings are invested. However, those who fail to exercise the initiative are not left behind (example, box 2-1).

Several findings suggest the potential of automatic 401(k)s to increase retirement saving:[2]

—Automatic enrollment has been shown to raise 401(k) participation rates dramatically when it is applied to new hires, especially to new hires who are female, members of minority groups, low earners, or some combination thereof (figure 2-1).[3] Automatic enrollment often cuts nonparticipation rates from roughly 25 percent to as little as 5 or 10 percent of newly eligible employees.

—Automatic escalation of contributions over time can raise overall contributions to 401(k)s as employees become accustomed to deferring receipt of a portion of their pay. Escalation also helps ensure that inertia does not keep some employees at a default contribution rate lower than the rate they would have chosen, absent the default (box 2-2).[4]

—Automatic investment can direct assets into balanced, prudently diversified, and low-cost vehicles and can help discourage overconcentration in employer stock in money market or stable-value assets.[5]

— Automatic rollover can help participants retain previously accumulated retirement savings in the tax-favored retirement system when they change jobs.[6]

A strong case can also be made that automatic enrollment is good for employers (box 2-3). For example, plan sponsors have an incentive to use automatic enrollment and escalation insofar as they help employees save and tend to improve plans' performance on the 401(k) nondiscrimination tests. Under these tests, the greater the average contributions by the majority of eligible employees, the more the executives and owners can contribute.

Figure 2-1. *Increases in Participation Rates through Automatic Enrollment*[a]

Percent

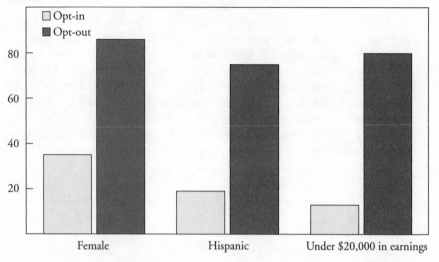

Source: Brigitte C. Madrian and Dennis F. Shea, "The Power of Suggestion: Inertia in 401(k) Participation and Savings Behavior," *Quarterly Journal of Economics* 116 (November 2001), pp. 1149–87.

a. Actual results from employees with between three and fifteen months of tenure.

Automatic 401(k)s and the Pension Protection Act of 2006

The Pension Protection Act of 2006 seeks to encourage 401(k) plan sponsors to adopt automatic features by addressing three significant concerns that have held many employers back and by attempting to provide a new incentive.[7]

Preemption of State Laws

Some firms considering automatic enrollment have been concerned that automatic payroll deductions might be prohibited by state antigarnishment laws, which require an employee's explicit written authorization for withholdings to prevent inappropriate and involuntary deductions from employee pay. The PPA provides that federal law preempts such state laws to the extent necessary to allow employers in all fifty states to automatically deduct 401(k) and similar retirement saving contributions from employees' paychecks.

"Unwind" of Automatic Enrollment

Another concern of plan administrators has been the risk that new, automatically enrolled participants might demand a refund of their automatic contributions,

Box 2-2. *Automatic Escalation*

Automatic escalation makes automatic enrollment more effective by gradually increasing employees' contribution levels over time, unless and until employees opt out of the increase. If automatic enrollment helps employees save by getting them into the plan, automatic escalation gives them a better chance of achieving adequate contribution levels. Escalation also helps employers do better on the 401(k) nondiscrimination tests and helps counteract the possible "drag-down" effect whereby automatic enrollment at a relatively low contribution level might induce some employees, who go with the default, to contribute less than they otherwise would have contributed.

Escalation could be fully automatic from the outset, so that all participants' contribution rates automatically increase by a specified amount (such as one or two percentage points) each year unless and until they opt out. (For example, new hires might be automatically enrolled at 3 percent; employees in their second year at 4 percent; in their third year at 5 percent, and so forth.) Alternatively, participants can be offered a one-time opportunity to elect annual escalation, so that the default is no escalation, but once elected, escalation continues automatically unless and until they opt out.

Increases in contribution rates could coincide with wage increases or raises (so employees never experience a decline in take-home pay) or could occur on a fixed date, such as the first day of the year or the anniversary of an employee's date of hire.[a] Escalation has been made a condition of the PPA 401(k) automatic enrollment safe harbor.

a. Under the "Save More Tomorrow" program proposed by Thaler and Benartzi, participants can agree that future pay increases will generate additional contributions. See Richard Thaler and Shlomo Benartzi, "Save More Tomorrow: Using Behavioral Economics to Increase Employee Saving," *Journal of Political Economy* 112, no. 1, pt. 2 (2004), pp. S164-S187. The IRS has explicitly approved both approaches mentioned here in a general information letter addressed to one of the authors. IRS General Information Letter dated March 17, 2004, to J. Mark Iwry.

claiming they did not read or understand the advance notice, and that 401(k) withdrawal restrictions would prevent the plan from honoring such requests. Moreover, even if refunds were permitted, they would ordinarily be subject to a 10 percent early withdrawal tax. The PPA addressed this concern by providing flexibility through a retroactive "unwind" provision; beginning in 2008, 401(k), 403(b), and 457 plans can return the full amount of automatic contributions without the 10 percent tax if an employee so requests within ninety days after the contributions begin.

Box 2-3. *Why Employers Use Automatic Enrollment: The Business Case*

Sponsors of 401(k) plans are increasingly adopting automatic enrollment and other automatic features, and surveys suggest the vast majority of employers that have used automatic enrollment have been satisfied with it.[a] Automatic features in retirement plans offer businesses several advantages.

Recruiting and Retaining Valued Employees. Automatic enrollment and escalation, together with appropriate default investments, tend to make 401(k) plans more effective in recruiting and retaining valuable employees. Accordingly, many plan sponsors no longer simply offer employees the opportunity to save. Companies sponsoring 401(k) plans are increasingly viewing automatic features as "the right thing to do" to help employees save.

Improving Nondiscrimination Results. By raising participation rates, contribution rates, or both among middle- and lower-income workers, automatic enrollment and escalation tend to produce better performance under the nondiscrimination standards.[b] By comparing the average contribution percentage for highly paid employees and those who are not highly paid, the nondiscrimination standards link executives' ability to enjoy larger tax-preferred benefits to the employer's success in encouraging or providing greater benefits for most employees. In addition, beginning in 2008, plans that opted to meet the conditions of a new PPA nondiscrimination safe harbor could avoid nondiscrimination and "top-heavy" testing altogether.

Mitigating the Loss of Defined Benefit Pensions. Some plan sponsors that have frozen or cut back defined benefit (DB) pensions have upgraded their 401(k)s through automatic features, seeking to mitigate somewhat the employees' loss of future DB benefits. By sparing employees the need to take the initiative to enroll and by simplifying their decisionmaking process (especially through appropriate default investments), automatic 401(k) features can replicate or approximate some valuable DB attributes, such as automatic coverage and professional investment management.

a. In one survey 96 percent of plan sponsors said they were satisfied with automatic enrollment. See Deloitte, "Annual 401(k) Benchmarking Survey, 2005/2006 Edition."

b. While most plan sponsors that use automatic enrollment told Deloitte they adopted it to increase participation or encourage retirement saving, the survey reports that 21 percent of sponsors said that their primary motivation for adding automatic enrollment was to improve nondiscrimination test results.

Fiduciary Relief for Specified Default Investments

Plan sponsors are protected to some degree from fiduciary liability for the consequences of investments elected by employees. However, until the PPA, this protection for "self-directed" investments did not extend to investments that employees "chose" by default (that is, without making an explicit election), as in the case of automatic enrollment. For many employers considering automatic enrollment, this was a concern, which the PPA has now addressed. The PPA directs the Department of Labor to issue regulations specifying certain default investments that give employers the same protection from fiduciary liability that they currently enjoy for employee-elected investments. This fiduciary protection is not total: plan fiduciaries still must be prudent in selecting the investment options on the menu they offer employees, while avoiding conflicts of interest and excessive fees.

Labor Department regulations, finalized in 2007, specified three types of default investments that entail asset allocation and that would qualify for this fiduciary protection.[8] These are life-cycle or target-maturity funds, balanced funds consisting of equities and fixed-income investments, and professionally managed accounts.

New Nondiscrimination Safe Harbors for Automatic Enrollment Plans

In addition to removing barriers, the PPA attempts to provide a new incentive to use automatic enrollment. As noted, 401(k) nondiscrimination standards seek to align management's interests with the interests of average employees and taxpayers who fund tax subsidies for 401(k) plans. These standards link executives' ability to enjoy larger tax-preferred benefits to the employer's success in encouraging or providing greater benefits for the majority of employees.

The PPA provides a new exemption from the 401(k) nondiscrimination standards that breaks and even reverses the linkage of interests between management and workers. As of 2008 a plan is exempt from the nondiscrimination (including the "top-heavy") standards if it applies automatic enrollment to new hires (and to existing nonparticipating employees who did not explicitly opt out) at 3 percent of pay (at least), escalating 1 percent a year up to at least 6 percent. Among other requirements, the plan must also offer specified employer matching contributions (conditioned on employee contributions) or make nonmatching contributions that in either case vest after two years.

This new exemption, however, is probably unnecessary and could even prove counterproductive. Although it provides a reminder that automatic escalation is permitted and desirable, the exemption as a whole could unfortunately remove an employer's financial incentive to encourage its lower-income employees to save. An employer exempted from compliance with the nondiscrimination standards not only loses its financial incentive to encourage participation but could actually acquire a financial incentive to discourage participation: the more employees save, the greater the matching contribution costs incurred by the employer without any countervailing benefit in the form of improved nondiscrimination testing. There is no evidence regarding the effectiveness of automatic enrollment when administered by an employer with a financial incentive to minimize participation, that is, in circumstances where greater participation increases the employer's matching costs without any compensating improvement in nondiscrimination results. An employer that administered automatic enrollment in a way that actually encouraged employees to opt out would be merely offering, not making, matching contributions.

Despite its questionable design, is it possible that, on balance, this new exemption will do more good than harm? Certainly. Experience will tell whether it ultimately advances retirement security, sets it back, or has no significant effect.

Automatic 401(k): Building Second-Generation Plans

In the wake of the PPA, much still remains to be done in Congress, the executive branch, and the market to expand and improve the automatic 401(k).

Plans that use automatic features need further encouragement to evolve from what we call "first-generation" to "second-generation" automatic features. A first-generation automatic 401(k) might typically automatically enroll only new hires at a 3 percent contribution rate, without escalation. Investments would be in a stable-value or money market fund. A second-generation automatic 401(k) improves on each of these default choices (table 2-1). It would automatically enroll both new hires and existing nonparticipating employees at a 5 or 6 percent automatic contribution, escalating automatically up to a significantly higher level. Assets would be invested automatically (that is, by default) in a low-cost, professionally managed account or life-cycle fund.

Initial Default Contribution Rates

More than 75 percent of plans with automatic enrollment have a default contribution rate of only 3 percent or less, which is less than half of the existing average pretax contribution rate of about 7 percent of pay.[9] Research has indicated that automatic enrollment can induce some employees to passively maintain the default contribution rate over time, including employees who might otherwise

Table 2-1. *Moving from First-Generation to Second-Generation Automatic 401(k)s*

Plan feature	First generation	Second generation
Initial contribution rate	3 percent	5–6 percent
Escalation of contributions	No	Annually, up to at least the match limit or higher (for example, 10–12 percent)
Investment allocation	Stable value	Managed account, life-cycle, or lifestyle (balanced) fund
Apply automatic 401(k) to	New hires	All covered nonparticipating employees
Plan size	Large	All sizes

Source: Authors.

have elected to contribute at a higher rate[10] and employees who would otherwise contribute less but could be induced by a higher default rate to contribute more. Setting and adhering to a very low default contribution rate can therefore significantly limit the power of the automatic 401(k) to increase retirement saving.

If automatic enrollment is to realize its full potential to increase saving, default contribution rates need to be substantially higher. A number of plans reportedly have moved to an initial default contribution rate of 5 or 6 percent of pay and have found that participant opt-out rates at these levels were not much higher than at 3 percent of pay.

Automatic Enrollment of Existing Employees

Most plan sponsors have applied automatic enrollment to newly hired employees only. However, increasing numbers of employers are extending automatic enrollment to existing employees who have not been participating in the 401(k) plan.[11] Typically, these are people who did not make a written election to stay out of the plan but often failed to join because of inertia or procrastination. Employers can communicate with these employees regarding the advantages of participation and inform them that they will be automatically enrolled unless they opt out. Automatic enrollment could be extended to these nonparticipants once or periodically (say, every two or three years).

Automatic Escalation

As discussed earlier, for automatic enrollment to realize its potential, default contribution rates also need to increase over time for employees who continue to participate; and if the plan starts with a low default contribution rate, it becomes even more important to raise that rate for continuing participants. Thus far, few plans (an estimated 15 percent of those that use automatic enrollment) have implemented such automatic escalation.[12] However, it appears that plan sponsors are increasingly considering this important technique.[13]

Automatic Investment

Labor Department regulations issued pursuant to the PPA should appropriately accommodate default investments that preserve principal (used by numerous plan sponsors that have adopted automatic enrollment), at least in the short term (for example, where a principal-preserving default automatically converts after a year or two to asset-allocated investments). In addition, the regulations' definitions of qualifying default investment alternatives might usefully be made more flexible to accommodate creative new investment products (such as life-cycle or balanced funds that include guarantees or other elements of principal preservation). The regulations also should give greater emphasis to the need for cost control in default investments, especially through the use of index funds or similar arrangements.[14]

In addition, the PPA did too little to discourage the overconcentration in employer stock that exposes participants to unnecessary risk. While there is a fine line to walk because matching employee saving with employer stock is better than no employer match at all, plan participants can be better protected from the risk that their employer's failure or financial difficulties will cost them both their jobs and their retirement savings. First, with policies that continue to encourage asset-allocated default investments (such as professionally managed accounts or life-cycle funds), overconcentration in employer stock should eventually give way to better asset allocation. Second, employers that recognize their employees are overexposed to company stock often fear that diversification could expose them to fiduciary liability or employee criticism if the stock price rises, could signal lack of confidence in the future of the enterprise, and in some cases could depress the market for the company's stock. Congress could address most of these concerns by giving fiduciary protection to plan sponsors that follow a safe-harbor "glide path" systematically, gradually diversifying participants' investments in company stock. Third, Congress could consider stronger measures that might require plans to offer employees asset-allocated investment options, the option to diversify out of employer stock on a "dollar cost averaging" basis, or even gradually diversify employees out of employer stock, as Congress did in the 1970s and 1980s by imposing a 10 percent limit on employer stock in defined benefit pension plans. Finally, Congress should remedy the PPA's failure to strengthen and rationalize the antiquated and ineffective diversification requirements applicable to employee stock ownership plans—tax-qualified retirement plans or employer contributions designed to be primarily invested in employer stock.

Automatic Rollover and Annuitization

Further work is also needed to determine how best to improve the 401(k) distribution phase by promoting both rollovers (to reduce the risk that retirement savings will be dissipated)[15] and annuitization (to reduce the risk of outliving one's retirement savings). Specifically, efforts are under way to explore means of expanding low-cost annuity options and promoting the appropriate use of longevity insurance and reasonably priced, portable annuity income that accumulates over time.

Expansion of Automatic 401(k)s to Midsize and Smaller Firms

Automatic 401(k)s have been expanding briskly. A recent study by Wells Fargo found that the proportion of employers offering automatic enrollment increased from 26 percent in 2006 to 44 percent in 2007.[16] Other studies have shown that larger employers are more likely to have adopted automatic enrollment. In 2005 over 34 percent of large 401(k) plans—those with 5,000 or more participants—used automatic enrollment, up from about 30 percent the year before and from virtually zero ten years earlier.[17] To date, however, automatic features have not caught on to any similar extent among 401(k) plans offered by midsize and small employers. Based on recent surveys, roughly 14 percent of firms with fewer than 5,000 participants have been using automatic enrollment.[18] Accordingly, to increase 401(k) participation among eligible nonparticipating employees, automatic 401(k)s not only need to continue spreading among larger plan sponsors but also need to make more significant inroads into the midsize and smaller employer market.

Continue Clarifying the Role of Federal Policies

The legislative preemption of state laws is unfortunately conditioned on automatic enrollment involving default investments described in Labor Department regulations. Automatic enrollment should be permitted without regard to state antigarnishment laws and without regard to whether a plan uses specified default investments.

Congress and the states, as appropriate, should also make clear that state antigarnishment laws do not preclude automatic enrollment in retirement savings plans such as Section 403(b) tax-sheltered annuities and Section 457 plans that are sponsored by states or nonprofit organizations. Many of these plans (as well as the Thrift Savings Plan covering federal government employees) could use automatic enrollment, but currently virtually none do.

In addition, Treasury should make clear that plans using the automatic enrollment nondiscrimination safe harbor should be free to escalate contribution rates to a level higher than 6 percent of pay, which is below the current average 401(k) contribution rate. Treasury should also make clear that contribution rates can be escalated to levels higher than 10 percent of pay.

Saver's Credit

Automatic features in 401(k) plans make participation easier, but effective financial incentives are also necessary. Federal tax preferences for retirement saving are quite costly, exceeding $100 billion per year. These subsidies, however, take the form of income tax deductions or exclusions, which deliver tax savings in proportion to one's marginal tax rate. This is an upside-down structure because it provides minimal incentives to the majority of American households (those that are in the 15 percent, 10 percent, or zero income tax brackets and that most need to save more to provide for basic needs in retirement) while reserving the largest incentives for the highest-income households. Moreover, as a strategy for promoting national saving, these subsidies are poorly targeted because higher-income taxpayers are disproportionately likely to respond not by increasing actual saving but by simply shifting existing assets from taxable to tax-preferred accounts.

The Saver's Credit, enacted in 2001, was designed to address these problems.[19] As the only major pension tax incentive targeted specifically to the majority of American households, it was designed to level the playing field by giving taxpayers earning less than $50,000 a tax credit for contributions to 401(k) plans, IRAs, and similar retirement savings vehicles. Although it was originally proposed as a permanent, 50 percent refundable tax credit, Congress sought to save revenue for other purposes by enacting the Saver's Credit as a nonrefundable credit with three income-based rates (only 10 percent for most of those eligible) and a 2006 sunset date.

The PPA began to restore the Saver's Credit to its intended design by making it permanent and indexing its income eligibility limits to inflation. However, the PPA leaves undone four major needed improvements to the Saver's Credit.

First, because the Saver's Credit is nonrefundable, it merely offsets a taxpayer's tax liability; it provides no saving incentive for some 50 million lower-income households that have no income tax liability. Making the Saver's Credit refundable would provide an important incentive to these households to save regularly and continually. It would also help secure the retirement of those with the lowest incomes, thus making them less dependent on Social Security income and means-tested government programs during their retirement years.

Second, the credit might have an enhanced incentive effect—and refundability might be more palatable to a bipartisan majority of Congress—if it took the form of an explicit government matching deposit to the contributor's IRA or 401(k) account rather than the current implicit match.[20]

Third, with 10, 20, and 50 percent credit rates and eligibility for each varying with income, the Saver's Credit is overly complicated and has inefficient "cliffs" at several income levels. It should be restored to its original design of a single, simple 50 percent credit, phased out smoothly above the income eligibility limit.

Fourth, the Saver's Credit still does not level the playing field for enough middle-income American families. Millions of households get little incentive from tax deductions because they are in the 15 percent income tax bracket, yet are ineligible for the Saver's Credit because they earn more than $50,000. A limit of about $70,000 per year would cover roughly those in the 15 percent or lower tax brackets, helping middle-class Americans save for a secure retirement.

Automatic IRA

The major unfinished business of the PPA is expanding coverage. Except by slightly improving the Saver's Credit, the legislation does not attempt to extend retirement savings coverage to workers who have no access to an employer-provided retirement plan. These workers currently number about 78 million, or about half of the U.S. workforce.[21] The Retirement Security Project and the Heritage Foundation have jointly proposed to build on the success of employer plans and the automatic 401(k) to extend payroll deposit savings to most of the 78 million through a proposed "Automatic IRA" (see chapter 4).

Under this proposal, which was introduced in the 110th Congress on a bipartisan basis,[22] a firm that is not ready to adopt a 401(k) or other retirement plan would offer its employees the ability to contribute to an IRA every payday by payroll deposit, much as millions of employees have their paychecks deposited directly to their bank accounts. It is easier to save small amounts on a regular basis, and once payroll deposits begin, they continue automatically unless the worker later opts out. Employers above a certain size (ten employees, for example) that have been in business for at least two years but that still do not sponsor any plan for their employees would be required to offer employees this payroll-deduction saving opportunity.

The Automatic IRA would involve no contributions or other outlays by employers, who would merely offer their payroll system as a conduit that employees could use to save part of their own wages in an IRA. Participating employers would receive temporary tax credits, would be required to obtain a written waiver from any employee who does not participate, would be encouraged to use automatic enrollment, and would be able to protect themselves from fiduciary liability. Employees, or the employer, could designate the IRA to receive the savings, including, as a fallback for those unable or unwilling to choose, a national-platform IRA that could be modeled on the federal employees' Thrift Savings Plan accounts. The default investment would be a diversified, low-cost, life-cycle fund, with other choices available (see chapter 4). The self-employed would be encouraged to save by extending payroll deposit to independent contractors, facilitating direct deposit of income tax refunds, and expanding access to automatic debit arrangements linked to IRAs, including online and traditional means of access through professional and trade associations.

Asset Tests

While automatic 401(k)s and an improved Saver's Credit encourage retirement saving, outdated asset tests in means-tested public assistance programs penalize lower- and moderate-income households that respond by saving.[23] Many low- and moderate-income families rely in times of need on public assistance programs such as food stamps, Temporary Assistance for Needy Families, Medicaid, and Supplemental Security Income. To be eligible, applicants generally must meet an asset test as well as an income test. While the asset tests usually do not count accrued benefits under a defined benefit plan as assets, too often they do count 401(k) or IRA balances or both. This has the effect of a steep implicit tax on 401(k) and IRA saving. As a result, families with incomes low enough to qualify for a means-tested program under the income test might respond by saving less.

Also, while some state programs have eliminated asset tests, or at least aligned the treatment of defined contribution plans with that of defined benefit plans, many have not. Asset tests treat retirement saving in a confusing and seemingly arbitrary manner, with different restrictions state by state and account by account. Congress and the states should therefore eliminate this implicit tax on retirement saving by mandating that retirement accounts such as 401(k)s and IRAs be disregarded for eligibility and benefit determinations in federal and state means-tested programs. Changing the law to exempt retirement accounts from being considered in means-tested programs would treat retirement savings fairly and consistently and would send an important signal to families that rely or might need to rely on means-tested programs in the future: you will not be penalized for saving for retirement.

Eliminating asset rules for retirement savings will have some short-term costs because additional lower-income households will qualify for and use means-tested benefit programs. However, these costs should be modest; and if moderate- and low-income households can save for a more secure retirement, fewer people will have to rely on public benefits in old age.

Conclusion

The Pension Protection Act of 2006 has taken significant steps to encourage the use of automatic 401(k) features and to consolidate the Saver's Credit. However, further legislative, regulatory, and corporate action is needed to make saving easier by expanding the use of the automatic 401(k), by improving the Saver's Credit, and by reforming the asset tests that currently penalize saving by those otherwise eligible for public assistance. Finally, Congress needs to complete the major unfinished business of the PPA and expand coverage to the half of the workforce that lacks access to any employer plan by instituting automatic, universal IRAs. Automatic IRAs will extend to tens of millions of workers the powerful mechanism of regular payroll deposit saving. Together, these measures compose a comprehensive and effective strategy to expand retirement saving: a strategy that particularly benefits those working Americans who currently lack sufficient opportunities or incentives to save and whose contributions are most likely to represent new savings.

Notes

1. See William G. Gale, J. Mark Iwry, and Peter R. Orszag, "The Automatic 401(k): A Simple Way to Strengthen Retirement Savings," Policy Brief 2005-1 (Washington: Retirement Security Project, 2005).

2. See generally J. Mark Iwry, William G. Gale, and Peter R. Orszag, "The Potential Effects of Retirement Security Project Proposals on Private and National Savings: Exploratory Calculations," Policy Brief 2006-2 (Washington: Retirement Security Project, 2006), who estimate that the automatic 401(k) could bring about a net increase of $44 billion a year in national saving.

3. Brigitte C. Madrian and Dennis F. Shea, "The Power of Suggestion: Inertia in 401(k) Participation and Savings Behavior," *Quarterly Journal of Economics* 116, no. 4 (2001), pp. 1149–87; and James Choi and others, "Defined Contribution Pensions: Plan Rules, Participant Decisions, and the Path of Least Resistance," in *Tax Policy and the Economy*, vol. 16, edited by James Poterba (MIT Press, 2002), pp. 67–113. Related approaches have also proven effective but generally are less powerful. One such approach is to require employees to make an explicit election so that inertia does not prevent them from participating or lead them to contribute less than they would if they were required to choose. Another approach presents employees with a presumptive contribution rate packaged together with an investment option—not as a default, but as an easy choice employees can make by checking a single box.

4. Richard Thaler and Shlomo Benartzi, "Save More Tomorrow: Using Behavioral Economics to Increase Employee Saving," *Journal of Political Economy* 112, no. 1, pt. 2 (2004), pp. S164–S187.

5. William G. Gale and J. Mark Iwry, "Automatic Investment: Improving 401(k) Portfolio Investment Choices," Policy Brief 2005-4 (Washington: Retirement Security Project, 2005); William G. Gale and others, "Improving 401(k) Investment Performance," Issue Brief 2004-26 (Boston College, Center for Retirement Research, 2004); J. Mark Iwry, "Promoting 401(k) Security" (Washington: Tax Policy Center, 2003).

6. William G. Gale and Michael Dworsky, "Effects of Public Policies on the Disposition of Lump-Sum Distributions: Rational and Behavioral Influences," Working Paper 2006-15 (Boston College, Center for Retirement Research, 2006).

7. The PPA, Public Law 109-280, was signed into law on August 17, 2006. This chapter addresses only the PPA provisions relating to automatic features in 401(k)-type plans and not the extensive PPA provisions relating to defined benefit plans and other pension issues. For further discussion of these provisions, see. J. Mark Iwry, "Analysis of the Pension Protection Act of 2006: Increasing Participation through the Automatic 401(k) and Saver's Credit" (Washington: Retirement Security Project, August 15, 2006).

8. Department of Labor Employee Benefits Security Administration, "Default Investment Alternatives under Participant Directed Individual Account Plans; Final Rule," *Federal Register* 72, no. 205 (October 24, 2007).

9. Hewitt Associates, Trends and Experiences in 401(k) Plans 2005 survey (referred to here as Hewitt survey) (Lincolnshire, Ill.); and the Profit Sharing/401(k) Council of America, PSCA's 49th Annual Survey of Profit Sharing and 401(k) Plans, 2006, (referred to here as PSCA survey) (Chicago).

10. James Choi and others "For Better or For Worse: Default Effects and 401(k) Savings Behavior," in *Perspectives in the Economics of Aging*, edited by D. Wise (University of Chicago Press, 2003), pp. 81–121.

11. Roughly three out of four plans targeted only new hires when they implemented automatic enrollment—81 percent in the Hewitt survey and 72 percent in a Deloitte 2005/06 survey (www.deloitte.com/dtt/cda/dcc/content/us_consulting_hc_401ksurveyresults_02008 06.pdf). According to Hewitt Associates' Hot Topics in Retirement 2007 survey of large plan sponsors, 55 percent of plan sponsors not currently offering automatic enrollment were "very likely" or "somewhat likely" to offer it for new hires in 2007. Only 26 percent indicated they would offer it to current nonparticipants as well.

12. The PSCA survey reports that 14.8 percent of plans with automatic enrollment also increase contribution rates over time. The Deloitte survey asks about "step-up" programs and finds that 16 percent of plans have a separate, stand-alone, step-up feature, while only 2 percent of plans (or 9 percent of those with automatic enrollment) have a step-up feature tied to automatic enrollment.

13. The Deloitte survey reports that 20 percent of plan sponsors are considering implementing automatic escalation features.

14. See letter from J. Mark Iwry, Principal, Retirement Security Project, to Department of Labor Employee Benefits Security Administration, dated November 13, 2006, commenting on the Department's proposed regulations.

15. Automatic rollover has the potentially valuable by-product of increasing use of IRAs and promoting retirement saving among middle- and low-income families that might no longer have access to a 401(k)-type plan.

16. See http://www.wellsfargo.com/downloads/pdf/com/bpsm/2007_survey_analysis.pdf.

17. PSCA survey.

18. Overall, 16.9 percent of plans in 2005 used automatic enrollment according to the PSCA survey. The Deloitte survey reported that 23 percent of all plans use automatic enrollment.

19. J. Mark Iwry, William G. Gale, and Peter R. Orszag, "The Saver's Credit," Policy Brief 2005-2 (Washington: Retirement Security Project, 2005); J. Mark Iwry, William G. Gale, and Peter R. Orszag, "The Saver's Credit: Issues and Options," *Tax Notes* (Washington: Tax Policy Center, May 3, 2004).

20. The explicit 50 percent credit is an implicit 100 percent match. For an example, consider a couple earning $30,000 who contribute $2,000 to a 401(k) plan. The Saver's Credit reduces that couple's federal income tax liability by $1,000 (50 percent of $2,000). The net result is a $2,000 account balance that costs the couple only $1,000 after taxes (the $2,000 contribution minus the $1,000 tax credit). This is the same result that would occur if the net after-tax contribution of $1,000 were matched at a 100 percent rate: the couple and the government each effectively contribute $1,000 to the account. While taxpayers should respond the same to equivalent implicit and explicit matches, empirical research provides evidence to the contrary. For a detailed discussion, see Esther Duflo and others, "A New Government Matching Program for Retirement Saving" (Washington: Retirement Security Project, 2005).

21. Craig Copeland, "Employment-Based Retirement Plan Participation: Geographic Differences and Trends, 2005," Issue Brief 299 (Washington: Employee Benefit Research Institute, 2006).

22. H.R. 2167 and S 1141.

23. For a detailed discussion of this issue, see Zoë Neuberger, Robert Greenstein, and Eileen P. Sweeney, "Protecting Low-Income Families' Retirement Savings: How Retirement Accounts Are Treated in Means-Tested Programs and Steps to Remove Barriers to Retirement Saving," Policy Brief 2005-6 (Washington: Retirement Security Project, 2005).

3

The Automatic 401(k):
Revenue and Distributional Estimates

CHRISTOPHER GEISSLER AND BENJAMIN H. HARRIS

O ne of the most promising aspects of retirement saving policy in recent years is the advent of automatic, or opt-out, features in 401(k) plans. Automatic 401(k)s enable saving even for workers who make no effort to participate in their 401(k) plan. In a 401(k) plan without automatic features, workers have to actively choose whether to sign up for the plan, how much to contribute to the plan, and what the investment allocation for their assets should be.[1] These decisions can be complex and daunting, and busy people often procrastinate or are unable to decide the best way to proceed. As a result, these workers do not participate in their 401(k) plan or make imprudent investment choices. By contrast, in a 401(k) with automatic enrollment, workers are automatically enrolled in their employer's plan at a default contribution rate, and funds are directed into balanced, prudently diversified investment accounts, unless participants affirmatively choose otherwise. Therefore, those who are unwilling or unable to make these complicated decisions would be saving through automatic 401(k)s.

Automatic 401(k) plans are beneficial to workers on several levels. First, they start workers on a saving path earlier than they otherwise might. Among employers with automatic enrollment, participation in 401(k)s increased from 75 percent to as high as 90 or 95 percent of newly eligible employees; the

We thank Lina Walker, Bill Gale, Mark Iwry, and David John for helpful comments, and Greg Leiserson for assistance with the Tax Policy Center model.

change was highest among lower-income and minority workers.[2] Second, workers will generally be invested in more appropriate and diversified funds in automatic 401(k)s than if they invest on their own.[3] Third, contributions to 401(k) plans are generally tax preferred relative to saving outside of 401(k)s because contributions to 401(k)s are tax deductible.

This chapter provides estimates of the effects—on federal revenue and the distribution of after-tax income—of a policy under which all 401(k) plans in the United States are converted to automatic 401(k)s. In recent years such plans have become more prevalent, in part because of the passage of the Pension Protection Act (PPA) of 2006, which provided new incentives for automatic 401(k) plans and addressed several employer concerns regarding them (see chapter 2). Between 2006 and 2007, the number of employers offering automatic enrollment increased from 26 percent to 44 percent among surveyed employers.[4] The chapter can help policymakers, analysts, and pension administrators evaluate the merits of automatic 401(k)s.

Because of the preferred tax treatment of 401(k) contributions, federal income tax revenues are expected to decline with any increase in 401(k) participation generated through higher enrollment rates and higher contribution rates. In addition, automatic 401(k)s will have different effects on workers at different income levels. Workers with higher marginal tax rates will receive a larger reduction in tax when they contribute to 401(k)s than will workers with lower marginal tax rates. At the same time, in practice, automatic features in 401(k)s disproportionately increase enrollment for workers with lower income, who face lower marginal tax rates. Furthermore, the default contribution rates are, for some workers, lower than they might have chosen in the absence of automatic features, a situation that lowers both their level of tax benefit and the revenue loss.

Our model finds the federal revenue costs to be modest over the ten-year budget window, particularly in relation to the revenue cost of providing saving incentives through employer-sponsored retirement saving plans. The revenue loss from making automatic enrollment in 401(k)s universal and implementing a default contribution rate is between $3.5 billion and $6.9 billion a year, with losses ranging between $35 billion and $69 billion over fiscal years 2008–17. The higher revenue estimates are associated with a model that escalates the default contribution rate over time.

We find that the distributional effects of making automatic enrollment in 401(k)s universal and implementing a default contribution rate are progressive relative to the current system. Specifically, we find the proportion of the benefit going to taxpayers in the bottom four income quintiles—taxpayers in the bottom 80 percent range of the income distribution—is larger than their share of the overall tax burden.

The next section describes our automatic 401(k) proposal. We then describe our modeling procedure and follow that with a discussion of the central results and some conclusions.

Description of Automatic 401(k) Plans

In traditional 401(k) plans, workers must make active decisions about whether to sign up, how much to contribute, how to allocate investment funds, how often to rebalance their portfolios, and what to do with the available funds when they change jobs and at retirement. These decisions can be difficult, and many workers either make poor choices or simply end up making no choice at all. In this system, a worker who is intimidated by the complexity remains outside of the 401(k) system and does not benefit from the tax-advantaged retirement saving opportunities that 401(k)s provide.

In contrast, with an automatic 401(k)—sometimes called an opt-out plan—the situation is reversed. Workers are automatically enrolled in the plan unless they actively choose not to participate; they are assigned a default contribution level, which may increase over time; and they are given a default investment allocation, all of which they can choose to change. That is, each stage of the 401(k) saving process is automatically set at a prosaving default. Workers who prefer different saving choices may opt out of the default but for others, the same force of inertia that stymied saving in a traditional 401(k) would promote saving under an automatic 401(k) plan.

In addition to the decision about whether to participate in a plan, workers in traditional 401(k) plans must also decide how much to contribute and how to invest their contributions. Automatic 401(k)s would set a default for these choices, which, like the decision about whether to participate, could be revised by the worker. The default contribution is determined as a proportion of earnings; for example, a company might set the default contribution as 3 percent of a worker's monthly earnings. Default contribution rates can either remain constant over time or increase gradually. In this chapter, we model three assumptions about default rates: one scenario where the default contribution rate remains constant at 3 percent of earnings, another scenario where the default contribution rate is initially set at 3 percent of earnings and gradually rises to 6 percent, and a third scenario where contribution rates gradually rise (as in the second scenario), but higher-income workers also contribute one and a half times the rate of other workers.

With traditional defined-benefit pensions, the decision about how to invest is made by a pension administrator, while 401(k)s require the worker to make the investment decision; this decision may be a difficult one for some 401(k) participants. An additional feature of automatic enrollment is that workers' contributions may be automatically invested in a diversified portfolio of assets (qualified default investment alternatives) suitable for retirement saving. This feature would prevent many workers from overinvesting in company stock, a common problem in 401(k) plans, while still allowing workers the option to make investment decisions.[5] We do not model the default allocation feature because portfolio allocation is beyond the scope of the Tax Policy Center model.[6]

Modeling the Impact of Automatic Enrollment

That model is a microsimulation model to estimate revenue and distributional effects of making automatic enrollment in 401(k)s universal and implementing a default contribution rate. It allows researchers to model the revenue and distributional effects of a change in tax policy. The primary data used by the model are tax returns, which are merged with demographic information provided by the federal government's Current Population Survey. The model, its capabilities, and a detailed description of our methodology are included in the appendix to this chapter.

Estimating the impact of automatic enrollment requires making assumptions about the number of workers eligible for automatic enrollment, the participation rates of eligible workers, and the contribution rates of those who participate.

We base our assumption about participation rates in automatic 401(k) plans on observed take-up rates reported in Madrian and Shea.[7] The authors study the changes in participation rates in a company before and after the adoption of automatic enrollment. We use Madrian and Shea's estimate of participation rates by age and income to simulate whether a worker subject to automatic 401(k) will elect to opt out of the program. Additional details of our simulation procedure, including modeling limitations, are provided in the appendix.

We employ three scenarios for contribution rates in automatic 401(k) enrollment programs:

—*Baseline:* Participants contribute 3 percent of earnings throughout the ten-year period (our budget window).

—*Baseline Escalating:* Participants contribute 3 percent of earnings in 2008. Contributions increase by 1 percent annually up to 6 percent in 2011 and remain at that level throughout the budget window.

—*Alternate Escalating:* Taxpayers with earnings under $100,000 (in 2008 dollars) contribute the same rate as in the baseline escalating scenario throughout the budget window. Taxpayers with earnings over $100,000 contribute 4.5 percent of earnings (one and a half times the rate in the baseline escalating scenario) throughout the budget window.

Simulating contribution rates presents a challenge because it is difficult to know how workers might contribute to accounts for which they were automatically enrolled given the wide variation in demographic and employment characteristics, employer-provided pension incentives, and default contribution rates. Several economists have studied the impact of automatic enrollment on contribution rates. Madrian and Shea, for example, find that the average contribution rate among participants drops with the initiation of an automatic enrollment program with a 3 percent default contribution rate, and that there are larger proportional decreases in contributions for participating employees at the lower end of the compensation scale.[8] Madrian and Shea also found that the average contribution rate for employees with higher compensation remained well above the default rate, while the average contribution rate for employees with less compensation approached the default rate as compensation decreased.[9] Other studies of default rates under automatic enrollment found that employees commonly contribute the default contribution rate and that raising default rates increases the contribution rates among participating employees.[10]

Still, it is difficult to generalize the results of these few studies to a larger population for a number of reasons. First, a complicating factor is the potential existence of automatic escalation, where default contribution rates are gradually increased over time to a set level; we do not know how workers would respond to such a policy. Second, while employee contribution levels are sensitive to default rates, they are also sensitive to other savings incentives, such as employer matching and tax benefits, which further complicate our ability to model worker contribution rates under automatic enrollment. Third, worker saving rates under automatic enrollment may also be sensitive to macroeconomic factors, such as wage growth, stock market activity, and employment security, all of which complicate assumptions about contribution rates.

Given the lack of empirical evidence measuring the impact of automatic enrollment on 401(k) contribution rates, particularly those that encompass automatic escalation of default rates, we present results under three scenarios of contribution rate trends. It is important to note that we are estimating only the participation rates of workers who are participating in a company 401(k) plan because of automatic enrollment, not the aggregate contribution levels of a cohort that includes workers who would have opted into a program without the existence of automatic enrollment.

Our baseline case corresponds to a constant default contribution rate equal to 3 percent, the most common default rate chosen by firms that already offer automatic enrollment. Moreover, studies of companies that adopted the 3 percent default rate found that employees in these plans frequently remained at this rate. Madrian and Shea, for example, studied a firm that implemented a 3 percent default contribution rate and found that 76 percent of automatically enrolled 401(k) participants contributed the default rate of 3 percent, as opposed to just 10 percent before automatic enrollment.[11] Because some employees are likely to contribute at a higher rate than the default rate, the average contribution rate will be higher, so this scenario represents a lower bound for the revenue costs of automatic enrollment.

The second scenario simulates a company plan with escalating default contribution rates. With the enactment of recent legislation, escalation of the default contribution rate is expected to become a more common feature among companies offering automatic enrollment. It is unclear how employees will respond to automatic escalation—some employees might opt to lower the contribution rate as it rises each successive year, others might opt to leave the contribution rate unchanged from the default rate, and another group may opt to contribute at a rate higher than the default. Here, we assume that workers do not opt out of the default escalating contribution rate throughout the budget window.

The third scenario combines the observation that automatic enrollees commonly contribute the default rate with the observation that high-income workers are more likely to opt out of the default contribution rate and adopt a higher contribution level. Madrian and Shea, for example, found that the average contribution rate for high-income workers was approximately 50 percent to 100 percent higher relative to other workers.[12] Here we assume that high-income workers opt to increase their contributions and contribute one and a half times the default rate, while all other workers remain at the default level.

Revenue and Distributional Estimates

This section presents revenue costs and distributional estimates of making automatic enrollment in 401(k)s universal and implementing a default contribution rate. Revenue costs are the change in net federal tax revenue as a result of the change in 401(k) contributions attributable to automatic features and can be considered the direct fiscal "cost" of implementing the policy. Distributional estimates measure how a reform affects taxpayers with different circumstances. In particular, we examine how automatic enrollment in 401(k)s would affect taxpayers with different incomes, where income is defined in terms of "cash income," a broader measure than adjusted gross income and a better representation of economic status.[13]

Several factors influence the distributional results. The first concerns participation. Taxpayers with higher wages are more likely to be participating in a company 401(k) before the implementation of automatic enrollment, both because they are more likely to work at a company that offers 401(k)s to its workers and because higher-income workers are more likely to participate in a 401(k) if eligible.[14] This condition means that automatic enrollment is more likely to incorporate lower-wage workers into company retirement plans, because these workers are less likely to be enrolled in such plans (a worker who is already enrolled in a company 401(k) cannot benefit from automatic enrollment).

The second factor concerns contribution rates and tax benefits. Because we assume that workers will contribute the default rate, expressed as a percentage of earnings, newly enrolled workers with high wages will have higher contribution levels to their 401(k)s. In addition, the tax benefit for a contribution to a 401(k) increases with income, because marginal tax rates are higher for high-income workers. As an example, consider the benefits associated with a $1 contribution for a worker in the 15 percent tax bracket compared with a worker in the 35 percent tax bracket. The $1 contribution by the worker in the lower bracket will drop that worker's taxable earnings by $1, which will result in a reduction of 15 cents in taxes paid. In contrast, the $1 contribution for the high-income worker, resulting in a $1 drop in taxable earnings, will produce a 35-cent drop in taxes paid. The end result is that relative to lower-income workers, wealthier taxpayers will have higher contributions because of their higher wages and will have larger tax benefits because of their elevated marginal tax rates.

Table 3-1 presents the revenue costs of automatic 401(k)s under the baseline, escalating, and alternate escalating scenarios; table 3-2 presents distributional effects by cash income percentile under the baseline scenario. Distributional results by income level are presented in the appendix.

Revenue Costs

The revenue costs of the automatic 401(k) proposal are modest relative to the total value of tax expenditures for retirement saving. For the baseline case, we find that the proposal would reduce revenues by an average of about $3.5 billion a year over the ten-year budget window, for a total ten-year cost of $35.1 billion. As a benchmark for the relative magnitude of these costs, the Joint Committee on Taxation estimates that the total value of tax expenditures for contributions to employer-sponsored retirement plans is $498.7 billion over 2008–11.[15] This suggests that automatic enrollment would increase total federal outlays for employer-sponsored retirement plans by approximately 2.2 percent. For the escalating case, where the default contribution rate is increased by 1 percent annually until it reaches 6 percent, we estimate the average annual cost to be $6.4 billion, with a ten-year cost of $63.6 billion over 2008–17. For the alternate escalation case, where the default rate is increased and we assume higher contribution rates for high-income workers, the average annual cost would be about $6.9 billion and the ten-year cost is $68.9 billion over 2008–17.

Table 3–1. *Static Revenue Effect from Automatic Enrollment in 401(k)s, 2008–17*[a]
Billions of dollars

Revenue effect	2008	2009	2010	2011	2012	2013	2014	2015	2016	2017	2008–17
Fiscal year revenue[b]											
Baseline[c]	–1.9	–2.7	–2.9	–3.2	–3.5	–3.8	–4.0	–4.2	–4.4	–4.6	–35.1
Escalating[d]	–1.9	–3.3	–4.5	–6.1	–6.9	–7.3	–7.8	–8.2	–8.5	–9.0	–63.6
Alternate escalating[e]	–2.1	–3.6	–4.9	–6.6	–7.5	–7.9	–8.4	–8.8	–9.3	–9.8	–68.9
Calendar year liability											
Baseline[c]	–2.5	–2.7	–3.0	–3.3	–3.6	–3.8	–4.0	–4.2	–4.4	–4.7	–36.2
Escalating[d]	–2.5	–3.6	–4.9	–6.6	–7.0	–7.5	–7.9	–8.3	–8.6	–9.1	–65.9
Alternate escalating[e]	–2.8	–3.9	–5.3	–7.1	–7.6	–8.1	–8.5	–8.9	–9.4	–9.9	–71.4

Source: Urban–Brookings Tax Policy Center microsimulation model.
a. The proposals are effective January 1, 2008. Estimates are static and do not account for any potential microeconomic behavioral response.
b. Fiscal year revenue numbers assume a 75–25 split. The actual effect on receipts could differ.
c. Baseline is current law. The proposal would automatically enroll all eligible workers in an automatic 401(k) plan unless they choose to opt out. We assume taxpayers that enroll contribute 3 percent of their earnings, subject to contribution limits. For more on how this proposal is modeled, see the description in the paper.
d. Same as baseline except contributions increase 1 percent each year from 3 percent in 2008 to 6 percent in 2011. After 2011, contributions remain at 6 percent.
e. Same as "escalating" scenario except individuals earning more than $100,000 in 2008 dollars are assumed to contribute 50 percent more.

Table 3-2. Distribution of Federal Tax Change from Automatic Enrollment in 401(k)s, by Cash Income Percentile, 2012[a]

Cash income percentile[b]	Percent of tax units[c]		Percent change in after-tax income[d]	Share of total federal tax change	Average federal tax change		Share of federal taxes		Average federal tax rate[e]	
	With tax cut	With tax increase			Dollars	Percent	Change (percentage points)	Under the proposal	Change (percentage points)	Under the proposal
Lowest quintile	1.8	0.3	0.0	3.9	−4	−0.6	0.0	0.8	0.0	5.4
Second quintile	5.3	0.1	0.1	19.3	−23	−0.6	0.0	4.5	−0.1	13.0
Middle quintile	5.7	0.0	0.1	26.4	−34	−0.3	0.0	11.2	−0.1	19.2
Fourth quintile	5.7	0.0	0.1	27.4	−43	−0.2	0.0	18.6	0.0	22.3
Top quintile	4.3	0.0	0.0	23.1	−41	−0.1	0.1	64.9	0.0	28.6
All	4.4	0.1	0.0	100.0	−26	−0.1	0.0	100.0	0.0	24.0
Addendum										
80–90	4.9	0.0	0.0	11.3	−39	−0.1	0.0	14.3	0.0	25.0
90–95	4.2	0.0	0.0	6.0	−44	−0.1	0.0	10.2	0.0	26.1
95–99	3.4	0.0	0.0	5.0	−45	0.0	0.0	15.7	0.0	28.1
Top 1 percent	2.1	0.0	0.0	0.7	−25	0.0	0.0	24.7	0.0	33.2
Top 0.1 percent	1.8	0.0	0.0	0.1	−33	0.0	0.0	12.4	0.0	35.7

Source: Urban–Brookings Tax Policy Center microsimulation model.

a. Calendar year. Baseline is current law. See table 3-1 for definition.

b. Tax units with negative cash income are excluded from the lowest income class but are included in the totals. The cash income percentile classes used in this table are based on the income distribution for the entire population and contain an equal number of people, not tax units. The breaks are (in 2008 dollars): 20 percent, $19,740; 40 percent, $38,980; 60 percent, $69,490; 80 percent, $117,535; 90 percent, $169,480; 95 percent, $237,040; 99 percent, $619,561; 99.9 percent, $2,832,449.

c. Includes both filing and nonfiling units but excludes those that are dependents of other tax units.

d. After-tax income is cash income less individual income tax net of refundable credits, corporate income tax, payroll taxes (Social Security and Medicare), and estate tax.

e. Average federal tax (includes individual and corporate income tax, payroll taxes for Social Security and Medicare, and the estate tax) as a percentage of average cash income.

Distributional Effects

We find the distributional effects to be progressive relative to the current system, with low- and middle-income taxpayers receiving a disproportionately larger benefit relative to their existing tax burdens than higher-income taxpayers. Specifically, we find the proportion of the benefit going to taxpayers in each of the bottom four income quintiles—taxpayers in the bottom 80 percent range of the income distribution—to be larger than their share of the overall tax burden. For example, taxpayers in the middle income quintile receive 26.4 percent of the overall benefit of the automatic 401(k) proposal but pay only 11.2 percent of the aggregate tax burden. Taxpayers in the top income quintile receive a lower share of the benefit (23.1 percent) relative to their share of the federal tax burden (64.9 percent).

We find the automatic 401(k) participation rates across the top four income quintiles to be relatively constant at approximately 5 percent, and that the average benefit increases with income. Our results for 2012—the midpoint of the ten-year budget window—show that taxpayers in the middle quintile receive an average benefit of $34 annually, which indicates that the mean benefit for participating taxpayers in that quintile is approximately $600 per year.[16] Taxpayers in the top income quintile receive an average benefit of $41 annually, or approximately $950 per participating taxpayer. Taxpayers in the bottom income quintile are less likely to contribute to a 401(k) as the result of automatic enrollment and also receive fewer tax benefits when they do participate. However, given the uneven distribution of current tax incentives for retirement saving, these estimates suggest that the automatic 401(k) plan is a useful mechanism for distributing the benefits of these incentives across income groups.

We also estimate the distributional effects under the escalating scenario and alternate escalating scenario and present distributional effects by cash income level. These estimates are presented in the appendix; distributional patterns are not markedly different under these alternate scenarios.

Conclusion

As the notion of automatic 401(k) enrollment gains traction in the policy arena and on Capitol Hill, it is important to understand the distributional and revenue effects of such reforms. Using the Tax Policy Center's microsimulation model, we find that the distributional effects of making automatic enrollment in 401(k)s universal and implementing a default contribution rate are progressive relative to the current system, and that low- and middle-income taxpayers receive a disproportionately larger benefit relative to their existing tax burdens than higher-income taxpayers. Specifically, we find the proportion of the benefit going to taxpayers in each of the bottom four income quintiles—taxpayers in the bottom 80 percent range of the income distribution—to be larger than their share of the overall tax burden.

We find the revenue costs to be modest over the ten-year budget window, particularly in relation to the total revenue cost of providing saving incentives through employer-sponsored retirement saving plans. We estimate the annual average cost to be between $3.5 billion and $6.9 billion, and the ten-year cost of fully implementing the automatic 401(k) to be between $35.1 billion and $68.9 billion over fiscal years 2008–17.

Appendix: Methodology

Model Description and Data

We use the Tax Policy Center microsimulation model to estimate revenue and distributional effects of making automatic enrollment in 401(k)s universal and implementing a default contribution rate.[17] The Tax Policy Center has developed a large-scale microsimulation model of the U.S. federal income tax system to produce revenue and distribution estimates of tax policy changes. The model is similar to those used by the Congressional Budget Office, the Joint Committee on Taxation, and the Treasury's Office of Tax Analysis. The model consists of three components: a database of tax returns from 2004 supplemented with demographic information; a statistical routine that "ages" or extrapolates the data to create a representative sample of filers and nonfilers for future years; and a detailed tax calculator and set of incidence assumptions that computes tax liability and tax burdens for filers under current law and alternative proposals.

The tax model uses two data sources: the 2004 public-use file (PUF) produced by the Statistics of Income Division of the Internal Revenue Service, and the 2005 Current Population Survey (CPS). The PUF contains approximately 150,000 income tax records with detailed information from federal individual income tax returns filed in the 2004 calendar year. It provides key data on the level and sources of income and deductions, income tax liability, marginal tax rates, and use of particular credits, but it excludes most information about pensions and individual retirement accounts (IRAs) as well as demographic information such as age.

To model retirement saving,[18] we supplement the PUF and CPS data described above with information from the 2004 Federal Reserve Board of Governors' Survey of Consumer Finances (SCF) and the Survey of Income and Program Participation (SIPP). Our principal data source for type of pension, pension participation, and contributions by employers and employees is the

SCF, a stratified sample of about 4,400 households with detailed data on wealth and savings. For the purposes of this paper, income is defined in terms of "cash income," a broader measure than adjusted gross income and a better representation of economic status.[19]

Imputing 401(k) Eligibility

To measure the effect of automatic saving plans, the first step is to impute automatic 401(k) eligibility for individuals in the model. Because the automatic 401(k) program targets those taxpayers who are eligible to participate in a 401(k), but chose not to, it was necessary to impute values for 401(k) eligibility, as well as participation.

We adopted earlier techniques used by Tax Policy Center researchers and used the probit maximum likelihood estimator to estimate the likelihood of being eligible for the automatic 401(k) program. Under the probit model, the coverage is observed if and only if $X1\beta1 + \epsilon1 > 0$, where $\epsilon1$ is assumed to be a standard normal random variable with mean 0 and variance 1, X is a vector of exogenous variables, and β is a vector of parameters to be estimated.

The list of exogenous variables for each probit regression is designed to be an exhaustive set of relevant variables that exist on both the SCF and the PUF. These variables include number of dependents, age (included as ten-year bracket dummies), income, and the following components of income: income from a farm or business, tax-exempt interest income, taxable interest income, rental income from schedule E, pension income, taxable dividends, and realized capital gains (all defined as the natural logarithm of the sum of one plus the income item). We include dummies for negative income from a business or farm and negative capital income. In addition, we include dummies for whether the individual itemizes deductions on his or her federal tax return, and dummies for whether certain federal tax schedules are filed (C for business income, E for rental income, and F for farm income). The list of exogenous variables is identical for each equation. Equations are estimated separately for head of household and spouse,[20] but are based on household-level values for the exogenous variables with the exception of age and earnings.[21]

Given the estimates of coverage and eligibility from the SCF, we impute values to tax-filing units in the PUF/CPS database. Imputation is done in two steps. First, we simulate whether the taxpayer is eligible for an employer-sponsored pension. For consistency, pension contributions are attributed only to tax returns that are not shown to be ineligible by virtue of their IRA contributions.[22] Using the estimated coefficients from the probit estimation for 401(k) eligibility and values of exogenous variables in the tax model database, we calculate $Xb1$ (where $b1$ refers to the probit estimate for $\beta1$). We then calculate the threshold probability, $z = \phi_{-1}(X1b1)$, where ϕ is the cumulative standard normal probability distribution, and draw a uniform random number, p, between 0 and 1. If $p < z$, we assign a nonzero value for the item.[23] Second, we adjust the imputed aggregates to match SCF totals. After the adjustment, the number of participants in employer-sponsored pension plans and eligible taxpayers for automatic enrollment programs match approximately the totals reported in the SCF.

It should also be noted that the statutory eligibility in the model complements the imputed eligibility calculations discussed above. That is, a taxpayer may be deemed "eligible" to receive an automatic 401(k) but is still subject to the statutory limits of the tax benefits associated with those pensions.

Modeling Automatic 401(k) Take-up Rates

After imputing values for automatic 401(k) eligibility, we modeled take-up rates for eligible taxpayers using estimates derived from Madrian and Shea.[24] They studied the experience of employees at a company that adopted automatic enrollment and measured the program's effects on take-up rates by gender, race, age, and compensation. Because the PUF/CPS data do not contain information on gender or race, we only used estimates of the age and compensation effects on take-up rates. We adjust the aggregate mean estimates in Madrian and Shea to calculate each taxpayer's probability of taking up a pension under an automatic enrollment plan, given that the taxpayer has already failed to opt in to a 401(k) or IRA pension. Specifically, Madrian and Shea calculate the following probabilities:

p_i = the probability of an employee in age group i participating before the advent of automatic enrollment
p_j = the probability of an employee in compensation group j contributing before automatic enrollment
p'_i = the probability of an employee in age group i contributing after automatic enrollment
p'_j = the probability of an employee in compensation group j contributing after automatic enrollment
$\bar{p}$ = the average participation rate before automatic enrollment
$\bar{p}'$ = the average participation rate after automatic enrollment

We calculate the expected probability of participation for each age and compensation profile:[25]

$$p_{ij} = \frac{(\bar{p}' - \bar{p})}{(1 - \bar{p})} + \frac{(p'_i - p_i)}{(1 - p_i)} + \frac{(p'_j - p_j)}{(1 - p_j)}.$$

Table 3A-1. *Distribution of Federal Tax Change from Automatic Enrollment in 401(k)s, by Cash Income Level, 2012*[a]

Cash income level (thousands of 2008 dollars)[b]	Percent of tax units[c]		Percent change in after-tax income[d]	Share of total federal tax change	Average federal tax change		Share of federal taxes		Average federal tax rate[e]	
	With tax cut	With tax increase			Dollars	Percent	Change (percentage points)	Under the proposal	Change (percentage points)	Under the proposal
Less than 10	0.3	0.6	0.0	-0.2	0	0.1	0.0	0.2	0.0	5.4
10–20	2.9	0.2	0.1	4.2	-7	-0.8	0.0	0.7	0.0	5.4
20–30	5.3	0.1	0.1	9.6	-20	-0.7	0.0	1.9	-0.1	11.0
30–40	5.6	0.0	0.1	10.8	-29	-0.5	0.0	2.8	-0.1	15.2
40–50	6.2	0.0	0.1	10.1	-34	-0.4	0.0	3.4	-0.1	18.0
50–75	5.3	0.0	0.1	19.4	-36	-0.3	0.0	9.7	-0.1	20.1
75–100	5.9	0.0	0.1	15.6	-43	-0.2	0.0	9.8	-0.1	21.9
100–200	5.0	0.0	0.0	22.2	-41	-0.1	0.0	26.2	0.0	24.8
200–500	3.7	0.0	0.0	7.2	-45	-0.1	0.0	17.8	0.0	27.5
500–1,000	2.5	0.0	0.0	0.7	-27	0.0	0.0	7.6	0.0	29.2
More than 1,000	2.0	0.0	0.0	0.4	-28	0.0	0.0	19.8	0.0	34.2
All	4.4	0.1	0.0	100.0	-26	-0.1	0.0	100.0	0.0	24.0

Source: Urban–Brookings Tax Policy Center microsimulation model.

a. Calendar year. Baseline is current law. See table 3-1 for description.

b. Tax units with negative cash income are excluded from the lowest income class but are included in the totals. See text for a description of cash income.

c. Includes both filing and nonfiling units but excludes those that are dependents of other tax units.

d. After-tax income is cash income less individual income tax net of refundable credits, corporate income tax, payroll taxes (Social Security and Medicare), and estate tax.

e. Average federal tax (includes individual and corporate income tax, payroll taxes for Social Security and Medicare, and the estate tax) as a percentage of average cash income.

Then, in a technique similar to that used in the imputation process, we calculate the threshold probability, $z = \phi - 1(p_{ij})$, where ϕ is the cumulative standard normal probability distribution, and draw a uniform random number, p, between 0 and 1. If $p < z$, we model that taxpayer as having automatically enrolled in a 401(k) plan.

Notes

1. For additional background, see William G. Gale, J. Mark Iwry, and Peter R. Orszag, "The Automatic 401(k): A Simple Way to Strengthen Retirement Saving," Policy Brief 2005-1 (Washington: Retirement Security Project, 2005).

2. Brigitte C. Madrian and Dennis F. Shea, "The Power of Suggestion: Inertia in 401(k) Participation and Savings Behavior," *Quarterly Journal of Economics* 116, no. 4 (2001), pp. 1149–87.

3. For a general discussion of the benefits of a diversified 401(k) portfolio, see William G. Gale and J. Mark Iwry, "Automatic Investment: Improving 401(k) Portfolio Investment Choices," Policy Brief 2005-4 (Washington: Retirement Security Project, 2005). James M. Poterba, "Employer Stock and 401(k) Plans," *American Economic Review* 93 no. 2 (2003), pp. 398–404, and Lisa K. Meulbroek, "Company Stock in Pension Plans: How Costly Is It," Working Paper 02-058 (Harvard Business School, 2002), discuss the problem of overinvestment in own company stock.

4. Wells Fargo, "Strategic Initiatives in Retirement Plans: 2007 Survey Analysis," www.wellsfargo.com/downloads/pdf/com/bpsm/2007_survey_analysis.pdf. Furthermore, of the employers who offer automatic 401(k)s, 42 percent used 3 percent as the default contribution rate, while 20 percent use a default rate that is higher than 3 percent. About one quarter of employers who offer automatic enrollment also automatically escalate contributions.

5. Shlomo Benartzi, "Excessive Extrapolation and the Allocation of 401(k) Accounts to Company Stock," *Journal of Finance* 56, no. 5 (2001), pp. 1747–64; Gale and Iwry, "Automatic Investment."

6. Assumptions regarding portfolio allocation and the subsequent rates of return on those portfolios do not apply to the Tax Policy Center model, which does not model the retirement decision by workers; for more documentation, see Leonard Burman and others, "Distributional Effects of Defined Contribution Plans and Individual Retirement Accounts," Discussion Paper 15 (Washington: Tax Policy Center, 2004).

7. Madrian and Shea, "The Power of Suggestion."

8. Ibid.

9. These conclusions are confined to cohorts with between three and fifteen months of tenure at the company. The company that was studied provided a 50 percent match on the first 6 percent of compensation after the first year, so many of these employees were not eligible for a company match. Madrian and Shea also control for demographic and employment differences and find that automatic enrollment with a default rate decreases contributions rates by 2.2 percent for employees with three to fifteen months' tenure.

10. James Choi and others, "For Better or for Worse: Default Effects and 401(k) Savings Behavior," in *Perspectives in the Economics of Aging,* edited by David A. Wise (University of Chicago Press, 2004); John Beshears and others, "The Importance of Default Options for Retirement Savings Outcomes: Evidence from the United States," Working Paper 12009 (Cambridge, Mass.: National Bureau of Economic Research, 2006),

11. Madrian and Shea, "The Power of Suggestion."

12. Ibid.

13. For a complete description of the definition of cash income, see note 19.

14. For a description of trends concerning participation in company retirement plans, see Craig Copeland, "Employment-Based Retirement Plan Participation: Geographic Differences and Trends, 2006," Issue Brief 311 (Washington: Employment Benefit Research Institute, 2007).

15. Joint Committee on Taxation, "Estimates of Federal Tax Expenditures for Fiscal Years 2007–2011" (Government Printing Office, 2007).

16. The Tax Policy Center model presents mean benefit for all taxpayers in a given quintile. We calculate average benefit for participating taxpayers by dividing the total tax benefit for taxpayers in the quintile by the number of taxpayers in the quintile participating in automatic enrollment.

17. For documentation, see Jeffrey Rohaly, Adam Carasso, and Mohammed Adeel Saleem, "The Urban–Brookings Tax Policy Center Microsimulation Model: Documentation and Methodology for Version 0304," http://taxpolicycenter.org/UploadedPDF/411136_documentation.pdf.

18. For a more complete description of the data and methods used in modeling the revenue and distributional effects of retirement saving accounts, see Burman and others, "Distributional Effects of Defined Contribution Plans and Individual Retirement Accounts."

19. Cash income includes wages and salaries, employee contributions to tax-deferred retirement savings plans, business income or loss, farm income or loss, Schedule E income, interest income, taxable dividends, realized net capital gains, Social Security benefits received, unemployment compensation, energy assistance, Temporary Assistance for Needy Families, worker's compensation, veteran's benefits, Supplemental Security Income, child support, disability benefits, taxable IRA distributions, total pension income, alimony received, and other income including foreign earned income. Cash income also includes imputed corporate income tax liability and the employer's share of payroll taxes. This puts the income measure on a pretax basis. See www.taxpolicycenter.org/TaxModel/income.cfm for more discussion of income measures. Note that because cash income is a broader measure than adjusted gross income (AGI), some people with low reported AGI actually appear in higher-income quintiles because they have other income such as pension contributions or tax-exempt bond interest that does not appear in AGI. As a result, some people in higher-income quintiles are eligible for income-tested tax benefits, and more people in the bottom quintile of cash income are subject to income tax than in the bottom quintile of AGI.

20. The SCF is a household-based survey that records only total income and wealth items for all individuals in the "primary economic unit" (PEU); it does not attribute shares of those amounts to individuals within the PEU. This provides a slight complication for those PEUs that consist of two unmarried individuals living together (with or without other financially interdependent members of the PEU). These individuals will show up in the income tax file as two single tax returns but will show up in the SCF as one unit. We assume that an unmarried couple living together with shared finances behaves like a married couple and thus include them in the married category when running the regressions. The results do not change significantly if these individuals are dropped from the analysis.

21. It is not appropriate in the SCF to simply run regressions or probits on the entire data set because of its approach to missing variables. The SCF imputes missing values for a number of fields. To reflect the variance introduced by that process, the SCF database includes five replicates of each observation. Missing values are drawn randomly for each replicate from

the estimated probability distribution of the imputed value, whereas nonmissing values are simply repeated. We estimate coefficients by computing each estimate separately for each sample replicate and then averaging the coefficient estimates.

22. Tax returns include data on contributions to traditional IRAs. Since taxpayers above certain AGI thresholds may not make contributions to IRAs if their employers offer a pension, any in those categories who report IRA contributions must not participate in an employer plan. For a discussion of taxpayer eligibility for IRAs, see Christopher Geissler and Benjamin H. Harris, "Taxpayer Eligibility for IRAs," *Tax Notes* 118, no. 13 (2007), p. 739.

23. Without adjustment, this process can produce too many or too few individuals with pension contributions in the PUF dataset. We force the numbers to match published totals by shifting the threshold probabilities by a constant (up or down) so the simulated number of contributors matches the estimates on the SCF.

24. Madrian and Shea, "The Power of Suggestion."

25. The mean aggregate participation rate in Madrian and Shea, "The Power of Suggestion," for workers eligible for automatic 401(k) plans is 85.9 percent (our value of $\bar{p}'$ above) , compared to 37.4 percent (our value for $\bar{p}$ above) for workers who are not automatically enrolled. Each age-compensation profile yields an expected participation rate in (0,1), indicating that all age-compensation profiles are naturally constrained to this interval.

4

Pursuing Universal Retirement Security through Automatic IRAs

J. MARK IWRY AND DAVID C. JOHN

Roughly half of all working Americans work for employers that offer no retirement plan. Thus about 78 million workers have no way to save on the job for the day when they stop collecting a paycheck. This circumstance, combined with a national saving rate that has been declining steadily for most of the past twenty years and the unlikelihood that Social Security will be able to provide increased benefits, makes inadequate retirement saving a major national problem.

This chapter spells out an ambitious yet practical set of initiatives to expand retirement saving dramatically. We propose making saving automatic—and hence easier, more convenient, and more likely. This strategy has been shown to be remarkably effective at boosting participation in workplace-based 401(k) retirement savings. We would extend this strategy to most employees who have no access to 401(k) plans by combining several key elements of our current system: payroll-deposit saving; automatic enrollment; low-cost, diversified default investments; and individual retirement accounts (IRAs).

Automatic IRAs would not crowd out or compete with 401(k) plans. To the contrary, we would hope that successful experience with the new, Automatic IRAs would lead more employers to step up to 401(k)s and then to match

The authors thank Bill Gale and many other individuals for helpful comments and Jaime Matthews and Spencer Walters for outstanding assistance.

45

employee contributions—if not dollar for dollar, then perhaps fifty cents on the dollar or some other ratio. *Automatic* would be the operative word for the new IRAs. Once all the automatic processes described in this and other chapters have been developed and implemented, every step in the process, from saving for retirement to withdrawing the savings upon retirement, would occur automatically unless the individual employee or employer stepped in and affirmatively chose a different course.

How People Would Save

The Automatic IRA approach, which was touted by President Barack Obama in his first address to a joint session of Congress, has been included in the president's proposed budget and has been endorsed by such diverse publications as the *New York Times* and the *National Review*.[1] It offers most employees not covered by an employer-sponsored retirement plan the opportunity to save through the powerful mechanism of regular payroll deposits that continue automatically. This is an opportunity now limited mainly to 401(k)-eligible workers. Under this approach:

—Employers above a certain size (at least ten employees, for example) that had been in business for at least two years and did not sponsor any plan for their employees would allow employees to use their payroll system to channel their own money to an IRA.

—Employers would retain the option at all times of setting up a 401(k), a SIMPLE IRA, or other retirement plan instead of a payroll-deposit IRA. Those retirement plans offer employer contributions, much higher employee contributions, and larger tax credits for employers.

—These employers, as well as smaller or newer firms that voluntarily offered payroll deposit as a conduit for employee contributions, would receive a small, temporary tax credit based on the number of employees who participated.

—For most employees, payroll deductions would be made by direct deposit, similar to the common practice of depositing paychecks directly into employees' bank accounts.

—The arrangement would be market-oriented, with IRAs provided by the same private financial institutions that currently provide them.

—Each employer would send all deposits to a single IRA provider of its choice, unless it also chose to send deposits to IRAs already held by its employees.

—As a fallback, individuals and employers that could not find an acceptable IRA on the market could use ready-made, low-cost Automatic IRA accounts through an online clearinghouse that connected employers with financial providers serving as IRA trustees or custodians. If that did not work, an IRA of last resort would be made available by a financial services industry consortium or nonprofit risk-pooling arrangement, with investment management contracted out to the financial services industry.

—Enrollment would be automatic; employees would save a proportion of their pay in an IRA unless they affirmatively chose to opt out.

Employers not wishing to use this method with their employees could likewise opt out and instead have every employee make an explicit choice. In all events, while no employee would be required to participate, no employee could be left out simply because of inattention. Automatic enrollment would thus harness the power of inertia to increase saving in sensible default investments.

Any employee declining to contribute would need to sign a waiver. If possible, the election form would be added or attached to IRS Form W-4, which new employees complete to make elections regarding payroll tax withholding. Evidence from the 401(k) universe strongly suggests that high levels of participation tend to result not only from automatic enrollment but also from the practice of requiring each eligible employee to decide explicitly whether to participate.

A national website would give firms a standard notice for informing employees of the payroll-deduction IRA option. It would include standard employee election forms and enrollment procedures. The website would also promote best practices as they evolve (about automatic enrollment, for example, and, potentially, automatic annuitization) and employee education regarding saving and investment. Finally, for employers that cannot find an acceptable IRA provider in their area, the website would connect them with interested IRA providers.

Employers that offer automatic payroll deposit would be protected from potential fiduciary liability for investment performance and from having to choose or arrange default investments. Instead, whether the IRA provider was designated by employees or their employer, workers' contributions would automatically be directed to a diversified investment (such as a life-cycle fund) unless the employees chose a principal-preservation investment alternative or a different option. Initially, however, when accounts were very small, the automatic investment might be designed with a view to simplicity and to avoiding short-term losses (for example, using Treasury securities or special retirement bonds). Payroll deduction contributions would be transferred, at the employer's option:

—To IRA providers designated by the employer;

—To IRAs designated by employees (if the employer allowed employees to choose their own provider in addition to the provider that the employer had selected); or

—To a fallback collective retirement account if the employer or employee failed to designate a provider.

The proposal is designed to minimize the employer's administrative functions and should involve little if any out-of-pocket employer cost. Many firms already offer their workers direct deposit of paychecks. Many use automatic or electronic payroll arrangements (some of which are web-based) or payroll software, or they outsource to a payroll service provider. Virtually all make payroll deposits to comply with income tax withholding (federal and state) and withholding for such things as Social Security, Medicare, and unemployment insurance. Payroll deposit to IRAs would not require much more effort from employers. They would facilitate employee saving by forwarding employees' contributions to their IRAs without having to sponsor a plan; make any matching or other employer contributions; comply with federal plan qualification or retirement insurance security requirements; select investments for employees; set up IRAs or other accounts for employees; or determine employees' eligibility to contribute to an IRA.

Many employers that still process payroll by hand would be exempted under the exception for very small employers. Firms not exempted could have the option of piggybacking the payroll deposits to IRAs onto the federal tax deposits they currently make online, by mail, or by delivery to the local bank.

The self-employed and other workers without employers would be encouraged to contribute to IRAs by automatic debit. Professional and trade associations could arrange the automatic debit and the IRAs themselves. The self-employed could also send deposits to IRAs in conjunction with their quarterly estimated taxes or instruct the IRS to make direct deposit to IRAs of part or all of their income tax refunds. Independent contractors receiving regular payments from a business could arrange for automatic payroll deduction to an IRA in the same way as employees.

Automatic IRAs would be carefully designed to avoid competing with or crowding out employer-based retirement plans and employer contributions for employees. In fact, for several reasons, extensive use of Automatic IRAs can be expected to expand opportunities to market 401(k), SIMPLE, and other tax-favored plans to employers.

—The maximum permitted annual contribution to IRAs (currently $5,000 with an additional $1,000 for those age 50 or older) exceeds employees' average 401(k) contribution but is not enough to satisfy the appetite for tax-favored saving of business owners or decisionmakers. They would still have an incentive to adopt a SIMPLE plan, which allows tax-favored employee contributions of up to $11,500, or a 401(k), whose limit is $16,500. Together with employer contributions, which are allowed in the 401(k) and required in the SIMPLE, total contributions to a 401(k) can reach $49,000 (and $5,500 higher for employees 50 or older).

—The Automatic IRA tax credit would be smaller than the tax credit small employers receive when adopting new retirement plans.

—To encourage employer retirement plans, firms would not be asked (or allowed) to contribute to Automatic IRAs. Employers interested in contributing for their employees or saving more for themselves would have to adopt 401(k)s or other plans.

Thus the proposal steers clear of discouraging employers from sponsoring actual retirement plans. In fact, the intended indirect effect of the proposal is to draw small employers into the private pension system by demonstrating the power and convenience of tax-preferred payroll deposit saving and whetting employees' appetite for it.

Within either the online clearinghouse that links employers with IRA providers or, if necessary a fall-back investment platform, investment management, record-keeping, and other administrative functions would be contracted to private financial institutions to the fullest extent practicable. Costs would be minimized through a no-frills design relying on index or other similarly low-cost investment funds, economies of scale, and maximum use of electronic technologies. The investment menu would be kept simple: money would go to a low-cost, diversified, asset-allocated fund unless the individual instead selected from among a few low-cost, diversified alternatives (probably including Treasury inflation-protected securities).

In addition, a powerful financial incentive for individuals to contribute might be provided by matching deposits to their IRAs. Employers could offer no such match, but the private financial institutions that maintain the accounts could deliver matching contributions and be reimbursed through federal tax credits. Alternatively, the Saver's Credit for voluntary contributions might be expanded to provide a match. Matching deposits are not, however, part of the basic Automatic IRA proposal.

The rest of this chapter explains in some detail each of the main points in our proposal.

Saving Up Is Hard to Do

Many American families, especially those with lower or middle incomes, find it hard to save, especially for retirement or other long-term needs. In 2004 half of all households headed by people aged 55 to 59 had $13,000 or less in employer-based 401(k)-type plans or tax-preferred saving plans.[2] The personal saving rate in the United States has declined steadily over the last two decades and in recent years has hovered around zero.[3] Moreover, traditional corporate defined-benefit pension plans are becoming rarer, and few expect Social Security to provide increased benefits in the future.

In general, those who tend to be in the best financial position to confront retirement are the 41 percent of the workforce that participate in employer-sponsored retirement plans.[4] About seven or eight of every ten workers who are

Figure 4-1. *The Power of Automatic Retirement Saving*[a]

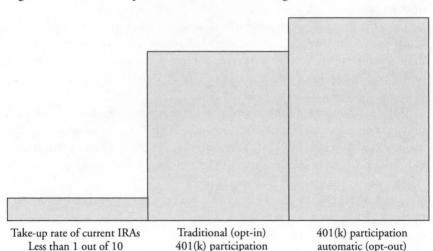

| Take-up rate of current IRAs
Less than 1 out of 10 | Traditional (opt-in)
401(k) participation
3 out of 4 | 401(k) participation
automatic (opt-out)
More than 9 out of 10 |

Source: Brigitte C. Madrian and Dennis F. Shea, "The Power of Suggestion: Inertia in 401(k) Participation and Savings Behavior," *Quarterly Journal of Economics* 116 (November 2001): 1149–87; Craig Copeland, "401(k)-Type Plans and Individual Retirement Accounts (IRAs)," EBRI Notes 28, no. 10 (October 2007), http://www.ebri.org/pdf/EBRI_Notes_10a-2007.pdf.

a. The Automatic IRA proposal would extend payroll-based saving to the 78 million American workers not covered by an employer-based retirement plan. Participation in IRAs would increase if payroll deduction were used and automatic enrollment encouraged.

eligible participate in employer-sponsored 401(k) plans, while the corresponding take-up rate for IRAs (which typically have no connection to the workplace or payroll system) tends to be less than one in ten. Moreover, an increasing share of 401(k) plans include automatic features that, by applying to all workers except those who explicitly choose an alternative, make saving easier and raise participation to rates often exceeding nine in ten (figure 4-1).

Yet among 155 million working Americans, some 78 million—about half—work for an employer that does not offer a 401(k) or any other type of employer-sponsored plan. Another 16 million fail to participate in or are not eligible for their employer's plan. Among the approximately 94 million full-time, full-year wage and salary workers aged 21 to 64, 63 percent work for an employer that sponsors a plan, and 55 percent participate.[5]

These facts reveal a major gap between our public policy goals relating to retirement security and the market's ability to meet those goals. The major federal tax expenditures and associated regulation of private pensions attest to a recognition of some need for public intervention to address this shortfall.

The causes of inadequate saving for retirement are several. Many people find it difficult to plan for retirement and to defer consumption. For many if not most, the necessary financial sophistication and self-discipline do not come naturally or easily. Many people do not exercise the initiative required to save in an IRA.

Our approach is intended to help households overcome these barriers by building on the successful use in 401(k) plans of automatic features that lead employees toward sensible decisions while allowing them to make alternative choices. Since their inception, 401(k) plans have encouraged contributions through payroll deposits that continue automatically ("set it and forget it") unless the employee takes the initiative to stop or modify them. Starting in 1998, the U.S. Treasury Department and the Internal Revenue Service (IRS) have issued a series of rulings defining, permitting, and encouraging the automatic initiation of those payroll deposits (which they called "automatic enrollment") and automatic rollover in 401(k) and other salary-reduction retirement saving plans.[6] Over time, the 401(k) market has responded by moving to automatic enrollment, automatic investment choices, and related automatic features. In 2006 Congress added its voice to this process by eliminating or reducing several barriers to the adoption of automatic 401(k) features (see chapter 2).[7]

Although workplace saving through employer contributions or regular payroll deposits tends to be the most effective vehicle for building retirement savings, a majority of small employers do not offer a retirement plan. Many of them, unaware of the low-cost, simplified 401(k) and SIMPLE IRA plan options now available (often online), mistakenly perceive plan sponsorship as a complex and costly undertaking.[8] Small business owners may be concerned that they have no one on staff with the knowledge and time to sort through the options for plan adoption and to administer the plan on an ongoing basis. In addition, small businesses, unlike larger firms, cannot spread fixed plan administration and investment costs across a large number of employees to make per capita costs more manageable. They also lack the economies of scale and bargaining power of a large employer when negotiating fees and expenses with financial services providers.

Our proposal is designed to reduce the transaction costs for small employers that adopt and maintain an Automatic IRA for their employees by using the spare capacity for saving that is inherent in employer payroll systems. By taking smaller employers and their employees part of the way down the path toward plan sponsorship and participation, the Automatic IRA approach would open up this market more widely to the financial providers, third-party administrators, and professionals who market, provide, and help administer employer plans.

Widespread use of payroll deposit to contribute to IRAs would lay the groundwork for a far deeper penetration of the small business market by 401(k) and SIMPLE plans. Either at the outset or after a year or two, many small business owners will ask how they or a key manager can save more for themselves than only $5,000 a year, the general 2009 IRA limit. Some will be interested in exploring how they could make a very modest matching contribution for their employees, at least in years when business has been good.

The answer to both questions is that the Automatic IRA is designed with a modest contribution limit and no employer contributions to induce employers to graduate to a 401(k) or SIMPLE plan. Even when firms did not choose to sponsor 401(k)-type plans, however, the Automatic IRA proposed here would apply the key lessons learned from 401(k) plans so that more workers could enjoy automated saving to build assets, without imposing any significant burden on employers.[9] Employers could help their employees save simply by transferring a portion of their pay to an IRA, preferably by direct deposit, at little or no cost.

Another reason that employer plans are less prevalent in the small business market is that many financial providers have found it less profitable or unprofitable to serve plans with a small average account size. Many small workforces have lower-wage employees with less ability or desire to contribute, and it can be difficult to find larger accounts to cross-subsidize the costs of servicing smaller accounts. However, many financial providers might be interested in receiving rollovers from such accounts if and when they have grown to a profitable size.

Our proposal seeks to address this concern by providing a backstop arrangement contracted to the private sector that would give an option to those employee groups that the financial services industry is not interested in serving. As described below, pooling of contributions in a standard, low-cost, automatic investment and a limited number of investment alternatives would lower costs through economies of scale, standardization, and elimination of most sales and marketing expenses. Once accounts had grown sufficiently, they could be automatically reinvested or could be rolled over, substantially increasing the financial services industry's assets under management.[10]

The Proposed Solution

The Automatic IRA is a means of facilitating direct deposits to a retirement account, giving employees access to the power of direct-deposit saving. In much the same way that millions of employees have their pay directly deposited to their account at a bank or other financial institution, and millions more elect to contribute to 401(k) plans by payroll deduction, employees would have the choice to have their employer send an amount they select directly from their paychecks to an IRA. Employers generally would be required to offer their employees the opportunity to save through such direct-deposit or payroll-deduction IRAs.

Payroll deposit to IRAs is not new. In 1997 Congress encouraged employers not ready or willing to sponsor a retirement plan to at least offer their employees the opportunity to contribute to IRAs through payroll deduction.[11] Both the IRS and the Labor Department have issued administrative guidance to publicize the payroll-deduction or direct-deposit IRA option for employers and to "facilitate the establishment of payroll deduction IRAs."[12] This guidance has made clear that employers can offer direct-deposit IRAs without having the arrangement treated as employer sponsorship of a retirement plan, which would subject it to federal Employee Retirement Income Security Act (ERISA) or qualified-plan requirements.[13] However, it appears that few employers actually have direct-deposit or payroll-deduction IRAs—at least in a way that actively encourages employees to take advantage of the arrangement. After some years of encouragement by the government, payroll-deposit IRAs have simply not caught on widely among employers and offer little opportunity for employees to save.

Our Proposal from the Employer's Perspective

Our strategy is designed to induce employers to offer, and employees to take up, direct-deposit or payroll-deduction saving. To the fullest extent possible, the arrangement would be structured to avoid imposing costs and responsibilities on employers.

Under our proposal, firms that do not offer employees a qualified retirement plan, such as a defined-benefit pension, profit-sharing, or 401(k) plan, would receive a temporary tax credit if they let their employees use their payroll system to make payroll-deduction contributions to IRAs. For the larger and more established small businesses that would be required to offer employees this opportunity, the tax credit would represent a small recognition that the employer is being asked to institute a new procedure, albeit one that involves little if any out-of-pocket cost.

To help firms meet those costs, the tax credit would be available for the first two years that its payroll-deposit saving program was in operation. This Automatic IRA credit would be designed to avoid competing with the tax credit available under current law to small businesses that adopt a new employer-sponsored retirement plan such as a 401(k) or other qualified plan or a SIMPLE IRA. Under current law, an employer with 100 or fewer employees can generally claim a tax credit of half the cost of establishing and administering a new retirement plan (including educating employees about the plan) up to $500 a year for each of the first three years of the plan.

The Automatic IRA tax credit could be set, for example, at $25 per employee enrolled, and it could be capped at $250 a year for its two years of availability. That would make it meaningful only to very small businesses. The larger credit for establishing a new employer plan would still favor 401(k) and SIMPLE plans over Automatic IRAs.

Employers could not claim both the 401(k) plan start-up credit and the proposed Automatic IRA credit; otherwise, some employers might exclude some employees from a new 401(k) plan to earn an additional credit for providing them with an Automatic IRA. Employers also would be ineligible for the Automatic IRA credit if they had sponsored a retirement plan during the preceding three years for substantially the same group of employees.

Employers that sponsor a retirement plan for their employees would generally be unaffected by the Automatic IRA provision. But an employer that offered the retirement plan only to employees in a particular subsidiary or division or other business classification would be required to make an Automatic IRA available to the others (except for employees who may be exempted under qualified plan coverage standards, specifically employees under age 18, those represented by unions, nonresident aliens, and those who work only a few hours a week or have not completed a year of service).

Thus the arrangement would be structured to avoid, to the fullest extent possible, employer costs or responsibilities. The tax credit would be available both to those firms that are required to offer payroll deposit to all of their employees and to the small or new firms that are not required to offer the Automatic IRA but do so voluntarily. The intent would be to encourage, without requiring, the smallest employers to participate.

For example, assume that Joe employs ten people in his auto body shop and does not sponsor a retirement plan for his employees. If he chooses to adopt a 401(k) or SIMPLE IRA plan, he and each of his employees generally can contribute up to $16,500 for a 401(k) or $11,500 for a SIMPLE each year, and the business might be required to make employer contributions. Joe can claim a start-up tax credit of half of his costs over three years, up to $500 a year. Alternatively, if Joe decides only to offer his employees payroll deposits to an IRA, the business will not make employer contributions, and Joe can claim a tax credit for each of the next two years of $25 for each employee who contributes out of his own salary (in this case up to the maximum Automatic IRA tax credit of $250 a year).

For many if not most employers, offering payroll-deposit IRAs would involve little or no cost. Unlike a 401(k) or other employer-sponsored retirement plans, the employer would not be maintaining a plan but simply acting as a forwarding agent for employee contributions. Employer contributions to payroll-deposit IRAs would not be required or even permitted. Employers willing to make retirement contributions for their employees would continue to be able to do so by sponsoring a retirement plan, such as a SIMPLE IRA, 401(k), or pension plan.

Employer-sponsored retirement plans are the saving vehicles of choice and should be encouraged; payroll-deposit IRAs are a fallback designed for employees not fortunate enough to be covered by an actual employer retirement plan. They are also intended to encourage more employers to decide, whether immediately or eventually, to sponsor a plan of their own.

Payroll-deposit IRAs also would minimize employer responsibilities. Firms would not be required to

—Comply with plan qualification or ERISA rules

—Establish or maintain a trust to hold assets (because the IRAs would receive the contributions)

—Determine whether employees were eligible to contribute to IRAs

—Select investments for employee contributions

—Select among IRA providers

—Set up IRAs for employees

Employers would be required simply to allow employees to make payroll-deduction deposits to an IRA, with a standard notice informing employees of the Automatic IRA saving option and a standard form eliciting each employee's decision to participate or opt out. Employers would then implement deposits elected by employees. Employers would remit the direct deposits to their IRA providers on the schedule they were already following for federal payroll and withholding tax deposits—usually biweekly or monthly.

Thus a requirement to offer to forward employee contributions to an IRA by payroll deduction would not be onerous but would dovetail neatly with what employers already do. The employee's payroll-deposit IRA election might be made on an attachment or addendum to the federal income tax withholding form. Because employees' salary reduction contributions to IRAs would ordinarily receive tax-favored treatment, the employer would report on Form W-2, the federal salary and wage reporting form, the reduced amount of the employee's taxable wages together with the amount of the employee's contribution.

Direct Deposit

Our proposal seeks to capitalize on the rapid trend toward automated or electronic fund transfers. With the spread of new, low-cost technologies, employers are increasingly using automated systems to manage payroll. Many employers hire a payroll service provider to perform these functions, including direct deposit of paychecks to accounts designated by employees or contractors. Some keep their payroll-tax and related functions in house but use readily available software or largely paperless online means of making federal tax deposits and perhaps other funds transfers, just as increasing numbers of households pay bills and manage other financial transactions online.

For the many firms that already offer their workers direct deposit, including many that use outside payroll providers, direct deposit to an IRA would entail no additional cost, even in the short term, insofar as the employer's system has unused fields that could be used for the additional direct deposit destination. Other small businesses still write their own paychecks by hand, complete the federal tax deposit and reporting forms by hand, and deliver them to employees and to the local bank or other depositary institution. Our proposal would not require these employers to incur the cost (if any) of transitioning to automatic payroll processing or using online systems, although it might have the beneficial effect of encouraging such transitions.

At the same time, we would not be inclined to deny the benefits of payroll deduction savings to all employees of employers that do not yet use automatic payroll processing (and we would not want to give small employers any incentive to drop automatic payroll processing). These employees would benefit from the ability to save through regular payroll deposits at the workplace whether the deposits are made electronically or by hand. Employees would still have the advantages of tax-favored saving, which, once begun, continues automatically, and is more likely to begin because of workplace enrollment arrangements and peer group reinforcement, and need not cause a visible reduction in take-home pay if begun promptly when employees are hired.

For employers that do not use automatic payroll processing, we contemplate a three-pronged strategy. First, a large proportion of the employers that still process their payroll by hand would be exempted as very small employers. Our proposal would focus on employers that already offer their employees direct deposit of paychecks but have not used that technology to provide employees with a convenient way to save for retirement.

Second, employers would have the option of piggybacking their payroll deposits to IRAs onto their federal tax deposits. The process, including timing and logistics, for both sets of deposits would be the same. Accompanying the existing federal tax deposit forms would be similar payroll deposit savings forms enabling employers to send all payroll deposit savings to a single destination. Small employers that mail or deliver their federal tax deposit checks and forms to the local bank would add another check and form to the same mailing.

Third, the existing convenient, low-cost, online system for federal tax deposits could be expanded to accommodate a parallel stream of payroll-deduction saving payments.

The cost to employers making payroll deduction savings available to their employees would be minimal. Employers would not be required to make contributions or to comply with plan qualification or federal requirements with respect to these arrangements. Implementing employee decisions to participate or to opt out might occasionally require employers to address mistakes or misunderstandings regarding payroll deductions and deposit directions. The time and attention required of employers could generally be expected to be minimized through orderly communications, written or electronic, between employees and employers, facilitated by the use of standard forms that piggyback on the existing IRS forms such as the W-4 used by individuals to elect levels of income tax withholding.

The requirement to offer payroll deposits to IRAs as a substitute for sponsoring a retirement plan would not apply to the smallest firms (say, those with fewer than ten employees) or to firms that have not been in business for at least two years. However, even exempt firms would be encouraged to participate. A possible alternate approach to implementation of this program would be to require payroll deposit for the first year or two only by employers above a slightly larger size. This tryout of the new system could identify improvements before broader implementation began.

Employees who do not work for an employer that offers a payroll-deposit system would be able to use other mechanisms to facilitate saving. These include instructing the IRS to deposit a portion of an income tax refund into an IRA, setting up an automatic debit arrangement for IRA contributions from employees' bank accounts (perhaps with the help of a professional or trade association), and making IRA contributions together with quarterly estimated tax payments.

The Proposal from the Employee's Perspective

In the case of an employer that does not sponsor a retirement plan, employees eligible for payroll-deposit savings might be, for example, all employees who have worked for the employer on a regular basis (including part-time) for a specified period of time (such as three months), which would exclude the highest-turnover employees and seasonal workers, As noted, if an employer sponsored a retirement plan, it would not be required to provide payroll deposits to Automatic IRAs unless its plan excluded a portion of the work force (such as a division or subsidiary).

Like a 401(k) contribution, the amount elected by the employee as a salary reduction contribution generally would be tax favored. If channeled to a traditional IRA, the contribution would be excluded from taxable income when it was made, but it—and whatever earnings it generated—would be taxed upon withdrawal from the IRA. A Roth IRA is quite different. Funds deposited into a Roth IRA are taxed, but withdrawals—those representing earnings that meet certain conditions as well as deposits—are entirely tax free. The statute authorizing

Automatic IRAs could specify which type of IRA was the default. (Employees who did not qualify to make a deductible IRA contribution or a Roth IRA contribution (for example, because their income exceeded eligibility thresholds) would be responsible for making the appropriate adjustment on their tax return. The firm would have no responsibility for ensuring that employees satisfied the applicable IRA eligibility requirements or contribution limits.)

The choice between a traditional and a Roth IRA is another decision that can impede participation. For many individuals, making this choice based on an informed and rational analysis would not be easy. In the interest of sparing households the need to make the decision, we strongly believe that one or the other type of IRA should be automatically prescribed (with, perhaps, the choice to opt for the other). Many households would simply go along with the standard option, while others would try to figure out the better alternative for them.

A reasonable case can also be made for simply prescribing one or the other type of IRA as the only available receptacle for contributions to Automatic IRAs. We are tentatively inclined to make the Roth IRA the presumptive choice for Automatic IRA deposits, because the Roth may be more beneficial for lower-income and moderate-income workers who lack sufficient taxable income to take full advantage of the traditional IRA tax deduction at the time of contribution but who may expect to be in higher tax brackets late in their careers. In addition, the Roth is often thought to be preferable by those who expect high federal budget deficits to eventually drive up future tax rates. All other things being equal, the Roth's tax advantage for payouts would likely be more valuable than the traditional IRA's tax deduction for contributions.

A number of other factors may militate in favor of defaulting to the Roth. First, for many, it comes as an unpleasant surprise that the account balance they have accumulated for decades in a deductible IRA or a traditional deductible 401(k) is worth far less than expected because it cannot be drawn upon without losing a substantial portion to taxation. The Roth generally avoids this unpleasant surprise, permitting the individual to plan for retirement without having to adjust projected or actual savings for an uncertain future tax bite.

Second, the Roth IRA, by producing less taxable income in retirement years, could avoid exposing some individuals to a higher rate of income tax on Social Security benefits in retirement. Third, while it is hoped that few participants would choose to withdraw funds from their IRAs before they reach or approach retirement age, those who do withdraw from a deductible IRA not long after contributing generally will be subject to both income tax and a 10-percent early withdrawal penalty on the entire amount withdrawn. In contrast, withdrawals from a Roth IRA within a few years after contributions are made will not be subject to income tax or the 10-percent penalty on the withdrawal except to the extent that it consists of earnings (which are likely to make up a relatively small portion of the account of those who withdraw relatively soon).

Finally, the fact that all but very high-income employees are eligible to contribute to a Roth IRA may make the Automatic IRA program somewhat simpler to administer because virtually all of the target population would be eligible. Individuals saving in a deductible IRA may need to be mindful of their possible eligibility for a qualified plan in another, concurrent job or of their spouse's eligibility. Some may be ineligible to make deductible contributions but permitted to make nondeductible contributions to a traditional IRA, which could be viewed as an advantage or as a drawback because of the additional layer of complexity it entails.

The Automatic IRA

Even if employers were required to offer direct deposit to IRAs, various impediments would prevent many eligible employees from taking advantage of the opportunity. To save in an IRA, individuals must answer at least five key and often thorny questions:

—Should they participate at all?

—At which financial institution should they open an IRA (or, if they have an IRA already, should they add to it or open a new one)?

—Should the IRA be a traditional or a Roth?

—How much should they contribute?

—How should they invest their IRA money?

Once these decisions have been made, the individual must still take the initiative to fill out the requisite paperwork to participate. Even in 401(k) plans, millions of employees are deterred from participating because inertia prevents them from making these important financial decisions or from getting around to enrolling.

These obstacles can be overcome by making participation easier and more automatic, in much the same way as is being done increasingly in the 401(k) universe. The employer or other 401(k) plan sponsor sets up an account in the plan for each participating employee, making a savings vehicle ready to receive regular payroll deductions from the employee. Once the employee has elected to participate, deposits continue to occur automatically and regularly, without the need for any action by the employee. To get the ball rolling, an increasing percentage of 401(k) plan sponsors are using automatic enrollment.[14]

Automatic enrollment, which typically has been applied only to newly hired employees, rather than to all nonparticipating employees, has produced dramatic increases in 401(k) participation, especially by lower-income and minority workers.[15] In view of the basic similarities between employee payroll-deduction saving in a 401(k) and a direct-deposit IRA arrangement, federal law should, at a minimum, explicitly permit employers to automatically enroll employees in direct-deposit IRAs.[16]

The conditions imposed by the Treasury Department on 401(k) automatic enrollment would apply to payroll-deposit IRA automatic enrollment as well: all employees who could potentially be automatically enrolled must receive advance written notice (and annual notice) regarding the terms and conditions of the saving opportunity and the enrollment, including the procedure for opting out, and all employees must be able to opt out at any time.

It is not at all clear, however, whether simply *allowing* employers to use automatic enrollment with payroll deposit IRAs would prove effective. A key motivation for using it in 401(k) plans is to improve the plan's performance under the 401(k) nondiscrimination test by encouraging moderate- and lower-paid ("non-highly compensated") employees to participate and to contribute as much as possible. That in turn increases the permissible level of tax-preferred contributions for highly compensated employees. This employer self-interest is absent from payroll-deposit IRAs, which lack nondiscrimination standards.

Similarly, the absence of such standards in payroll-deposit IRAs gives the employer less incentive than a 401(k) sponsor to provide automatic increases in the initial contribution rate. Gradual automatic increases in 401(k) contribution rates have been found to make automatic 401(k) enrollment more effective. The automatic contribution rate can increase, unless the employee opts out of the increase, either on a regular, scheduled basis, such as 4 percent of salary in the first year, 5 percent in the second, and so forth, or in coordination with future pay raises.[17]

A second major motivation for using 401(k)-style automatic enrollment in many companies is management's sense of responsibility or concern for employees' retirement security. Many executives involved in managing employee plans and benefits have opted for automatic enrollment and other automatic 401(k) features (such as asset-allocated default investments) because they believe far too many employees are saving too little and investing unwisely and need a strong push to "do the right thing." Closely allied to this motivation is the employer's interest in recruiting and retaining valuable employees.

There is reason to believe, however, that employers impelled by these interests tend to be those that have already chosen to sponsor a 401(k) or other retirement plan. By contrast, those that have not sponsored a plan are more likely to be among the group of employers that have a more laissez-faire approach. These include many smaller employers that may not feel that encouraging employees to save is their role. Some may offer health insurance, and both employees and employer might regard contributions to employees' share of health premiums as a higher-priority use for employees' limited resources than retirement saving contributions, especially in view of the rising cost of health insurance.

Third, in the case of payroll-deposit IRAs, employers might have greater concern about potential employee reaction to automatic enrollment because there is no employer matching contribution. With 401(k) plans, the employer match gives the appearance of a high rate of return on the employees' investment. That gives confidence to 401(k) sponsors that automatic enrollment does right by their employees and that they need not worry unduly about potential complaints from workers who fail to read the notice informing them that they would be automatically enrolled unless they opted out.

On the other hand, some employers might be more inclined to use automatic enrollment with payroll-deposit IRAs because greater employee participation would not increase the employer's matching costs. In addition our proposal provides that the amount of the two-year tax credit for employers using Automatic IRAs would rise with the number of employees participating.

A good case can be made for requiring, rather then merely allowing, employers to use automatic enrollment and automatic contribution increases for their direct-deposit IRAs. Automatic enrollment would probably increase participation sharply while leaving employees the option to decline enrollment. But employers that do not offer a qualified plan or a match are unlikely to use automatic enrollment voluntarily.

The arguments against such a requirement include the concern that a workforce whose demand for a qualified retirement plan was too weak to get one might react unfavorably to being automatically enrolled in direct-deposit savings without a matching contribution. In addition, some small-business owners who have only a few employees and work with all of them every day might regard automatic enrollment as unnecessary because of the constant flow of communication between owner and employees.

It is noteworthy, however, that public opinion polling shows strong support among registered voters for making saving automatic: 71 percent of respondents favored automatic enrollment, investment, and contribution increases, with the opportunity to opt out at any stage.[18] A vast majority (85 percent) said that if they were automatically enrolled in a 401(k), they would not opt out. And 59 percent preferred a workplace IRA with automatic enrollment to one without.

AUTO ENROLLMENT OR REQUIRED RESPONSE. Short of automatic enrollment in an IRA, employees could be required to explicitly accept or decline enrollment in an IRA. With 401(k) plans, evidence suggests that this approach can raise participation nearly as much as automatic enrollment does. Requiring an explicit choice picks up many who would otherwise fail to participate because they did not complete and return the enrollment form either because they could not decide on contribution levels or investments or because they just did not get around to it.

Accordingly, a possible strategy for increasing participation in payroll-deposit IRAs would be to generally require employers to obtain written or electronic notification from each eligible employee—an explicit up-or-down election— either accepting or declining the direct deposit to an IRA. Employers that chose to enroll their employees in the direct deposit IRAs automatically would be excused from the requirement because all employees who failed to elect would automatically participate.

What if an employer that opted for this up-or-down election procedure was unable for some reason to obtain an election from a particular employee? Under our approach, the employer would inform the employee that failure to respond would lead to automatic enrollment at the specified automatic contribution rate and in the specified investment and would give the employee a final election opportunity.

This might be viewed as tantamount to requiring all employers to use automatic enrollment. After all, it carries out what is arguably the primary function of automatic enrollment: ensuring that mere inertia, procrastination, or indecision does not keep anyone from participating. However, an up-or-down election procedure may not frame the choice for the employee in a manner that tilts in favor of participation, does not convey the same implicit employer endorsement of participation that automatic enrollment does, and does not necessarily steer individuals to an automatic contribution rate and investment because it does not frame the choice around a presumptive package unless employees initially fail to elect.

This exemption—treating an employer's use of automatic enrollment as an alternative means of satisfying its required-response obligation—would add an incentive for employers to use automatic enrollment without requiring them to use it. Any firms that preferred not to use automatic enrollment would simply obtain a completed election form from each employee. And under either approach, participation would likely increase significantly, perhaps even approaching the level that might be achieved if automatic enrollment were required for all payroll-deposit IRAs.

This combined strategy for promoting payroll-deposit IRA participation could be applied separately to new hires and existing employees. An employer that automatically enrolled new hires would be exempted from obtaining completed elections from all new hires but not from existing employees. An employer that automatically enrolled both new hires and existing employees would be excused from having to obtain elections from both groups.

Employers would not be obligated to obtain a new election from each employee every year. As in most 401(k) plans, the initial election would continue unless the employee chose to change it. Similarly, an employee who failed to submit an election form and was automatically enrolled by default in the payroll-deposit IRA would continue to be enrolled until the employee took action to make an explicit election.

After some period of time, however, employees could be offered automatic increases in their Automatic IRA contribution rates, on terms similar to those applicable to the initial automatic contributions. Employers would be able to use flexible automatic enrollment with respect to these increases, either obtaining an election regarding increases from each employee or providing that employees who did not submit elections would be deemed to have elected to increase their Automatic IRA contributions at a specified gradual rate.

To maximize participation, employers would receive a standard enrollment module reflecting current best practices in enrollment procedures. A national website would provide firms with standard employee notice and election forms as well as standard enrollment procedures. The website and the fallback Automatic IRA platform would promote employee education and best practices as they evolved, such as automatic enrollment and, potentially, automatic annuitization. Especially with the decline of traditional defined benefit pension plans, the need is increasing for readily available, low-cost, guaranteed lifetime income—and for innovative ways of delivering it—in individual account saving vehicles. The fallback Automatic IRA account would provide a national platform that could facilitate innovation and development of annuity products suitable for IRAs and other account-based retirement vehicles.

The use of automatic enrollment would be encouraged in several ways. First, the standard materials provided to employers would be framed to present auto enrollment as the presumptive or perhaps even the default enrollment method, although employers would be able to opt out easily in favor of simply obtaining an up-or-down response from all employees. In effect, such a "double-default" approach would use the same principle at both the employer and employee level, automatically enrolling employers into automatically enrolling employees.

Second, as noted above, employers using automatic enrollment to promote participation would not need to obtain responses from unresponsive employees, and the ultimate outcome for an employee who failed to submit a required election would be automatic enrollment. Finally, the employer tax credit would give employers a modest incentive to encourage participation, which auto enrollment is likely to do.

COMPLIANCE AND ENFORCEMENT. Employers' use of the required elections by employees would help solve an additional problem: enforcing compliance with the requirement that employers offer direct-deposit savings. As a practical matter, many employers might question whether the IRS would ever really be able to monitor and enforce such a requirement. Employers might believe that, if asked by the IRS why none of its employees used direct-deposit IRAs, they could respond that their employees were told about the option but were not interested. However, if employers had to obtain a signed election from each eligible employee who declined the payroll-deposit option, the IRS could audit their files for each employee's election. This by itself would likely improve compliance.

In fact, a single paper or e-mail notice could advise the employee of the opportunity to engage in payroll-deduction savings and elicit the employee's response. The notice and the employee's election might be added or attached to the IRS tax-withholding form that new hires must complete. If the employer chose to use automatic enrollment, the notice would also inform employees of that feature (including the automatic contribution level and investment and the procedure for opting out), and the employer's records would need to show that employees who failed to submit an election were in fact participating in the pay-roll-deduction savings.

Employers would be required to certify annually to the IRS that they were in compliance with the payroll-deposit savings requirements. This might be done in conjunction with the existing IRS Form W-3 that employers file annually to transmit W-2 forms to the government. Failure to offer payroll-deposit savings would, if necessary, trigger an excise tax on the employer for each employee affected by the violation. This sanction would be less than the one employers face if they violate the federal requirement (known as COBRA) to offer certain employees who lose their health benefits to continue their coverage, and would be subject to exceptions and opportunities for mitigation and relief that are gen-erally based on the corresponding COBRA exceptions.

In addition, employees would be protected from an employer's failure to remit employee payroll-deduction contributions by a compliance and enforce-ment regime substantially similar to the one that applies to an employer's failure to remit payroll tax deductions.

IRAs are inherently portable. Unlike a 401(k) or other employer plan, an IRA survives and functions independently of the individual saver's employment status. Thus the IRA owner is not at risk of forfeiting or losing the account or of suffering an interruption in the ability to contribute when changing or losing employment. As a broad generalization, the Automatic IRAs outlined here pre-sumably would be freely transferable to and with other IRAs and qualified plans that permit such transfers, although, as discussed below, there may be a need for some restrictions on those transfers.

How They Would Invest

Most current direct deposit arrangements use a payroll-deduction savings mech-anism similar to the 401(k); unlike the 401(k), however, the employee does not have a ready-made vehicle or account to receive deposits. The employee must open a recipient account and must identify the account to the employer. However, where the purpose of the direct deposit is saving, it would be useful to many individuals who would rather not choose a specific IRA to have a ready-made fallback or default account available for the deposits.

Under this approach, modeled after the SIMPLE IRA, which currently is estimated to cover some 3 million employees, individuals who wish to direct their contributions to a specific IRA would do so. The employer would follow these directions as employers ordinarily do when they make direct deposits of paychecks to accounts specified by employees. At the same time, the employer could simplify its task by remitting all employee contributions in the first instance to IRAs at a single private financial institution that the employer designates.[19] However, even in this case, employees would be able to transfer the contributions, without cost, from the employer's designated financial institution to an IRA provider chosen by the employee.

By designating a single IRA provider to receive all contributions, the employer could avoid the potential administrative hassles of directing deposits to a multitude of different IRAs for different employees, while employees would be free to transfer their contributions from the employer's designated institution to an IRA provider of their own choosing. Even this approach, though, still places a burden on either the employer or the employee to choose an IRA. For many small businesses, the choice might not be obvious or simple. In addition, the market may not be very robust because at least some of the major financial institutions that provide IRAs may well not be interested in selling new accounts unless they seem likely to grow enough to be profitable within a reasonable time. Some of the major financial firms appear to be motivated at least as much by the objective of maximizing the average account balance as by the goal of maximizing aggregate assets under management. They therefore may shun small accounts.

The current experience with automatic rollover IRAs is a case in point. Firms are required to establish these IRAs as a default vehicle for 401(k) and other qualified plan participants whose employment terminates with an account balance of not more than $5,000 and who fail to provide any direction regarding rollover or other payout. The objective is to reduce leakage of benefits from the tax-favored retirement system by stopping involuntary cash-outs of account balances between $1,000 and $5,000.[20] Because plan sponsors are required to set up IRAs only for "unresponsive" participants—those who fail to give instructions as to the disposition of their benefits—these IRAs are presumed to be less likely than other IRAs to attract additional contributions. Accordingly, significant segments of the IRA provider industry have not been eager to cater to this segment of the market.

Automatic IRAs differ importantly from automatic-rollover IRAs, however. Even if they start small, they are likely to experience continuing growth. In contrast to automatic-rollover IRAs, whose owners have failed to respond to the plan sponsor's notices, there is no reason to expect Automatic IRA owners generally to be unresponsive or unlikely to continue contributing. Accordingly, the Automatic IRAs hold much more promise for financial providers.

In addition, to benefit the financial institutions that serve as IRA trustees and custodians, the fallback Automatic IRA arrangement outlined below might ultimately serve as both a source of rollovers to the financial services industry and a potential receptacle for their small and inactive or orphan IRAs. The path between industry and a collective standard IRA arrangement could be a two-way street. Pursuant to appropriate standards, IRA providers might be given the opportunity to "dump" a certain number of very small IRAs that are unprofitable because they have been inactive (not receiving contributions) for an extended period (in some cases, because the owner is deceased). These IRAs could be transferred to the central arrangement, which could serve as a low-cost incubator of small inactive accounts. At the same time, owners of IRAs within the arrangement that have grown to a profitable size could roll them over to private-sector providers.

A Standard Automatic Account

The prospect of tens of millions of relatively small personal retirement accounts with a likelihood of relatively meager growth suggests that the market might need to be encouraged to develop widely available, low-cost IRAs. Otherwise, for small savers, fixed-cost investment management and administrative fees might consume an unacceptably large share of earnings and even erode principal.[21]

We believe that a strong case can be made for a standard IRA that would be automatically available to receive direct-deposit contributions after either the employee or the employer had a chance to choose among IRA providers. We recognize, however, that some geographic areas or small business segments may be underserved by locally available IRA providers. For that reason, we propose that one of two national platforms be made available to any small business that has trouble finding an acceptable IRA.

The first and preferable approach would be the creation of at least one national website that could match employers with IRA providers interested in their business. Employers that went to the site would enter in basic information about their company and its workforce, and the site would connect the firm to providers willing to provide IRAs to the firm's employees. Ideally, the site would then allow the employer to set up accounts and a method to transfer IRA contributions from its employees to their Automatic IRAs.

However, if it proved impossible to find IRA providers interested in serving all small employers that are required to offer Automatic IRAs to their employees, then (and only then) the contributions would go to standard IRAs in a platform maintained and operated by private financial institutions under contract with the federal government. To the fullest extent practicable, the private sector would provide the investment funds, investment management, record-keeping, and related administrative services.

Although this arrangement resembles the federal Thrift Savings Plan (the 401(k)-type retirement savings plan for federal government employees) in certain respects, other ways to manage standard accounts to receive direct deposits that have not been directed elsewhere by employers or employees are equally possible, and the accounts need not be maintained by a governmental entity. Given sufficient quality control and adherence to reasonably uniform standards, various private financial institutions could contract to provide the default accounts, on a collective or individual institution basis, more or less interchangeably—perhaps allocating customers on a geographic basis or in accordance with other arrangements based on providers' capacity. These fund managers could be selected through competitive bidding.

Cost Containment

Both the direct-deposit IRAs expressly selected by employees and employers and the standardized direct-deposit IRAs would be designed to minimize the costs of investment management and account administration. It should be possible to realize substantial cost savings through economies of scale in asset management and administration, uniformity, electronic technologies, and investments in index funds or other low-cost funds.

In accordance with statutory guidelines for all direct-deposit IRAs, government contract specifications would call for a no-frills approach to participant services in the interest of minimizing costs. By contrast to the wide-open investment options provided in most current IRAs and the high (and costlier) level of customer service provided in many 401(k) plans, the standard account would provide only a few investment options (patterned after the Thrift Savings Plan and possibly more limited). It would permit individuals to change their investments only once or twice a year and would emphasize transparency of investment and other fees and other expenses.[22]

Specifically, costs of direct-deposit IRAs might be reduced by federal standards by, to the extent possible,

—Limiting the investment menu under the Automatic IRA to a standard default investment and only two or three alternatives

—Allowing individuals to change their investments only once or twice a year

—Specifying a low-cost automatic investment option and providing that, if any of an individual's account balance is invested in that option, all of it must be

—Prohibiting loans from the employee account (IRAs do not allow them in any event)

—Limiting, perhaps, preretirement withdrawals

—Limiting access to customer service call centers

—Contemplating moderate fees instead of large commissions

—Making compliance testing unnecessary

—Giving account owners only a single account statement a year, possibly delivered electronically (especially if daily valuation is built into the system and such valuation reports are available through some other means to account owners)

—Encouraging the use of online, electronic, and other new technologies for enrollment, fund transfers, record-keeping, and communications among IRA providers, participating employees, and employers. Electronic administration has considerable potential to cut costs.

The availability to savers of a major low-cost personal account alternative in the form of the standard account may even help, through market competition, to drive down the costs and fees of IRAs offered separately by private financial institutions. Through efficiencies associated with collective investment and greater uniformity, the standard account should help make smaller accounts more feasible by creating a low-cost alternative to the retail-type cost structure characteristic of current IRAs. It should also help create a broad infrastructure of individual savings accounts that would cover most of the working population.[23]

In conjunction with these steps, Congress and the regulators may be able to do more to require simplified, uniform disclosure and description of IRA investment and administrative fees and charges by building on previous work by the Labor Department and trade associations relating to 401(k) fees. Such disclosure should help consumers compare costs and thereby promote healthy price competition.

Another approach would begin by recognizing the trade-off between asset management costs and investment types. As a broad generalization, asset management charges tend to be low for money market funds, certificates of deposit, Treasury bonds, and certain other relatively low-risk, low-return investments that generally do not require active management. However, it appears that limiting individual accounts to these types of investments, at least over the long term, would be unnecessarily restrictive. As discussed below, passively managed index funds such as those used in the Thrift Savings Plan are also relatively inexpensive.[24]

A very different approach to cost containment would be to impose a statutory or regulatory limit on investment management and administrative fees.

One example is the United Kingdom's limit on permissible charges for management of "stakeholder pension" accounts—an annual fee cap of 150 basis points for five years that is scheduled to drop to 100 basis points thereafter.[25] Another example is the limit the U.S. Labor Department has imposed on fees charged by providers of automatic-rollover IRAs established by employers for terminating employees who fail to provide any direction regarding the disposition of account balances of up to $5,000. These labor regulations provide a fiduciary safe harbor for these IRAs that preserves principal and that does not charge fees greater than those charged by the IRA provider for its other IRAs.

Presumably, a mandatory limit would give rise to potential cross-subsidies from products that are free of any limit on fees to the IRAs that are subject to the fee limit, a result that could be viewed either as an inappropriate distortion or as a necessary and appropriate allocation of resources. The U.K. cost cap is widely considered to be a major reason for the failure of stakeholder pensions to attract support from financial firms. It could have a similar impact in the United States. We would view a mandatory limit as a last resort, preferring the market-based strategies outlined above.

Automatic Investment Fund Choice

Automatic IRAs would serve the important purpose of providing low-cost professional asset management to millions of savers, presumably improving their aggregate investment results. To that end, all of these accounts would offer an automatic investment fund for all deposits unless the individual chose otherwise. The standard automatic investment would serve several key purposes. First, it would encourage employee participation in direct-deposit savings by enabling employees who are satisfied with the default to simplify what may be the most difficult decision they would otherwise be required to make as a condition of participation—how to invest. Second, the automatic investment should encourage more employers to use automatic enrollment (and thereby boost employee participation) by saving them from having to choose a standard investment. This, in turn, would make it easier to protect employers from responsibility for IRA investments, especially employers using automatic enrollment (as discussed below).

We would not fully specify the automatic investment by statute. It is desirable to maintain a degree of flexibility in order to reflect a consensus of expert financial advice over time. The advisability of such an approach has become more evident in view of the nearly unprecedented fall in equity values and worldwide recession in 2008–09, which has sparked fresh differences of opinion concerning the prospects for realizing an "equity premium" over medium- and longer-term time horizons and the extent to which it may be advisable to invest

retirement funds in diversified equities or in investments that emphasize mini-
mization of risk. Whatever one's views on the merits of these issues, the fact that
many 401(k) and IRA participants have seen a decade worth of gains evaporate
during the past year has made many U.S. households far more risk averse than
they were before the recession, leading to a general loss of confidence. At least
for some time to come, many may be reluctant to contribute to an Automatic
IRA arrangement that does not guarantee a return of principal. Accordingly,
general statutory guidelines would be fleshed out at the administrative level after
regular comment by and consultation with private-sector investment experts.[26]

At least initially, we contemplate that this automatic investment choice would
be a highly diversified "target asset allocation" or life-cycle fund comprising a
mix of equities and fixed-income or stable-value investments and probably relying heavily on index funds or other low-cost alternatives. (The life-cycle funds
that are offered by the federal Thrift Savings Plan are one possible model.) A portion or all of the fixed-income component could consist of Treasury inflation-
protected securities (TIPS) to guard against the risk of loss and inflation.

The mix of diversified equities and fixed income would be designed to reflect
a degree of consensus among personal investment advisers for sound asset allocation and diversification of investments, including exposure to equities and
perhaps other assets that have higher risk and greater potential return. This
strategy recognizes the foundation of retirement income already provided by
Social Security and would apply to IRAs that will not shortly be needed for
expenses. The use of index funds would be one way to avoid the costs of active
investment management while promoting wide diversification.[27]

This automatic investment would actually consist of several different funds,
depending on the individual's age, with the more conservative investments
(such as those relying more heavily on TIPS) applicable to older individuals
who are closer to the time when they might need to use the funds. Individuals
who selected the automatic fund or whose contributions were automatically
placed into it would have their account balances entirely invested in that fund.
However, they would be free to switch at specified times to a different investment option among those offered within the IRA.

A variation on the automatic investment fund may be worth considering. A
temporary guarantee of principal—as might be provided by a bond similar to a
Treasury savings bond or TIPS—might ease some households, especially those
that have no investment experience, into the process of saving and investing.
Behavioral research has produced evidence that many smaller savers—the
2008–09 market downturn aside—are particularly averse to losses of principal
and weigh the risk of loss far more heavily than the prospect of gain.

On the other hand, a "safe" investment, with no risk of loss but no significant potential for growth over time, raises concerns about the adequacy of the

likely long-term accumulation. Some evidence suggests that favorable investment returns over the long term are attributable not so much to successful selection of individual stocks or other investments but to judicious asset allocation—an appropriately balanced and diversified mix of asset types and classes (including substantial exposure to diversified equities or other assets with growth potential) that have risk characteristics designed to be uncorrelated with one another.[28] Accordingly, we contemplate that the automatic investment could take the form of a balanced "asset-allocated" fund either from the start or after a limited transition period, while giving risk-averse individuals the ability to choose a principal-preserving investment as an alternative.

Another intriguing possibility might be to offer a variation on the life-cycle fund that guarantees that the investor will not lose money on a nominal or even a partly inflation-adjusted basis. This variation would be intended to help induce participation by those who are risk-averse but still hope for growth. The key question would be the extent of the limitation on the upside potential of the investment that would be required by a guarantee of principal.

Yet another possibility worth exploring would be the inclusion of some form of annuity purchase as part of the life-cycle fund, perhaps as a replacement for the bond component. This option would allow savers to ensure that their accounts could provide some level of guaranteed lifetime income, thus helping to address longevity and investment risks, regardless of the rises and falls of the stock market and of interest rates. Because balances in Automatic IRAs are likely to be smaller on average than balances in 401(k) plans, annuity purchases might have to be phased in as the account grew, or perhaps balances could be transferred at regular intervals from the bond component into an annuity. Other technical and policy questions, such as portability of such annuities, would need to be examined before such an approach could be fully recommended.[29]

Certain IRA savers will have lower-than-average earnings and thus fairly low balances in their accounts. These accounts will be both less attractive to IRA providers and more likely to be seriously eroded by administrative fees. A potential strategy for handling these low balances would be to place them in a short-term transitional guaranteed investment, such as a government bond or a bank certificate of deposit (CD), until balances reached a specified level, at which point they would be automatically transferred into the standard automatic investment option.

The transition account could be either a standard bank savings or short-term CD account, or it could begin as a principal-preservation fund in much the same way that the federal Thrift Savings Plan began with the G (government securities) Fund.[30] In either case, the account would include the same early withdrawal disincentives as any other IRA account. When the account balance reached a specified level, it would be automatically rolled over into the standard automatic investment option, with all future contributions going directly into that standard option.

Other Investment Options

An additional, major design issue is whether the standard, limited set of investment options for payroll-deposit IRAs should be only a minimum set of options in each IRA, allowing the IRA provider to offer any additional options it wished. Limiting the IRAs to these specified options would best serve the purposes of containing costs, improving investment results for IRA owners in the aggregate, and simplifying individuals' investment choices. Behavioral research has suggested that eligible employees or other consumers who are confronted with numerous choices often tend to avoid the decision (here, participation in saving) or revert to relatively arbitrary decision rules.[31] At the same time, such restrictions would constrain the market, potentially limit innovation, and limit choice for individuals who prefer other alternatives.

One of the ways to resolve this trade-off would be to limit the prescribed array of investment options to the "backstop" Automatic IRAs, in which individuals would invest when neither the employee nor the employer had affirmatively elected another IRA. While all Automatic IRAs would be required to offer the default investment, the only ones constrained to offer the limited list of other fund options would be the "backstop" automatic IRAs. Alternatively, all Automatic IRAs could be made subject to the limited list of investment alternatives in addition to the default option.

In either case, no comparable limits would be imposed on other IRAs, and owners of the default IRAs or all payroll-deposit IRAs would be able to transfer or roll over their account balances between the various classes of accounts. Under this approach, the owner of an Automatic IRA could transfer the account balance to other unrestricted IRAs that were willing to accept such transfers (but perhaps only after the account balance reached a specified amount deemed sufficient to overcome profitability concerns for most IRA providers). While a system that permitted transfers to an unrestricted IRA would deprive the owner of the cost-saving advantages of the no-frills, limited-choice model, such a system would still leave individuals free not to make such a transfer and instead to retain the efficiencies and cost protection associated with the standard low-cost model.[32]

Protecting Employers

Employers traditionally have been particularly concerned about the risk of fiduciary liability associated with their selection of retirement-plan investments. This concern extends to the employer's designation of default investments that employees are free to decline in favor of alternative investments. In the IRA universe, employers transferring funds to automatic-rollover IRAs and employer-sponsored SIMPLE IRAs retain a measure of fiduciary responsibility for initial investments.

By contrast, under our proposal, employers making direct deposits would be insulated from such potential liability or fiduciary responsibility for the manner in which direct deposits are invested in Automatic IRAs, regardless of whether the IRA provider is selected by the employer or the employee. Nor would employers be exposed to potential liability with respect to any employee's choice of IRA provider or type of IRA. This employer protection would be facilitated by regulatory designation of standard investment types, an approach that would reduce the need for continuous professional investment advice.

ERISA protects plan fiduciaries from liability for losses that result directly from employees' investment choices. Labor Department regulations, in accordance with the 2006 Pension Protection Act, extended this protection from fiduciary liability under ERISA to certain types of employer-chosen investments that employees select by default, without making an affirmative election. Regulatory designation of a life-cycle or balanced fund as the default investment for Automatic IRAs would be consistent with these ERISA fiduciary regulations, which extend this type of fiduciary protection to default life-cycle funds, balanced funds, and professionally managed accounts. The regulatory approach to the design of the Automatic IRA default investment could reflect any modifications to these ERISA fiduciary regulations.

In addition, employers providing payroll-deposit IRAs would be able to avoid fiduciary responsibility even for the selection of an IRA provider for their employees either by allowing each employee to designate a preferred provider or by specifying the government-contracted default Automatic IRA. An employer that wished to choose the IRA provider for its employees would be responsible for doing so prudently. Another possible alternative would be for the regulators to specify an approved list of providers (based on capital adequacy, financial soundness, and other criteria) from which employers could choose if they wished to have another means of avoiding any fiduciary responsibility.

Public opinion polling has shown overwhelming support for payroll-deduction, direct-deposit saving. Among workers surveyed in 2007 who would be eligible for an Automatic IRA, 86 percent said that it would be a useful way to save, and 83 percent found the proposal easy to understand.[33]

Another poll shows very strong support for a requirement that every company offer its employees some kind of retirement plan, such as a pension or 401(k), or at least an IRA to which employees could contribute. Among registered voters surveyed in August 2005, 77 percent supported such a requirement (and 59 percent responded that they were "strongly" in support).[34]

PROTECTING EMPLOYER PLANS. Employer-sponsored pension, profit-sharing, 401(k), and other plans tend to be far more effective than IRAs in accumulating benefits for employees. For one thing, pension and profit-sharing plans, for example, are funded by employer contributions that are made automatically for the benefit of eligible employees without requiring the employees to take any initiative to participate. For another, essentially all tax-qualified employer plans must abide by standards that either seek to require reasonably proportionate coverage of rank-and-file workers and management or give the employer a distinct incentive to encourage widespread participation by employees. This encouragement typically takes the form of both employer-provided retirement savings education efforts and employer matching contributions. The result is that the naturally eager savers, who tend to be in the higher tax brackets, tend to subsidize or bring along the naturally reluctant savers in the lower brackets.

Employer-sponsored retirement plans also have other features that tend to make them effective in providing or promoting coverage. And our proposal seeks to transplant some of these features to the IRA universe. These include the automatic availability of a saving vehicle, the use of payroll deductions, matching contributions (which could be provided by the saver's credit, especially if expanded as proposed elsewhere), professional investment management, and peer group reinforcement of saving behavior.

Our approach to providing for payroll deposit contributions to IRAs is therefore designed carefully to avoid competing with or crowding out employer plans such as pension, profit-sharing, 401(k), or SIMPLE plans. Business owners and others who control the decision whether to adopt or maintain a retirement plan for employees should continue to have incentives to sponsor such plans, which require that coverage for lower-income workers be proportionate, to some degree, to coverage for highly paid employees. Payroll-deduction direct-deposit savings as envisioned here would promote wealth accumulation for retirement by filling in the coverage gaps around employer-sponsored retirement plans. Moreover, as described below, the arrangements we propose are designed to set the stage for small employers to graduate from offering payroll deduction to sponsoring actual retirement plans.

Probably the single most important protection for employer plans is to set maximum permitted contribution levels to the Automatic IRA so that they will be sufficient to meet the demand for savings by most households but not high enough to satisfy the appetite for tax-favored saving of business owners and decisionmakers. The average annual contribution to a 401(k) plan by a non-highly compensated employee is less than $3,000 (7.5 percent of pay for a $40,000-a-year family, and 6 percent of pay for a $50,000-a-year family), and average annual 401(k) contributions by all employees are on the order of 7 percent of pay.[35]

IRA contribution limits are already higher than these contribution levels. Accordingly, at the most, payroll-deposit IRAs should not permit contributions above the current IRA dollar ceilings and could be limited to a lower amount such as $3,000. (Only at incomes of $100,000 or more would employees who contributed 3 percent of pay bump up against such a ceiling.) Imposing a lower limit on the payroll-deduction IRA would reduce to some degree the risk that employees would exceed the maximum IRA dollar contribution limit because of automatic enrollment and possible other contributions to an IRA.[36] That is already a risk under current law, but automatic enrollment increases the risk, especially in combination with automatic escalation of contributions. There is a trade-off between the desirability of limiting the contribution amount (to reduce both this risk and the danger of competing with employer plans) and the simplicity of using an existing vehicle (the IRA) "as is."

In any event, employees, not employers, would be responsible for ensuring that all their IRA contributions comply with the maximum limit. The ultimate reconciliation would be made by the employees in their federal income tax returns.

In addition, the Automatic IRA is designed to avoid reducing ordinary employees' incentives to contribute to employer-sponsored plans such as 401(k)s. If workers perceived a direct-deposit savings to IRAs to be more attractive than an employer-sponsored plan (for example, because of tax treatment, investment options, or liquidity), they could be diverted from employer plans. This in turn could have a destabilizing effect by making it difficult for employers to meet the nondiscrimination standards applicable to 401(k)s and other plans and therefore potentially discouraging employers from continuing the plans or their contributions.

PROMOTING EMPLOYER PLANS. Our approach is designed not only to avoid causing any reduction or contraction of employer plans, but actually to promote them. Consultants, third-party administrators, financial institutions, and other plan providers could be expected to view this proposal as providing a valuable new opportunity to market 401(k)s, SIMPLE IRAs, and other tax-favored retirement plans to employers. Firms that, under this proposal, were about to begin offering their employees payroll-deduction saving or had been offering their employees payroll-deduction saving for a year or two could be encouraged to "trade up" to an actual plan such as a 401(k) or SIMPLE IRA.

Especially because these plans can now be purchased at very low cost, it would seem natural for many small businesses to graduate from payroll-deduction savings and complete the journey to a qualified plan in order to obtain the added benefits in terms of recruitment. The results could include improved employee relations and larger tax-favored saving opportunities for owners and managers. Table 4-1 compares the maximum annual tax-favored contribution levels for

Table 4-1. *Retirement Plan Contribution Limits*
Dollars

Age	IRA tax-favored contribution limit	401(k) contribution limit (employee plus employer)	401(k) employee contribution limit	SIMPLE IRA employee contribution limit
Under age 50	5,000	49,000	16,500	11,500
Age 50 and older	6,000	54,500	22,000	14,000

Source: 2009 IRA Contribution and Deduction Limits: http://www.irs.gov/retirement/article/0,,id=202510,00.html; 401(k); Resource Guide: http://www.irs.gov/retirement/sponsor/article/0,,id=151925,00.html.

IRAs, SIMPLE IRA plans. and 401(k) plans in effect for 2009. In addition, as noted, small employers that adopt a new plan (including qualified plans and SIMPLEs) would for the first time be entitled to a tax credit of up to $500 each year for three years, while the Automatic IRA tax credit for employers would be half that amount for two years. This too maintains the incentive for employers to go beyond the payroll-deposit IRA and adopt an actual plan. (As noted, the tax credit for new qualified plans could be increased, which would permit a larger Automatic IRA credit while still maintaining a substantial edge in favor of the qualified plan credit.)

Encouraging Contributions by Nonemployees

The payroll-deposit system outlined thus far would not automatically cover self-employed individuals, employees of the smallest or newest businesses, or certain unemployed individuals who can save. But a strategy centered on automatic arrangements could also make it easier for these people to contribute to IRAs.

For individuals who are not employees or who otherwise lack access to payroll deduction, automatic debit arrangements can serve in its stead. Automatic debit enables individuals to make payments on a regular and timely basis by having them automatically charged to or deducted from an account—such as a checking or savings account or credit card—at regular intervals. The individual generally gives advance authorization to the payer that manages the account or the recipient of the payment, or both. The key is that, as in the case of payroll deduction, once the initial authorization has been given, regular payments continue without requiring further initiative on the part of the individual. For many consumers, automatic debit is a convenient way to pay bills or make payments on mortgages or other loans without having to remember to make each payment when due and without having to write and mail checks.

Similarly, as an element of an Automatic IRA strategy, automatic debit can facilitate saving while reducing paperwork and cutting costs. For example, households can be encouraged to sign up online for regular automatic debits that direct funds from a checking account or credit card to an IRA or other saving vehicle. With online sign-up and monitoring, steps can be taken to familiarize more households with automatic debit arrangements and, through Internet websites and otherwise, to make those arrangements easier to set up and use as a mechanism for saving in IRAs.

Professional and trade associations could facilitate the establishment of IRAs and the use of automatic debit and direct deposit to them. Independent contractors and other individuals who do not have an employer often belong to such an association. The association, for example, might be able to make saving easier for those members who wish to save by making available convenient arrangements for automatic debit of members' accounts. Association websites can make it easy for members to sign up online, monitor the automatic debit savings, and make changes promptly when they wish to. Although such associations generally lack the payroll-deduction mechanism that is available to employers, they can help their members set up a pipeline involving regular automatic deposits (online or by traditional means) from their personal bank or other financial accounts to an IRA established for them.

Another major element of a strategy to encourage contributions outside of employment would be to allow taxpayers to deposit a portion of their income tax refunds directly into an IRA by simply checking a box on their tax returns.[37] Beginning in 2007 (tax year 2006), the IRS made it possible to split refunds among different accounts. Allowing households to split their refunds and deposit a portion directly into an IRA could make saving simpler and, thus, more likely. Federal income tax refunds total nearly $230 billion a year (more than twice the estimated annual aggregate amount of net personal savings in the United States), so even a modest increase in the proportion of refunds saved every year could bring about a significant increase in savings.

Millions of Americans are self-employed as independent contractors. Many of these workers receive regular payments from firms, but because they are not employees, they are not subject to income- or payroll-tax withholding. These individuals might be included in the direct-deposit system by enabling them to request that the firm receiving their services deposit a specified portion of their compensation directly into an IRA.

Compared with writing a large check to an IRA once a year, this approach has several potential advantages to independent contractors, which might well encourage them to save. These include the ability to commit themselves to save a portion of their compensation before they receive it (which, for some people, makes the decision to defer consumption easier); the ability to avoid having to make an affirmative choice among various IRA providers; remittance of the funds by the firm by direct deposit to the IRA; and, where payments are made to the independent contractor on a regular basis, an arrangement that, like regular payroll withholdings for employees, automatically continues the pattern of saving through repeated automatic payroll deductions.

In many cases, the independent service provider and the hiring firm may not have a sufficient connection, or may be unwilling, to enter into a payroll-deposit arrangement. In such instances, the independent contractor could contribute to an IRA by using automatic debit or by sending the contribution together with the estimated taxes that the self-employed generally are required to pay quarterly.

MATCHING DEPOSITS. A powerful financial incentive for direct-deposit saving by those who are not in the higher tax brackets (and who therefore derive little benefit from a tax deduction) would be a matching deposit to their direct-deposit IRA. One means of delivering such a matching deposit would be through the bank, mutual fund, insurance carrier, brokerage firm, or other financial institution that provides the direct-deposit IRA. For example, the first $500 contributed to an IRA by an individual who is eligible to make deductible contributions to an IRA might be matched by the private IRA provider on a dollar-for-dollar basis, and the next $1,000 of contributions might be matched at the rate of 50 cents on the dollar. The financial provider would be reimbursed for its matching contributions through federal income tax credits.[38]

Recent evidence from a randomized experiment involving matched contributions to IRAs suggests that a simple matching deposit to an IRA can make individuals significantly more likely to contribute and more likely to contribute larger amounts.[39]

Matching contributions, similar to those provided by most 401(k) plan sponsors, not only would help induce individuals to contribute directly from their own pay, but also, if the match were automatically deposited in the IRA, would add to the amount saved in the IRA. The use of matching deposits, however, would make it necessary to implement procedures designed to prevent gaming—contributing to induce the matching deposit, then quickly withdrawing those contributions to retain the use of those funds. Among the possible approaches would be to place matching deposits in a separate subaccount subject to tight withdrawal rules and to impose a financial penalty on early withdrawals of matched contributions.

Conclusion

American households have a compelling need to increase their personal saving, especially for long-term purposes such as retirement. This chapter proposes a strategy that would seek to make saving more automatic, and thus easier, more convenient, and more likely to occur. Our strategy would adapt to the IRA universe the same practices that have proven successful in promoting 401(k) participation. In our view, the Automatic IRA approach outlined here holds considerable promise of expanding retirement savings for millions of workers.

Notes

1. Obama's Republican rival, Sen. John McCain, also expressed support for the concept during the campaign.

2. Even among those households that had savings in 401(k)s or IRAs, the median account balance was only $69,000. Authors' calculations using the Federal Reserve Board 2004 Survey of Consumer Finance.

3. As measured in the National Income and Product Accounts, www.bea.gov/national/nipaweb/index.asp.

4. Craig Copeland, "Employment-Based Retirement Plan Participation: Geographic Differences and Trends, 2005" Issue Brief 299 (Washington: Employee Benefit Research Institute, November 2006), fig. 1, p. 7.

5. Ibid.

6. Rev. Rul. 1998-30 clarified that automatic enrollment in 401(k) plans was permissible for newly hired employees. Treasury and the IRS ruled in 2000 that automatic enrollment was allowed for current employees as well (Rev. Rul. 2000-8). Later rulings also extend IRS-Treasury approval to 403(b) and section 457 plans.

7. Pension Protection Act of 2006 (Public Law 109-280), Section 902.

8. The SIMPLE IRA is essentially a payroll-deposit IRA with an employee contribution limit that is in between the IRA and 401(k) limits and with employer contributions, but without the annual reports, plan documents, nondiscrimination tests, or most of the other administrative requirements applicable to other employer plans.

9. See, for example, Alicia H. Munnell and Annika Sunden, *Coming Up Short: The Challenge of 401(k) Plans* (Brookings Institution Press, 2004).

10. The preceding discussion draws on Section 1.02(3), J. Mark Iwry, "Growing Private Pensions: A Supporting Role for the States," *Tax Management Compensation Planning Journal 34* (Dec. 1, 2006).

11. In the conference report to the Tax Reform Act of 1997, Congress stated that "employers that choose not to sponsor a retirement plan should be encouraged to set up a payroll deduction [IRA] system to help employees save for retirement by making payroll-deduction contributions to their IRAs." It encouraged the Treasury secretary to "continue his efforts to publicize the availability of these payroll deduction IRAs." See H. Rept. 220, 105 Cong. 1 sess. (1997), p. 775.

12. Department of Labor, "Interpretive Bulletin 99-1," 29 Code of Federal Regulations 2509.99-1(b) (June 18, 1999); IRS Announcement 99-2, 1999-2 I.R.B. 44 (January 11, 1999), http://www.irs.gov/pub/irs-drop/a-99-2.pdf.

13. Neither the IRS nor the Labor Department guidance addressed the possible use of automatic enrollment in conjunction with direct-deposit IRAs.

14. William G. Gale, J. Mark Iwry, and Peter R. Orszag, "The Automatic 401(k): A Simple Way to Strengthen Retirement Savings," Policy Brief 2005-1 (Washington: Retirement Security Project, 2005).

15. Brigitte C. Madrian and Dennis F. Shea, "The Power of Suggestion: Inertia in 401(k) Participation and Savings Behavior," *Quarterly Journal of Economics* 116 (November 2001), pp. 1149–87; James Choi and others, "Defined Contribution Pensions: Plan Rules, Participant Decisions, and the Path of Least Resistance," in *Tax Policy and the Economy,* vol. 16, edited by James Poterba (MIT Press, 2002), pp. 67–113; Sarah Holden and Jack VanDerhei, "The Influence of Automatic Enrollment, Catch-Up, and IRA Contributions on 401(k) Accumulations at Retirement," Issue Brief 283 (Washington: Employee Benefit Research Institute, July 2005); and Cass R. Sunstein and Richard R. Thaler, *Nudge: Improving Decisions about Health, Wealth, and Happiness* (Yale University Press, 2008).

16. Any such statutory provision could usefully make clear that automatic enrollment in direct-deposit IRAs was permitted irrespective of any state payroll laws that prohibit deductions from employee paychecks without the employee's advance written approval. Assuming that most direct-deposit IRA arrangements are not employer plans governed by the federal Employee Retirement Income Security Act (ERISA), such state laws, as they apply to Automatic IRAs, may not be preempted by ERISA because they do not "relate to any employee benefit plan."

17. In 2004 the IRS affirmed that plans are permitted to increase the automatic contribution rate over time in accordance with a specified schedule or in connection with salary increases or bonuses. See letter dated March 17, 2004, from the Internal Revenue Service to J. Mark Iwry. The idea of coordinating automatic contribution increases with pay increases was developed by Richard Thaler and Shlomo Benartzi, "Save More Tomorrow: Using Behavioral Economics to Increase Employee Saving," *Journal of Political Economy* 112, no. 1, pt. 2 (2004), pp. S164–87.

18. Between August 28 and 31, 2005, in a survey commissioned by the Retirement Security Project, the Tarrance Group, in conjunction with Lake, Snell, Mermin/Decision Research, interviewed 1,000 registered voters nationwide about retirement security issues. A full report of the survey findings can be found at www.retirementsecurityproject.org.

19. Employers that sponsor a SIMPLE IRA plan may deposit all employee contributions in IRAs at a single designated financial institution selected by the employer (IRS Notice 98-4, 1998-2 I.R.B. 25).

20. Plan sponsors continue to have the option to cash out balances of up to $1,000 and to retain in the plan account balances between $1,000 and $5,000 instead of rolling them over to an IRA.

21. Considerable challenges are involved in building and implementing a workable universal saving system based on employer direct deposits of contributions to IRAs. These challenges include dealing with the contingent workforce, with employees who have multiple jobs, work part-time, and tend to earn relatively low wages, and with small employers. A somewhat different and thoughtful approach to designing such a system can be found in the evolving work of the Conversation on Coverage, a collaborative effort among individuals (including one of the authors) drawn from a diverse range of stakeholder organizations. A final report from the Conversation on Coverage was published in 2007: see www.conversation oncoverage.org/about/final-report/covering-the-uncovered.pdf. For an analysis by a nonpartisan expert panel (including one of the authors) of the issues involved in designing arrangements for distributions from individual accounts, see National Academy of Social Insurance, *Uncharted Waters: Paying Benefits from Individual Accounts in Federal Retirement Policy* (Washington: 2005). Although various other efforts have been made to design such systems or programs, this chapter does not attempt to catalogue them.

22. For some years, the federal Thrift Savings Plan had five investment funds: three stock index funds (S&P 500, small- and mid-capitalization U.S. stocks, and mostly large-capitalization foreign stocks); a bond index fund consisting of a mix of government and corporate bonds; and a fund consisting of short-term, nonmarketable U.S. Treasury securities. Effective August 1, 2005, the plan added a set of life-cycle funds, each one of which is composed of a mix of the other five investment funds.

23. This was part of the impetus behind the 2001 statutory provision to the effect that the secretaries of Labor and Treasury may provide, and shall give consideration to providing, special relief with respect to the use of low-cost individual retirement plans for purposes of automatic rollovers and for other uses that promote the preservation of assets for retirement income; see Economic Growth and Tax Relief Reconciliation Act of 2001, Public Law 107-16, 115 Stat. 38, Section 657(c)(2)(B). In a similar vein, one of the authors has proposed a strategy for states to act as catalysts in expanding coverage under standardized, low-cost payroll-deposit IRAs, SIMPLE IRA plans, and 401(k) plans by facilitating the pooling of small businesses to offer these vehicles. See J. Mark Iwry, "Expanding Retirement Savings at the State Level," written statement to the Legislature of the State of Washington (April 2003). The proposal has been described in oral testimony by Iwry to the Michigan Senate and to the Maryland House of Delegates, written testimony before the U.S. Senate Committee on Finance Subcommittee on Long-Term Growth and Debt Reduction (June 29, 2006), and is more fully described in J. Mark Iwry, "State K: A New Strategy for Using State-Assisted Saving to Expand Private Pension Coverage," *NYU Review of Employee Benefits and Executive Compensation* (2006), and in "Growing Private Pensions: A Supporting Role for the States," *Tax Management Compensation Planning Journal* (Bureau of National Affairs) 34 (December 1, 2006).

24. The difference in expense between passively managed index funds and actively managed mutual funds has been estimated to be, as a broad generalization, roughly 100 basis points (1 percent) a year; see William F. Sharpe, "Indexed Investing: A Prosaic Way to Beat the Average Investor," paper presented at the Spring President's Forum (Monterey Institute of International Studies, May 2002).

25. One of the authors has testified before Congress regarding the British retirement plan system and has been critical of the United Kingdom's attempt to impose a limit on charges. See David C. John, testimony before the Subcommittee on Social Security of the Committee on Ways and Means, U.S. House of Representatives (June 16, 2005). See also chapter 5 for a discussion of this issue.

26. For example, some contend that a balanced fund reflecting the participant's appetite for risk is preferable to a life-cycle fund because the latter tends to transition to a relatively low percentage of equities by age 60 or 65, even though the participant might continue to hold the investment for another three decades. However, for the presumably large numbers of the population who can be expected not to take the initiative to adjust their asset allocation as they age, some automatic adjustment might be preferable to no adjustment. In addition, the prospect that participants will make explicit choices may be far greater as they confront retirement, when they might be able to focus on a one-time basis sufficiently to adjust a life-cycle fund to suit their preferences, taking into account when they expect to draw down the funds.

27. As noted, the federal Thrift Savings Plan consists mainly of index funds, which are the building blocks for the recently added life-cycle funds. The Thrift Savings Plan informational materials state that the life-cycle funds "provide a way to diversify your account optimally,

based on professionally determined asset allocations. This provides you with the opportunity to achieve a maximum amount of return over a given period of time with a minimum amount of risk. . ." (see www.tsp.gov). A professionally run "managed account" that could achieve similar results at no greater cost might be another attractive option, and managed accounts are growing in popularity as an option in 401(k) plans. A question may be raised as to whether managed accounts are a better fit for 401(k) plans than for Automatic IRAs, because 401(k)s tend to have more substantial account balances and greater flexibility to accommodate individual preferences while allocating costs to individuals who opt for costlier alternatives.

28. Gary P. Brinson, L. Randolph Hood, and Gilbert L. Beebower, "Determinants of Portfolio Performance," *Financial Analysts Journal* 42 (July/August 1986): 39–48.

29. For additional information about strategies for the expanded use of annuities in connection with retirement savings, see chapters 6 and 7.

30. The Federal Employees' Retirement System Act of 1986 (Public Law 99-335) established the Thrift Savings Plan as of January 1, 1987, with a government securities fund. The initial legislation called for two additional funds—fixed income and stock index—to become available on January 1, 1988.

31. Particularly concerning 401(k) trading behavior, see, for example, Takeshi Yamaguchi and others, "Winners and Losers: 401(k) Trading and Portfolio Performance," Working Paper 2006-26 (University of Pennsylvania, Wharton School Pension Research Council, November 2006), and Shlomo Benartzi and Richard Thaler, ""Naïve Diversification Strategies in Defined Contribution Saving Plans," *American Economic Review* 91 (March 2001), pp. 79–98.

32. The question of how best to fit direct-deposit IRAs, with their improved and simplified investment structure, into the larger IRA universe is related to a broader issue: the potential simplification of IRAs. We favor simplification and revision of the current array of IRA options. However, the specifics of any such proposals are beyond the scope of this chapter.

33. Prudential, "Saving for Retirement at Work: Employee and Business Reactions to the Automatic IRA Concept" (Newark, N.J.: January 2008).

34. See Gale, Iwry, and Orszag, "The Automatic 401(k)," for a full report of the survey findings.

35. Craig Copeland, "Retirement Plan Participation and Retirees' Perception of Their Standard of Living," Issue Brief 289 (Washington: Employee Benefit Research Institute, January 2006), pp. 1–6, fig. A4.

36. It is conceivable that the risk of exceeding the IRA dollar limit could be mitigated to some degree by capping automatic enrollment at, say, $250 a month (for an annual total of $3,000) or $300 a month. However, because automatic enrollment would be administered at the employer level and might be based on paychecks provided weekly or every two weeks, the maximum dollar amount would need to be adjusted accordingly (say, $60 if weekly, $120 if every two weeks, or $250 if monthly).

37. J. Mark Iwry, "Using Tax Refunds to Increase Savings and Retirement Security," Policy Brief 2006-1 (Washington: Retirement Security Project, January 2006).

38. Among the issues such an approach would need to address is the means of reimbursing private financial institutions that have no federal income tax liability to offset because they are tax exempt or in a loss position. A proposed alternative mechanism would convert the existing Saver's Credit (a federal income tax credit to households with joint income below $55,500 for contributing to an IRA or employer plan) to a direct matching deposit to an IRA or other savings account. As currently structured, the Saver's Credit reduces the household's

federal income tax liability and is nonrefundable; thus, it is not automatically saved. A variation would have such a direct matching deposit delivered by the financial institution that sponsors the IRAs or that serves as financial provider to the 401(k) plan to which the individual contributes. One of the authors was involved in developing the Saver's Credit and, in congressional testimony and writings, has advocated its extension and expansion. See, for example, William G. Gale, J. Mark Iwry, and Peter R. Orszag, "The Saver's Credit: Expanding Retirement Savings for Middle- and Lower-Income Americans," Policy Brief 2005-2 (Washington: Retirement Security Project, March 2005). This proposal has been essentially incorporated in President Barack Obama's budget for fiscal 2010. Another significant asset-building approach targeted to lower- and moderate-income households is reflected in individual development accounts (IDAs). See, for example, Michael Sherraden, *Assets and the Poor: A New American Welfare Policy* (Armonk, N.Y.: M. E. Sharpe, 1992), and Ray Boshara, "Individual Development Accounts: Policies to Build Savings and Assets for the Poor," Policy Brief (Brookings, March 2005).

39. Esther Duflo and others, "Saving Incentives for Low- and Middle-Income Families: Evidence from a Field Experiment with H&R Block," *Quarterly Journal of Economics* 121 (November 2006), pp. 1311–46.

5

National Retirement Savings Systems in Australia, Chile, New Zealand, and the United Kingdom: Lessons for the United States

DAVID C. JOHN AND RUTH LEVINE

Financial security in retirement is not just an important goal for working families in the United States. Retirees across the globe typically rely on a combination of public pensions (such as the U.S. Social Security system), private savings, and corporate pensions to pay their way after their paychecks have stopped. Modern industrialized countries, embracing the three-pillar philosophy advocated by the World Bank and others, have created complex pension landscapes that combine public and private provision of old-age income.[1]

However, achieving this security is an increasing challenge at a time when structural and demographic trends are putting ever-rising strains on government-paid income programs for the retired. Over the last several decades, many national pension systems have shifted some of the financial risk of retirement from society to the individual. Employers have shifted from defined benefit pensions, which guarantee retirees a regular payment every month no matter how long they live, to defined contribution retirement savings plans, which leave it to retirees to put aside enough money during their working lives to last them through their retired years.

Demographically, multiple factors are at play. As life expectancy increases, pension accumulation must be larger to fund longer retirement. Entrance into

The authors thank Catherine Lee, former research assistant with the Retirement Security Project, for her extensive work in initiating the chapter.

the labor force is increasingly delayed by prolonged higher education, thus shortening the number of years that a worker saves for old age. Although a good argument can be made for restoring those lost years by delaying retirement, such a move is controversial and in many countries has yet to be effectively implemented. In the United States pressures on the pension system began to grow as the oldest of the baby-boomer generation (those born between 1946 and 1964), became eligible for early retirement in January 2008. The number of boomers who reach retirement will steadily increase until 2030, when the entire boomer generation will be eligible for full Social Security retirement benefits. Because succeeding generations will be smaller, there will be fewer workers to pay boomers all promised Social Security and health care benefits at the same time that health care and other costs are growing.

As a result, Americans today face precarious retirement prospects that have only been made worse by the recession that began in 2007. In 2008, 64 percent of Social Security recipients depended on the program for half or more of their income.[2] The program provided 90 percent or more of income for about one-third of recipients. Facing both funding pressures on Social Security and the results of the shift from defined benefit to defined contribution plans, it is only logical that a growing proportion of Americans lack confidence in their ability to live comfortably in retirement. The Gallup Economy and Personal Finance Poll indicates that only 46 percent of American workers in 2007 expected to have sufficient funds to live comfortably in retirement, compared with 59 percent five years earlier.[3]

These trends are not unique to the United States. Facing similar dilemmas, the rich countries of the Organization for Economic Cooperation and Development (OECD) have cut their public pension promises by an average of 22 percent since 1990 through various pension reforms.[4] These cuts have been implemented in a variety of ways, many of which are so complex that their full effect will not be apparent to workers until they retire.

A few countries have coped with projected rises in public pension costs by adding a personal savings element that either supplements or in a few cases replaces the tax-financed public pension. The rationale behind these savings systems is that individuals should bear a greater portion of the cost of their own retirement. Because it is naïve to expect every worker to become a financial expert, these countries have created systems that make it easier for workers both to participate in investment decisions and to make appropriate investment choices. Using either mandatory participation or automatic enrollment, the national savings systems studied in this chapter attempt to ensure that individuals will see their savings grow without having to acquire extensive knowledge or pay for expensive individualized investment advice.

This chapter examines the current and planned retirement savings plans of four countries with unique pension systems—Chile, Australia, New Zealand,

and the United Kingdom—and attempts to draw lessons for U.S. policymakers to use in their efforts to build a more sustainable pension system that can provide increasing retirement security for future generations.

Chile

In 1981 Chile replaced its pay-as-you-go Social Security system with a fully funded private pension system based on individual accounts managed by private pension fund managers known as AFPs (Administradoras de Fondos de Pensiones). All new wage and salary workers joining the workforce after 1981 had to join the AFP system, while existing workers as of that date had the option of either moving to the new system or accepting whatever benefit the old system would be able to pay. Aided by major incentives to switch to the post-1981 system, 97 percent of Chileans who contributed to a pension plan were in the new system by 2004.

Structure of the System

In the individual accounts system, all formally employed workers are required to have 10 percent of their earnings automatically deducted to fund their retirement as well as disability and survivor insurance. Workers have an additional 2–3 percent of pay deducted to cover administrative costs of their accounts, for a total deduction of 12–13 percent.[5] Employers are required to send the employees' contributions to the pension administrator of the employee's choice, which in turn credits it to the fund or funds chosen by the employee. Currently employees can choose from among five pension fund administrators, each of which offers the four types of funds that are approved by the government regulator.[6]

In addition to the mandatory contribution, workers are allowed to make voluntary contributions to either their AFP account or another voluntary retirement savings account. Only about 10 percent of workers make voluntary contributions.[7] Employers are not required to make any contribution. Self-employed workers may participate in the system but are not required to.

The transition to the fully funded system in Chile was aided by a fiscal surplus resulting in large part from the sale into the private sector of companies that had formerly been nationalized and by the large number of working people relative to retirees.[8] The government continued to fund the defined benefit pensions of the workers who chose to remain in the old system and gave recognition bonds to the workers who switched to the new system. These bonds, which mature when the individual reaches retirement age, pay a lump sum into their account that is based on their last twelve monthly contributions to the old system adjusted for both the number of years they participated in that system and an annuity factor.[9] The switch to the fully funded system is now nearly complete; by 2025 the defined benefit pensions will be fully phased out. However, to date, few if any retirees have financed their pensions solely through contributions. Almost all of those who have retired under the 1981 system had at least a portion of their pensions financed through recognition bonds.

Recent Changes

Until a reform enacted in 2008, the public pillar guaranteed a minimum pension for participants whose pension income after twenty years of contributions fell below 80 percent of the statutory minimum salary. The minimum pension was paid on top of the worker's regular pension to bring it to a certain level. In January 2009 the minimum monthly salary was 159,000 pesos ($254.40), and the minimum pension was 127,000 pesos ($203.50).[10] Additionally, for workers who did not qualify for the minimum pension, a means-tested basic pension, called PASIS, gave benefits equal to 50 percent of the minimum pension regardless of an individual's contributions to the system.

The 2008 reform came in response to concerns raised in a 2006 report about coverage of both private and public pensions, as well as about high administrative costs among the five pension administrators. Passed in March 2008, the Sistema de Pensiones Solidarias revamped the public pillar, increased participation in the AFP system, and addressed several other problems with the system. The basic PASIS pension, renamed the basic solidarity pension (Pensión Básica Solidaria), was increased from 48,000 to 60,000 pesos per month in 2008, and eligibility was broadened to workers in the bottom 40 percent of the income distribution with twenty years of residency in Chile. This new guarantee is a noncontributory, means-tested pension paid to workers who have no other pension.

The old minimum pension guarantee was replaced by the Aporte Previsional Solidario for those who have contributed to a pension plan. The new program removes the former requirement that a worker must contribute to a pension account for twenty years in order to qualify for the guarantee. The solidarity contribution provides up to 17,000 pesos a month for individuals who have a self-financed monthly pension of between 50,000 and 70,000 pesos in 2008.[11] That amount gradually rises to 255,000 pesos a month by 2012.

The new solidarity pension and other reforms are projected to cost 2.9 percent of GDP annually starting in 2008, falling to 1.3 percent of GDP by 2025. These costs are to be financed by a new pension reserve fund, which receives both part of the budget surplus (8.7 percent of GDP in 2007) and revenues from the production of copper. The fund had about 1.1 billion pesos in 2008.

Other reforms to the pension system passed in 2008 include mandating participation of the self-employed and eliminating monthly fixed administrative fees that exist in addition to earnings-based fees. The law also assigns new labor force entrants automatically to the fund with the lowest fees and allows funds to contract out the administration of individual accounts. To increase the number of funds and competition in the industry, insurance agencies will be able to set up pension fund administrators as subsidiaries. To encourage voluntary contributions to private accounts among middle-income workers, those who enroll in and contribute to voluntary accounts will be eligible for a subsidy of 15 percent of annual contributions up to 1.5 million pesos. Finally, a financial education fund was set up to create a network of advisers for account holders.

Participation and Coverage

A major criticism of the 1981 law was that the new system failed to cover significant portions of the Chilean workforce. Although the reform included a mandatory contribution rate for all wage and salary workers, only 55 percent of the labor force actively contributed in 2004, slightly below the pre-1981 participation rate of around 63 percent.[12] In both the old system as well as the 1981 savings-based system that replaced it, the self-employed, who had the option of participating or not, made up a significant share of the nonparticipants. In 2007 the self-employed constituted an estimated 28 percent of the workforce, but only about a quarter of them regularly contributed to an account managed by a pension fund administrator.[13]

In addition, many Chileans work in the formal economy for just part of the year or spend some time in the informal economy, and they do not contribute in months when they are not formally employed.[14] A growing proportion of the labor force is employed in temporary, seasonal, or part-time jobs rather than in year-round, full-time jobs for the same employer. Thus, while 55 percent of the labor force participated in 2004, it is unlikely that the same 55 percent contributed for all twelve months of that year. One study found that only 20 percent of workers contributed 90 percent of the time, while a similar proportion contributed only 10 percent of the time.[15]

Sporadic work histories also limited the effectiveness of the publicly financed safety net before the 2008 reforms. A large proportion of contributors to managed pension accounts had a pension financed by their savings that was lower than the minimum pension guarantee. Unfortunately, a large and growing number of these workers would also have fewer than the required twenty years of contributions, thus making them ineligible to receive the minimum pension even though it was designed to assist lower-income workers. In 2006 one study showed that 45 percent of pension fund contributors had savings that would result in a retirement benefit that was below the guaranteed level. The study further predicted that by 2025 virtually all workers with pensions below that level would not have accumulated the required twenty years of savings necessary to receive the guaranteed amount.[16]

Returns and Costs

Rates of return on pension fund assets have improved since the new system began in 1981. A 2006 study found that accounts managed by pension fund administrators had earned an annual average rate of return of 6.8 percent during the previous ten years.[17] When the system began in 1981, these funds were limited to investments in Chilean assets, with a large proportion going into Chilean government bonds. However, as the size of the funds grew, the supply of bonds and other domestic investments was unable to absorb all of the savings. As a result, allowable investments were liberalized to include non-Chilean assets, a development that contributed to increasing the return on the funds. However, investment regulations remain quite complex.

The pension funds are allowed to offer only four types of investment funds, which differ in the percentage of total assets that they may invest in equities and government bonds. Chilean workers are allowed to place their contributions in a maximum of two of the four funds. Each of the four types of funds has a performance standard equal to the average rate of return of all of the funds of that type over the previous three years. Each fund also has reserves it must use if it fails to meet the performance standard. The government dissolves any fund whose reserves are exhausted.[18]

Fees and other costs imposed on savers have been sources of controversy. Despite efforts to increase competitiveness of the pension funds, average costs rose 5 percent between 1982 and 2003.[19] Until 2008 two types of monthly fees were allowed—fixed administrative fees, and variable fees based on earnings—although only two funds maintained their fixed fee. As noted, the fixed fees were eliminated in the 2008 reforms. The average earnings-related fee in 2008 was 1.71 percent of a worker's salary, a rate that was higher than all but two of the Latin American countries with a Chilean-style individual accounts system.[20]

Because they compete by offering gifts and other incentives to potential members, the pension funds have had little incentive to lower fees. Fees have also remained high, because until 2008 it was very difficult for new funds to be formed, thus eliminating potential competition. The law requires that the funds charge the same fees to all members regardless of the size of their accounts, a structure that effectively subsidizes members with larger accounts. Until their elimination, the fixed fees also had a greater effect on the smaller account balances of low-wage earners. Decreasing costs and increasing administrative simplicity of the pension funds were among the main goals of the 2008 legislation.

Retirement Income

Despite problems with relatively low coverage and high administrative costs, the Chilean system's average income replacement rates are projected to be on par with OECD countries. Estimates show that after 2020, retirees will on average replace 44 percent of their preretirement income. These high average replacement rates are likely the result of the relatively high mandatory saving rate of 10 percent. However, because the same savings rate is applied to all income levels, the system has very limited progressivity. A more serious problem is that the average replacement rate for women is projected to be nearly twenty percentage points below that for males.[21] On the plus side, the 10 percent contribution rate may have contributed to the increase in national saving after the 1981 reform: as a proportion of GDP, national saving grew from less than 1 percent in 1981 to 25 percent in 1990 and more recently to 60 percent.[22]

Once pensioners reach retirement age, which is 65 for men and 60 for women, they can choose to annuitize their retirement immediately, take programmed withdrawals, or take a deferred annuity with programmed withdrawals in the interim. Early retirement is allowed for workers whose savings can fund a retirement benefit equal to a set proportion of their average earnings over the previous ten years. The benefit also must exceed the minimum pension by a certain level. Initially, workers had to have a retirement benefit equal to at least 50 percent of their earnings and 110 percent of the minimum guaranteed pension. Starting in 2004 these thresholds are gradually being raised; they will reach 70 percent and 150 percent by August 2010.[23] Previously nearly 65 percent of men took early retirement, with their average retirement age being 56.

Before 2004 high transaction costs may have discouraged some individuals from taking their income as an annuity, but even so in 2000, more than half of retirees chose annuities.[24] Retirees could purchase an annuity from either an insurance company or through an intermediary. Fees were unregulated and reached up to 6 percent of the value of the annuity.[25]

Reform in 2004 required providers to have an electronic bidding system so that the costs of different products were clear for retirees. In addition, fees were capped at a level that is reviewed every two years, a move that reduced the fees by more than half. Still, retirees who purchase annuities tend to have larger accounts than those who choose programmed withdrawals. This discrepancy occurs in part because individuals whose accounts near the minimum pension level are required to take a programmed withdrawal so that a small proportion of their accounts will be paid as fees rather than as retirement income.[26] Pension funds also charge a fee for programmed withdrawals.

Australia

Australia's mandatory Superannuation Guarantee (SG) retirement savings system requires employers to contribute an amount equal to 9 percent of employee earnings to individual retirement account funds. In addition, there is a means-tested, tax-financed Age Pension for all individuals whose income and assets are below certain statutory levels. The Age Pension has been in place since 1909, while the SG system's universal mandate for contributions was enacted in 1992. It was built upon a superannuation system created in 1986 through a centralized wage settlement that resulted in an employer contribution of 3 percent of earnings into individual retirement accounts.[27] Contributions to an SG account are taxed when money goes into the account, as earnings accumulate, and when savings are withdrawn before the worker reaches the minimum distribution age of 55 to 60 depending on a worker's birth year. Before 2007, all distributions were taxed, regardless of the worker's age when distribution began. By one estimate, taxes at various stages of the process effectively reduced the mandatory 9 percent contribution rate to 7.65 percent before 2007.[28]

How the System Works

Superannuation is required for all workers between the ages of 18 and 65 who earn more than $450 (in Australian dollars) per month, although employers can also choose to contribute on behalf of lower-earning workers. The earnings threshold for low-income workers was put in place to reduce the number of small accounts that would be subject to proportionally high administrative fees, although the threshold has not been changed since the SG system began. In 2006 only 7 percent of employees earned less than $450 per month.[29] Since 2007 annual tax-advantaged contributions have been capped at $50,000; individuals may also make additional voluntary contributions of up to $150,000 annually, but with no tax advantage. Individuals do not pay taxes on mandatory contributions, although the investment fund they go into pays taxes at a rate of 15 percent on both contributions and earnings. Contributions above $50,000 annually are taxed at a rate of 31.5 percent.

The system for choosing investment funds changed substantially in 2005, when employees were given the ability to choose which superannuation fund and investment portfolio to use. Employees were also allowed to decide whether to add voluntary savings over the 9 percent rate. If an employee fails to make an active choice, no additional savings are contributed, the money goes to a super-annuation fund determined by the relevant industry or employer, and an investment portfolio is chosen by a fund trustee.[30] The savings in all superannuation funds are fully vested, portable, and preserved until the contributor turns age 55, the earliest age at which they can be withdrawn.

The Age Pension, the public pillar of the Australian pension system, provides a means-tested benefit for all individuals of retirement age, regardless of their contributions history. The amount of the benefit is determined by both an asset and an income test. In addition, recipients must have lived in Australia for at least ten years and for five consecutive years prior to applying.[31] Workers who qualified for the full Age Pension received a maximum fortnightly payment in 2008 of $562 for singles and $939 for couples. This is equal to about 25 percent of average male earnings. Payments are indexed to inflation and are usually adjusted twice annually. In addition, if the maximum benefit falls below 25 percent of male weekly earnings, it is adjusted upward at the same time. Benefits are not taxed.

The income test reduces Age Pension payments by 40 cents for each dollar earned above the "free area" amount equal to $138 per fortnight for singles and 20 cents for each dollar of income above $240 per fortnight for couples. Adjustments are made for children.[32] The asset test differs for homeowners and non-homeowners, though 90 percent of the pensioners who did not receive the Age Pension in 2004 were made ineligible by their income rather than their assets. [33] Because home values are not part of the asset test, there have been charges that the system is tilted toward benefiting wealthier individuals who are more likely both to own a substantial home and to be able to adjust their assets to receive a benefit. Because receiving the Age Pension brings with it additional government-provided benefits, workers try to adjust their retirement incomes to qualify for at least a minimal amount.

Participation and Coverage

Roughly two-thirds of retirees currently receive the full value of the Age Pension, and just under 50 percent of all pension wealth is publicly provided.[34] These numbers, however, are expected to decrease over time as the Superannuation Guarantee system matures. The existing mandatory saving rate of 9 percent was reached only in 2002, and the proportion of Australian workers with superannuation guarantee accounts increased from under 50 percent in 1988 to over 90 percent in 2004.[35] As more of these accounts grow, the government expects fewer people to be eligible for the Age Pension, thus reducing government outlays.

In recent years, Australian pensioners have on average seen large increases in their account balances: by 49 percent between 2004 and 2006 for men; and by

30 percent for women. In the aggregate, superannuation funds increased from $135 billion in 1991 to $625 billion in 2004. Australia now has more money per capita invested in managed funds than any other country, in part because of the new system.[36] Projections show that by 2020 the total value of superannuation fund assets will exceed 110 percent of GDP.[37] However, these projections were made before the global financial outlook worsened, and in 2008, the average value of SG funds declined by about 19.7 percent.[38]

One weakness in the SG system is that the self-employed are exempt from the mandatory savings requirement. Policymakers hope that a new superannuation clearinghouse (discussed below) will help increase participation among these workers. Another problem is the large number of "lost accounts" created when participants switch jobs without consolidating their accounts. By 2008 there were over 6.4 million lost accounts containing $12.9 billion in assets, accounting for one in five SG accounts or one lost account for every two Australian workers.[39] A government discussion paper released in November 2008 seeking comments on how to reduce lost participants was the first step toward creating a system to track and automatically consolidate lost accounts.

Additionally, the mandatory nature of the system may mean that superannuation fund contributions crowd out private household saving. A study using annual data from 1966 to 2002 found that every dollar saved by households as part of the 9 percent mandatory contribution reduced voluntary saving by 38 cents. Therefore, net new saving as a result of the SG system is about 62 cents per dollar saved.[40]

Returns and Costs

Before the sharp drop in world markets that began in the second half of 2008, the average five-year nominal returns on balanced SG retirement funds in 2008 were roughly 8 percent, an increase over the 5 percent yields from 2004 and 2005.[41] But even before the market drop, some concerns were expressed that returns were too low. Although employees were given a choice, starting in 2005, regarding which superannuation fund to join, there remain no performance standards or regulations such as the U.S. qualified default investment alternative to specify how an employee's retirement savings in a 401k-type account should be invested if the employee does not designate a fund. Thus, each fund could have a different mix of investment types, making direct comparisons between funds difficult.

There are four major types of SG investment alternatives in the market:

—Industry funds, set up by unions and groups of employers, run by trustees, and open only to members

—Public-sector funds, limited to government employees

—Corporate funds, also known as wholesale funds, run by financial institutions for groups of employers

—Retail funds, open to individual investors

Individual retail funds have been available since the first superannuation reform in 1986. By 2008 self-managed and other retail funds held nearly 50 percent of all assets, while industry funds accounted for 17 percent of assets, public sector funds 15 percent, and corporate funds 5 percent.[42]

Administrative costs charged by these funds remain a concern. Annual expense rates on corporate funds between $50 million and $250 million in size were roughly 1 percent of assets in 2001, while smaller retail funds were more expensive at around 2 percent of fund assets. Retail funds have higher total administrative costs because many of them charge both entry and exit fees as well as additional annual management fees; these funds also pay more taxes than public sector funds.[43] Even today, fees are higher than those charged for comparable investments in other countries, averaging 1.25 percent of assets according to Sen. Nick Sherry, Australia's minister for superannuation and corporate law.[44] Sherry says that his government hopes to see fees decline over time to 1 percent or less.

The 2005 legislation allowing employees to choose their preferred superannuation fund and investment portfolio was intended in part to improve the net investment returns by using competition to put downward pressure on unnecessarily high fees. However, initial signs were discouraging. In a survey by the Australia and New Zealand Banking Group after the reform passed, only 55 percent of respondents were aware of their ability to choose a fund and investment portfolio. Additionally, while 77 percent of respondents could identify the best indicator of fund performance as returns minus fees, only 37 percent indicated that they would take fees and charges into account when choosing a fund.[45]

A new superannuation clearinghouse, scheduled to begin operation on July 1, 2009, may help to reduce fees and will almost certainly make it easier for employers to encourage their employees to choose which SG fund to join.[46] Employers will be able to send all of their employees' SG contributions to the clearinghouse, which will allocate the individual contributions to the individual employee's chosen fund. According to the government, use of the new clearinghouse will be optional and free to all employers with fewer than twenty employees.[47] Operation of the clearinghouse will be contracted out to the private sector.

Retirement Income

At the time of retirement, which is 65 years for men and 63 years for women, pensioners can choose to take their benefits as a lump sum or as an income stream.[48] Despite tax incentives for retirees to take an income stream, a large majority opt for a lump sum. Of those who retired in 2000, 75 percent of new retirees chose a lump sum.[49] Since July 1, 2007, retirees 60 or older may receive funds in any form from their account tax free if it was invested in an SG fund that paid taxes during the accumulation stage. Almost all SG funds are subject to these taxes. Workers who retire early can begin to receive SG funds as soon as age 55 if they were born before July 1, 1960. This minimum distribution age gradually increases for those born after that date until it reaches age 60 for those born after July 1, 1964.[50]

For the average male Australian earner in 2007, average retirement income was 43 percent of preretirement income, while the replacement rate net of taxes was 56.4 percent. This is somewhat lower than the OECD averages of 59 percent and 70 percent. Although cross-country comparisons of relative replacement rates are complex, Australians' retirement incomes on average are negatively affected by the degree to which they rely on the Age Pension. Two-thirds of retirees receive the full amount of the public benefit, and only 21 percent are able to live principally off the proceeds of their SG accounts, although this proportion mainly reflects the fact that the SG system is still relatively new. The net replacement rate of an average earner relying on the Age Pension is only 37 percent, so average replacement rates should clearly increase as the SG system continues to mature.[51]

The distribution of retirement wealth is also important in preventing old-age poverty. The OECD uses a measure of progressivity of the pension system that relates the distribution of pension earnings to the distribution of preretirement lifetime earnings.[52] On this measure the reference points are a pure basic scheme that would give a flat-rate pension to all retirees (100 on the index) and a pure insurance scheme that would simply aim to provide a 100 percent replacement rate of preretirement income (0 on the index). Australia scores a 73 on this measure, which compares favorably to the OECD average of 37 and the U.S. score of 51. The progressivity of the Australian system results in part from the size of the benefit given by the Age Pension; in 1991 Australia was surpassed only by Canada among the Group of Seven countries when minimum pension values are compared.[53]

Options for increasing retirement income through the SG system include encouraging higher workforce participation by reducing early retirement and increasing the number of hours worked among 55- to 64-year-olds. Currently labor force participation rates are ten percentage points lower for this age group than for the rest of the working-age population, and many older workers are part-time employees. Keeping contributors in the workforce until age 65 would increase their balances significantly, although nearly 40 percent of Australians aged 55 to 64 suffer from at least one major health problem, making it difficult to maintain working hours.[54]

This and other changes may be possible after an Australian government commission reviewing the nation's tax system reports in March 2009. That panel is charged with reviewing the SG system to determine if it meets the objectives of being broad and adequate; acceptable to individuals; "robust" in dealing with investment, inflation and longevity risk; simple and approachable; and sustainable.[55]

New Zealand

New Zealand's KiwiSaver program is the world's first nationwide, automatically enrolled, government-sponsored, voluntary retirement saving system. Launched on July 1, 2007, the program supplements the New Zealand superannuation system, which pays a flat-rate individual pension currently financed from general tax revenues to all who have lived in New Zealand for at least ten years. By using an automatic enrollment system based on behavioral economics, KiwiSaver takes advantage of workers' natural inertia to increase rates of retirement saving and direct workers into more appropriate investment choices than they might have made under a traditional savings system.

The Structure of KiwiSaver and New Zealand Superannuation

After KiwiSaver's launch, all employees were automatically enrolled in a saving plan upon starting a new job, while existing employees and self-employed individuals could join the plan voluntarily. Workers who are automatically enrolled may opt out of the system completely as long as they do so between the fourteenth and fifty-sixth day of their employment. Those who remain in KiwiSaver automatically save 4 percent of their income through April 1, 2009, and 2 percent after that date unless they choose a higher savings rate. In addition to the 2 percent and 4 percent savings rates, there is an 8 percent option. The plan does not allow any other savings levels, but a worker can change from one level to the other at any time.

Participants can direct their savings into any of the investment funds that have been registered with the government. Employees who do not actively make an investment choice are moved into an employer-chosen fund. If the employer has not selected an investment choice, the government randomly assigns the individual to one of six very conservatively managed default funds.[56]

The earnings on an individual's retirement contributions are taxed, although balances are not taxed upon removal. Contributions are locked into the system but are portable across jobs and funds. Early withdrawal of KiwiSaver funds is allowed only for serious illness, significant financial hardship, or absence from New Zealand (presumably on a semipermanent basis) for at least twelve months. In addition, after three years of contributions, a member can take a one-time withdrawal for the down payment on a first home.

In normal circumstances, KiwiSaver contributions may be removed at the later of either age 65 or five years after membership began. Members who have been participating for twelve months or longer may interrupt their contributions for anywhere from three months to five years as a "contributions holiday." Additionally, some employer-sponsored plans allow members to divert up to half of their contribution to pay a mortgage under the theory that mortgage-free homeownership contributes to future retirement wealth.[57]

Although participation in KiwiSaver initially was to be encouraged only through automatic enrollment techniques, the government later decided to add a series of financial incentives. Prior to April 1, 2009, the employee-targeted incentives were:

—A "kick-start," $1,000 tax-free government contribution to each KiwiSaver account upon enrollment

—A tax credit matching up to $20 of contributions per week between age 18 and retirement

—A fee subsidy of $20 every six months

—A first-home deposit (down payment) subsidy of up to $5,000 after three years of contributing to a KiwiSaver account

Beginning in April 2008 employers were also required to match employees' KiwiSaver contributions at a rate initially equal to 1 percent of income, scheduled to increase to 4 percent by 2011.[58] Employers are rewarded as well for both their compliance with the match and any optional additional contributions to KiwiSaver. Up to 4 percent of an employee's gross pay, when contributed to a KiwiSaver plan, is exempt from the Specified Superannuation Contribution Withholding Tax, which is paid by the employer. Through April 1, 2009, employers also received a tax credit of up to $20 a week per KiwiSaver employee.[59]

The public portion of the retirement saving system is called New Zealand Superannuation (NZS). This program aims to provide more than a basic pension but less than complete replacement of preretirement earnings. Put in place in 1977, the NZS provides a universal, flat-rate pension that is required to fall between 65 percent and 72.5 percent of the net average earnings of employed New Zealanders.[60] Eligibility is based simply on whether a worker has been a legal resident of New Zealand for ten years; there is no income or asset test used in determining eligibility. Benefits are subject to income tax. Because it continues for the entire life of a New Zealander after retirement, NZS also protects against the risk of outliving one's assets.

Faced with estimates that the cost of NZS will rise to a point that future governments will be unable to fund it through general revenues alone, New Zealand created a buffer fund in 2001 that is in theory much like the U.S.

Social Security trust fund. The government invests roughly $2 billion annually (in New Zealand dollars) into the fund. No withdrawals are to be made until 2027; thereafter the fund will begin to pay for roughly 15 percent of the cost of NZS benefits.

Changes as of April 1, 2009

On December 15, 2008, a newly elected government changed the incentives to savers in order to reduce the overall cost of the program. At the same time, minimum savings levels were changed to make it easier for lower-income workers to participate. The changes went into effect on April 1, 2009.[61]

The revised law eliminated the annual government subsidy of $40 to defray administrative charges on the KiwiSaver accounts, abolished the weekly $20 subsidy for employers, and reduced from 4 percent to 2 percent of gross pay the exemption from the Specified Superannuation Contribution Withholding Tax on contributions to a KiwiSaver plan. At the same time, the mandatory employer contribution was frozen at 2 percent of employee gross income, eliminating the scheduled rise to 3 percent in 2009 and 4 percent in 2011. Employers were also prohibited from reducing employees' pay to offset the matching contribution to KiwiSaver.

The December 2008 law lowered the default savings rate to 2 percent in response to concerns that the minimum savings rate of 4 percent discouraged lower-income workers from participating. Existing KiwiSaver members could reduce their savings to the 2 percent level at that time. Workers will be able to choose from three savings rates, with 2 percent joining the previously existing 4 percent and 8 percent options.

Participation and Coverage

Since KiwiSaver is still very young, it is difficult to say how the program will affect retirement saving patterns in the future. Thus far, however, it appears that the participation rates among workers are exceeding the assumptions made by the Treasury before the program began. At that time, the Treasury predicted only 7 percent participation among workers aged 18 to 64 in 2008, rising to 25 percent in 2014.[62] However, 39 percent of respondents to a survey conducted in June 2008 reported that they participated in some workplace saving scheme, an increase from 27 percent in October 2007.

Of the 500,000 KiwiSaver members as of March 20, 2008, approximately 32 percent had been automatically enrolled and another 16 percent had opted in through an employer. The remainder opted in through a financial services provider. An additional 99,000 people had been automatically enrolled but opted out of the system. Just over half of the members were female, and about 20 percent were 55 or older.[63]

There is some question about how much of the KiwiSaver accounts represents new saving or reduced consumption and how much substitutes for other forms of private saving.[64] Additionally, as a result of the contribution holiday, it is possible that some participants will contribute for only twelve months to receive the initial $1,000 kick-start incentive and then cease making any contributions for the following five years.

In 2007 NZS was still the primary source of retirement income for over 70 percent of the population aged 65 and up. Although that proportion is likely to drop as KiwiSaver accounts mature, the cost of providing NZS will not be affected since all workers are covered, regardless of income. Moreover, the proportion of the 65-and-over population is projected to double by 2050, so the cost of providing NZS will rise from its current level of 4.6 percent of GDP to over 6 percent of GDP. Options that have been mentioned to decrease the costs of the program include targeting benefits, increasing the residency requirement, increasing the eligibility age, or reducing the average replacement rate of benefits.

On top of the NZS, the cost of incentives for consumers to join KiwiSaver is projected to add roughly $2 billion (20 percent of the net costs of the NZS) to the cost of government retirement saving programs by 2016.[65] The high cost of incentives to encourage participation raises the question of whether KiwiSaver membership should be made compulsory, as is the Superannuation Guarantee in Australia, or whether the NZS and KiwiSaver should be coordinated in some way that might allow some recapture of all or a portion of those incentives from upper-income workers. Another question is whether the incentives are really necessary in the long run, or whether automatic enrollment alone would be sufficient to ensure optimal participation.

Returns and Costs

Average five-year returns on balanced funds in New Zealand have been roughly 4.5 percent in nominal terms.[66] Currently, thirty KiwiSaver providers offer participants over 180 funds of varying investment strategies and risk. To be registered with KiwiSaver, a fund must meet certain regulations regarding asset allocation, but there are no performance guarantees. The government negotiates the level of fees and other costs funds may charge, but determining the cost for a particular fund can be complex, because up to ten different types of fees may be imposed. These include an annual fee measured as a percentage of the total assets in the fund, a membership fee, entry or exit fees, and occasional legal or audit fees. Multiple reported cost numbers may make choosing a preferred fund more difficult for employees. The Retirement Commission, an autonomous government entity that provides financial education and guidance, estimates that conservatively managed funds have total annual fees of between 0.3 percent and 0.6 percent of assets, while more actively managed funds have fees of around 1 percent.

The six government-designated default funds are required to be invested primarily in cash, with only about 20 percent of the total amount invested in growth assets. However, fees charged by the default funds vary, raising an equity question because workers who do not choose another investment option, are randomly assigned to a default fund.

Financial education in New Zealand, which has been used as a model for other countries, is important both for maximizing individuals' retirement incomes and for maintaining competition and low costs among the investment funds. The website "Sorted," started by the New Zealand government in 2001, provides a number of easy-to-use financial planning calculators and guides.[67] Additionally, there are plans to include financial education, already available in the workplace, in school curricula as well.

Retirement Income

Replacement rates in New Zealand are low relative to Australia and the OECD, at around 39.7 percent gross and 41.7 percent net of taxes.[68] A study done by the New Zealand Treasury suggests that under conservative assumptions about spending changes and consumption patterns after retirement, roughly 40 percent of couples and 30 percent of individuals aged 45 to 64 are not saving enough for retirement. Under less conservative retirement income assumptions (which require a lower saving rate to achieve), estimates show that closer to 20 percent of New Zealanders still have inadequate savings.[69] There are also concerns regarding the saving patterns of younger cohorts, although such patterns are difficult to measure empirically. Some analysts believe that younger New Zealanders have greater access to credit and thus will have more debt than did their parents' generation.

That said, labor force participation rates among those aged 50 and older have been increasing significantly, with workers in this category accounting for half of the total growth of the labor force from 1991 to 2005.[70] In 2006, 43 percent of men and 25 percent of women aged 65 to 69 were in the labor force, one of the highest participation rates among older people in the OECD.

In 2007 pension wealth contributed only 2 percent of total net wealth of couples aged 45 to 54. Other financial assets made up 44 percent of wealth and housing equity was 22 percent, with the value of NZS benefits making up the balance (32 percent).[71] The small role played by pension wealth helps to explain the paucity of annuities that are taken in New Zealand. Individual retirement accounts are also relatively small in size. The thin annuities market may begin to grow once KiwiSaver members start to accumulate significant levels of retirement savings and need a source of permanent retirement income. Several barriers to the development of the annuities market exist on both the supply and demand side. These include risks to the insurance companies that increasing life expectancies will make annuities more costly, the fact that annuity income is taxed at a higher rate than other income, the perception that the NZS provides annuities, and the fear of dying before receiving the full benefits of the annuity.

The distribution of retirement income in New Zealand is flat relative to preretirement income. The progressivity index calculated by the OECD is 100 for New Zealand, meaning that the income disparities between the highest and the lowest earners among retirees are among the lowest in the thirty OECD countries. Retirement income replaces 81 percent of preretirement income for New Zealanders who earned an average amount equal to half the country's average male earnings level, nearly double the replacement rate paid to retirees who earned average earnings. The degree of equity in retirement income is likely because pension wealth, which is linked to preretirement earnings, makes up such a small percentage of total retirement wealth, and because the NZS is universal.

United Kingdom

The pension system in the United Kingdom is exceptionally complex, with two levels of public pensions supplemented by a two-part, means-tested program. The interaction between the differing public programs is often confusing, especially when the worker also has additional personal or employer-sponsored defined contribution or defined benefit plans of some form. The one constant in the public pension system over the last several decades has been change. To some extent this is the result of the country's tax system, under which taxes and tax preferences appear, change, and disappear almost annually. In addition, over the last few decades, the benefits calculation under the two public pension benefits has changed several times, and the two means-tested benefits have been created. These changes have confused British workers, and the interaction between the various public plans has discouraged nongovernmental pension saving.

Now, the system is evolving again. If recently proposed reforms are put into place as planned, the United Kingdom will offer its citizens a major new pension saving system that should greatly increase retirement security. Recent history suggests that future governments may continue to tinker with the system.

Structure of the System

In the current public pension system, the first tier, known as the Basic State Pension (BSP), is a flat-rate pension. Men who make a National Insurance contribution (NIC) for at least forty-four years and women who contribute for thirty-nine years receive the full value of the pension, and those who contribute for fewer years receive a proportionally lower amount. [72] Through April 2009, a full basic weekly pension was 90.70 British pounds for individuals and 145.05 pounds for couples. [73]

Initially, the BSP was indexed to growth in average earnings, but in 1981 that was changed to indexation by inflation. The result has been a gradual but dramatic decline in the amount of preretirement income that the BSP replaces. At the time indexation was changed in 1981, the BSP amounted to just below 30 percent of average income at age 50. By 2000 it had declined to 20 percent, and if inflation indexation remains in place, it would reach 10 percent by about 2040. [74]

To supplement the BSP, a means-tested Pension Credit was introduced in 2003 to benefit pensioners with low or zero personal savings. The credit has two parts. First is a universal credit regardless of the amount or years of National Insurance contributions paid by the worker. It is intended to raise the pensioners' weekly income to roughly 20 percent of average wage and salary earnings, an amount equal to 124 pounds for individuals and 189 pounds for couples in 2008. Individuals over age 65 can also benefit from the second part of the Pension Credit: an additional payment known as the Savings Credit, which pays retirees an amount equal to the value of 60 percent of all their privately financed retirement income. [75] This second part of the Pension Credit, which in theory rewards retirees for having saved, pays up to 20 pounds a week for individuals and 26 pounds for couples.

The Pension Credit is controversial for several reasons. First, British workers must apply for it, and the application is somewhat detailed. At the time that it went into effect, there was concern that some older pensioners would be unable to understand the process or might be discouraged by the amount of information it required. Second, because the second part of the Pension Credit effectively reclaims about 40 pence per pound of savings, there were fears that in practice, it would discourage workers, and especially moderate-income workers, from saving for retirement. Finally, there were fears that because of the declining value of the BSP, an ever-growing proportion of future retirees would qualify for the Pension Credit. This last concern was potentially dealt with in the 2007 Pensions Act, which is intended to increase retirement savings.

In addition to the BSP, a second tier, now known as the State Second Pension (S2P), is the earnings-related portion of the public pension system. Initially created by a Labor Party government in 1978 and known then as the State Earnings Related Pension System, this program pays workers a benefit based on earnings between an upper and lower limit. In 2009 S2P benefits were based on annual earnings between 4,680 and 40,000 pounds, a range that is adjusted regularly. Before 2003 the S2P provided a replacement rate of 20 percent of average lifetime earnings for workers between the earnings limits.[76] That rate, set in 1988, was a reduction from the 25 percent replacement rate set when the program was adopted in 1978. Government actuaries belatedly discovered that using the 25 percent replacement rate would require payments far in excess of what the government would be able to pay.

Since 2003 S2P benefits have been based on wages. For purposes of calculating their eventual pension benefit, workers with 2009 earnings greater than 4,680 pounds but less than 13,500 pounds would be credited with a 40 percent replacement rate for earnings between those amounts. Workers would receive credit at a marginal 10 percent rate for earnings between 13,500 and 31,100 pounds, and at a 20 percent rate for earnings between 31,100 and 40,040. The same calculation would be made for each year of earnings to determine the S2P benefit. The 2003 reforms, which were intended to increase benefits for moderate-income workers, represent an intermediate stage before the S2P becomes a flat benefit. Starting in 2010, the upper two bands will merge and provide a 10 percent replacement rate, before it is replaced with a flat rate benefit by approximately 2030.[77]

Since its creation in 1978, one of the S2P's signature features has been the ability of participants to "contract out" through participation in an employer-sponsored retirement plan. If they do so, both the employer and the employee pay lower National Insurance Contributions (NIC). Individuals who are not covered by a pension plan or retirement saving plan at work may also contract out this part of the public system plan by choosing a stakeholder pension or a personal pension. In that case the NIC rates are not decreased, but the government rebates the contributions by placing them directly into the individual retirement account. All private retirement account contributions are pretax. Some individuals may choose to have a "rebate-only" private pension—that is, one that consists only of the NIC rebates and is worth roughly the same as the S2P.

The ability to contract out caused a major "mis-selling" scandal in the late 1980s and early 1990s after the government passed a law forbidding employers to require workers to participate in their pension plan. Instead, employees had the ability to withdraw from the employer's plan and start their own personal retirement savings plan. Companies immediately started to market to employees, urging them to join a personal plan, but failing in many cases to disclose that workers who did so would lose any contributions that the employer would have made, thus leaving the employee worse off. The ensuing scandal and several other similar scandals forced financial services companies to make reparations to affected workers and to greatly increase the advice given before a worker could invest with them. Although apparently caused as much by insurance and other sales agents who had previously sold other types of products and may have been honestly unfamiliar with the details of retirement savings products as by intentional deception, the scandals greatly weakened public trust in retirement savings plans.

At one time, the United Kingdom had a large system of employer-based retirement plans. In 1979 almost 65 percent of all workers were enrolled in an employer-based plan, but since then, the rate of participation has declined, falling to roughly 55 percent in 2004. There were 2 million fewer members in 2004 than in 2000.[78] This decline is closely related to the closure of many large and small defined benefit plans, in part because employers shifted to defined contribution plans to escape the increasing cost of defined benefit plans caused by rising life expectancies.

Previous reforms sought to increase retirement savings through a system of stakeholder pensions, which can be employer-based or owned by an individual whose employer does not offer any form of retirement plan.[79] Offered starting in 2001, stakeholder pensions are extremely simple and have administrative fees capped at a maximum of 1 percent of balances. Employers with more than five employees were required to offer their employees these accounts, but enrollment was not automatic and many employers did not promote them, so relatively few stakeholder accounts were opened. In addition, most financial institutions complained that the fee cap, which included all advertising costs, made stakeholder accounts unprofitable and so did not promote them. The failure of stakeholder pensions resulted in the personal accounts plan enacted in 2007.

Recent Reforms Taking Effect in 2010

In response to the continuing debate over pensions, the U.K. government passed the Pensions Act of 2007, which will make substantial changes beginning in 2010. The reforms are intended to simplify the private saving system, increase saving, and avoid undersaving among moderate and low earners. The law

—Reduces the number of years of contributions necessary to qualify for full Basic State Pension benefits to thirty years for both men and women

—Allows pensioners to claim state pension benefits based on their spouse's qualifying years of contributions and earnings at any time after retirement age, rather than only after the spouse claims his or her pension

—Indexes the basic state pension to average annual earnings rather than to prices (although the exact date that this will happen is uncertain)

—Simplifies the State Second Pension so that the lowest income band will accrue benefits at a flat rate of 1.40 pounds weekly and the top two bands of earnings will be combined so that they both accrue benefits at 10 percent of earnings

—Increases the state pension age by one year per decade between 2020 and 2050 (reaching 68 eventually) for everyone born after April 1959

—Abolishes contracting out the S2P into employer-sponsored defined contribution and stakeholder plans (but not defined benefit plans)

Personal Accounts

Perhaps most important, the 2007 law established a system of voluntary, automatic enrollment, private retirement accounts that will begin in 2012. The personal accounts system will enable all workers to have an occupational pension plan that has low fees and charges. The plan would be administered by an independent administrative body.

All employees and workers between age 22 and the state pension age who are not already in an occupational pension plan and whose annual earnings exceed a specified amount—5,035 pounds in 2007—will be automatically enrolled in an account.[80] Enrollees may opt out of the plan, subject to automatic reenrollment every three years. Nonworkers, below-threshold earners, and the self-employed may opt in but will not be eligible to receive an employer contribution. Employees will contribute an amount equal to 4 percent of pay, which will be combined with a mandatory 3 percent contribution by employers, while the government will provide roughly 1 percent through tax relief, for an overall default contribution of 8 percent.[81] Annual earnings over a specified limit—33,540 pounds in 2007—will not be subject to personal account contributions, and annual contributions are limited to not more than 5,000 pounds per year. Individuals may not consolidate other retirement savings into their personal accounts.

The personal accounts system is intended to increase private retirement saving, lower the government's liability for state pension payments, and raise average replacement rates. As is the case with automatic enrollment in New Zealand, the U.K. system intends to take advantage of employee inertia to increase participation rates. Estimates produced by the Department for Work and Pensions based on survey data of individuals' attitudes toward the new program suggest that nearly 70 percent of individuals are likely to remain in their employer's plan or participate in the personal accounts system.[82] If this participation rate is accurate, 6 million to 9 million workers would be saving more in their workplace pensions than they do now; 4 million to 8 million of these would be new savers. Evidence from other U.K. automatic enrollment schemes has shown that individuals who save as a result of the automatic feature tend to have lower-than-average incomes.

The new U.K. system will continue to use employer-based plans as its foundation. Employers with more than two employees and no other pension plan will be required to participate in the personal accounts system. At start-up, however, it would cover only large employers and then gradually be extended to small employers. Employers may be exempt from the personal accounts system and regulations associated with it if they choose to automatically enroll employees in a pension plan of equal or better value.[83]

Mandated matching employer contributions will increase costs for an estimated 670,000 employers that currently do not offer a pension plan and for an additional 240,000 employers that contribute at a rate below 3 percent of income. The total cost of additional employer contributions is projected to be between 1.8 billion and 2.9 billion pounds a year once the mandatory 3 percent level is fully phased in.[84] Some of these costs may be offset by lower National Insurance Contributions, although employers indicate that some of their costs may be covered by price increases or wage deductions.[85]

In the aggregate, the government projects that the reform will generate up to 10 billion pounds per year by 2015 in additional pension savings. Because of tax relief that is provided to savers, these additional savings will cost the government an estimated 1.3 billion pounds in 2020 and 2.4 billion pounds in 2050. Another cost will be corporate tax losses as a result of decreased corporate profits stemming from higher total employer retirement contributions. A portion of these tax expenditures and losses will be offset by higher receipt of taxes on pension income; the increase in self-provision for retirement will also decrease the cost of the means-tested Pension Credit.

These results are questioned by a number of private sector retirement professionals who believe that the personal accounts system will encourage employers that contribute more than 3 percent of workers' income to a retirement plan to reduce their contributions. Still other employers may choose to close their plans and to rely instead on the personal accounts system.

Returns and Costs

The administration of the personal accounts system will be centralized to keep costs low. A clearinghouse collects the contributions and allocates them to large aggregate investment funds, where they will be managed by private sector investment managers. A separate administrative body will manage the marketing, customer contact and information, and issues statements to participants.

The goal of the Pensions Commission is to run the entire personal accounts system at a total annual cost of 0.3 percent of assets. Regulating the types of funds that qualify under the personal accounts scheme will also help to ensure adequate returns. Low fees will especially help in early phases of the personal accounts system, when the funds are relatively small and low fees will translate into higher returns on investments.[86]

However, the 0.3 percent administrative fee is substantially lower than that charged by many retirement plans, and it may be difficult to achieve. Some studies suggest that an annual fee closer to 0.5 percent of assets is more realistic.

Retirement Income

Participants in both the BSP and S2P are eligible to retire at age 65 for men and 60 for women. Those ages are set to equalize gradually at 65 over the period of 2010–20 and then to rise to 68 by 2050. Deferral of a state pension benefit is also allowed, and additional benefits accrue from the statutory retirement age at a rate of 10.4 percent of earnings subject to National Insurance Contributions per year. Upon retirement, all balances in the public system (mainly those in the S2P) are automatically annuitized. Balances accrued in individual or occupational private accounts must be annuitized by age 75 to the extent that they are funded by NIC tax rebates. Seventy-five percent of any additional retirement contributions must also be annuitized by age 75, with the remaining 25 percent being available for withdrawal in a tax-free lump sum. Pension annuity income is taxed at the same rate as other income.

Although pensioner income in the United Kingdom has been increasing over the past forty years, 44 percent of retirees still rely almost entirely on state-provided benefits, and the old-age dependency ratio is projected to double by 2030. State pensions are likely to provide lower replacement rates in the future, and before the 2007 reform, declining participation in occupational plans further depressed projections of future retirement income. Without change, the participation-based state pensions would have led to very low retirement incomes for individuals who did not contribute consistently to an employer-based retirement plan over their working lives. Reliance on the means-tested Pension Credit would have created a higher implicit tax on saving for an increasing percentage of the population.[87] The gross replacement rate in 2007 for mean earners was only 30.8 percent, the lowest in the OECD. Net of taxes, the United Kingdom ranked a bit higher, with a replacement rate of 41.1 percent at the mean of earnings. The OECD pension progressivity index for the United Kingdom was relatively high at 81.1, although this is a result of the low levels of participation in occupational pensions.[88]

If the predicted levels of participation in the personal accounts system after it goes into effect in 2012 are accurate, they will translate into increased retirement saving for future retirees. Baseline predictions suggest that with the minimum automatic contribution levels, pension incomes for individuals aged 68 to 75 will have increased by 12 percent in 2050. The replacement rate for individuals who are 22 years old in 2012 will be roughly 68 percent by the time they reach retirement, and for those who are 40 years old in that year it will be roughly 40 percent.[89] If individuals contribute more than the automatic 4 percent of income into a personal account, their replacement rate will be higher; survey data suggests that nearly half of those who stay enrolled in a private pension plan will contribute at a higher rate than the minimum.

The impact of the reforms on pension progressivity will depend largely on participation rates among low earners. This group is the most likely to benefit from the automatic enrollment mechanism in the system. However, the contribution from the government based on tax relief will slightly disproportionately benefit higher-bracket earners.

The mandatory annuitization system aims to ensure that retirees' savings last for the remainder of their lives. The regulation seeks to overcome market barriers that otherwise might suppress the use of annuities: potential behavioral biases that lower demand and adverse selection, and changing mortality risks that would raise costs of annuities. Additionally, a portion of the retirement savings that must be used to purchase an annuity is funded by tax rebates, which the government believes should be used for income and not to fund bequests.

The annuities market in the United Kingdom tripled between 1991 and 2006 and is projected to increase further as private retirement funds shift toward defined benefit plans.[90] With the increase in demand has come an increase in flexibility for annuitants. Retirees are able to delay annuitization until age 75, and providers have developed numerous products that are specific to differing lifestyles, health statuses, and number of dependents. Additionally, retirees now have the ability to choose an open market option for purchasing an annuity. Under this option, they can use an online tool that lists all potential annuities that meet their personal conditions and are available to them, the costs of each option, and the weekly income each would provide. Retirees can now search for the best value on the market rather than being tied to the same company that handled their savings.[91]

Challenges Facing the U.S. Retirement Saving System

In the coming years, the United States is likely to grapple with a number of challenges as Social Security and private pensions evolve. Social Security has been technically insolvent for twenty of its nearly seventy-five years, and the

Social Security actuaries project that Social Security will be solvent only until 2016, after which it will spend more in benefits than it will receive in payroll taxes. [92]

Although the present value of total lifetime Social Security benefits will be higher under current law for future retirees than for current retirees, the share of preretirement income that Social Security will replace will decrease.

Social Security's impending insolvency highlights the increasing significance of retirement savings accounts for future retirees. Unfortunately, while participation in employer-sponsored plans has increased significantly over the last sixty years, from roughly 24 percent in 1950 to almost 50 percent in 2000, it has remained relatively stable since the late 1980s. Additionally, the creation of individual retirement accounts (IRAs) in 1974 and reforms in 2001 have made saving for individuals without an employer-sponsored plan feasible and attractive through tax incentives.[93] However, a large proportion of IRAs have been opened by workers rolling over a 401(k) plan sponsored by a former employer after leaving the job. Under 10 percent of workers whose employers do not sponsor a retirement plan regularly contribute to an IRA. About 37 percent of workers have neither an employer-sponsored retirement plan nor an IRA.[94] Coverage rates are lowest among low-income workers, younger workers, women, and members of minority groups. Many of these workers are employed in a small business. Involving these groups in retirement savings accounts is one of the main challenges for pension policy.

Employer-sponsored retirement plans have continued to shift toward defined contribution plans, in which workers contribute a portion of earnings into an investment account and receive benefits that are equal to their contributions plus investment returns. From 1975 to 2000 the number of defined contribution plans more than tripled, to almost 700,000 accounts, while the number of private-sector defined benefit plans fell from 170,000 to under 50,000. In 2003, 58 percent of workers with a retirement plan participated in a defined contribution plan, and that proportion is expected to increase as time goes on. Small employers with fewer than 250 employees account for a major part of the decline in defined benefit plans.[95] The shift to defined contribution plans combined with the need to increase participation and the recent drop in asset values during the recession will frame much of the coming discussion about the future of the U.S. retirement system.

Lessons for the U.S. System

The experiences of the four countries reviewed here offer some valuable lessons to U.S. policymakers as they address these challenges facing the country's retirement system.

Mandatory Savings vs. Automatic Enrollment

Increasing the participation rate in retirement savings accounts can be accomplished through either mandatory participation or automatic enrollment mechanisms. Evidence suggests that while mandatory systems clearly work, automatic enrollment may achieve similar participation rates at a lower political cost. Two of the four countries in this study (Australia and Chile) have a mandatory savings structure, while New Zealand uses automatic enrollment, and the United Kingdom is starting an automatic enrollment system.

Both countries with mandatory systems have the expected high participation rates. As noted above, Chile's participation rate is less than optimal, but this is explained more by the makeup of the workforce than by anything else. One disadvantage of the mandatory system is that it must allow people some ability to choose their own contribution rates. In Australia, the effort to find a least-common-denominator contribution rate has led to a decrease in savings rates for some participants.

It is too early to determine how the new automatic enrollment systems in New Zealand and the United Kingdom will work. However, evidence from the United States shows that automatic enrollment can boost participation of eligible employees from roughly 75 percent to between 85 and 95 percent.[96] The greatest increase comes from those with the lowest participation in the current system. One study shows that with automatic enrollment employees with under $20,000 in earnings increase participation rates from 13 percent to 80 percent, and Hispanic workers' rates increase from 19 percent to 75 percent.[97] Additionally, making enrollment eligibility universal would allow participation by the roughly 50 percent of workers who currently have no access to a 401(k) plan.[98]

Default Investment Choices

Setting appropriate default investment options is a critical part of improving retirement income. Overall, limiting investment options works much better than providing a long list of choices. Even in Chile, where there was a measure of consumer choice and competition among providers, the actual investments were limited to a select few fund types, and their structure was dictated by a government agency. Similarly, New Zealand randomly places participants who do not choose an investment fund into one of six default funds, and the coming personal accounts system in the United Kingdom will also have both a default and a very limited menu of other choices. This is also true in the industry funds of Australia, where most participants remain in a trustee-selected balanced portfolio of investment choices.

A Simple Savings Platform to Keep Administrative Fees Low

International experience shows that the best way to keep administrative costs low is to provide a simple investment platform with default investment funds and a high proportion of index-type funds. Chile, the only country studied in this paper without such a structure, has higher fees than its neighbors that have adopted similar individual account systems. While rival administrators in Chile do compete among themselves, they try to lure depositors with gifts rather than more economically priced services.

Costs in New Zealand, which does have a simple investment platform with a default investment option, appear to be fairly low, although that will be clear only after the system has been in operation for a longer time. Australia's super-annuation clearinghouse, which was slated to start operations on July 1, 2009, and will help to direct contributions to investments, was created in response to complaints about fee levels in that system.

Meanwhile, the personal accounts reform in the United Kingdom will use a centralized administrative body to help keep costs well below those that can be found in other parts of the country's financial system, but its target level for administrative costs of 0.3 percent of assets was chosen by a governmental body and may not be achievable for some time, if at all. A simple centralized investment mechanism appears to have a better chance of keeping fees low in much the same way as the U.S. Thrift Savings Plan (TSP) has kept costs down for federal employees. The TSP has a centralized administration and record-keeping agency that tracks participants' contributions and allocates them to chosen funds. Administrative costs for TSP funds have been very low since their inception; in 2007 costs averaged only .015 percent of assets.[99] Both New Zealand's KiwiSaver and the coming U.K. system are based on the TSP.

A simple retirement system also increases the ability of workers to understand it and to be able to predict their retirement income. An extremely simple system such as that in New Zealand is probably the easiest for participants to understand, while the very complex U.K. system has left many workers both confused and nervous that their retirement income will be inadequate.

Changeable Savings Systems

A clear lesson from the United Kingdom is the need to avoid constant changes in retirement savings systems. Since the creation in 1978 of what came to be known as the State Second Pension, successive governments have changed returns on contributions and the overall structure of the system itself. Returns were reduced for everyone in 1988 and then were changed into a progressive benefit system in 2003, with further changes coming that will turn the system into a flat benefit. Admittedly, the first change was necessitated by poor actuarial work that provided workers with more for their savings than the government could afford. But British governments have been unclear about the purpose of S2P and who should benefit from it. The result has been to confuse potential savers about what their retirement benefits will be and, in many cases, whether they should even save at all.

More recently, New Zealand's KiwiSaver plan had a series of incentives added to it just before the plan opened, only to have the incentives pared back and other changes made shortly after the government changed hands. If these sudden shifts continue, they could damage public support for the plan. On the other hand, recent reforms in Chile were only made after serious consideration of the plan's shortcomings. Clearly, plans must change with the nation's economy, but changes should come only after serious consideration of long-term consequences.

Ensuring an Adequate Safety Net

While augmenting public pensions with retirement income funded by private saving is both desirable and necessary, adequate income guarantees remain crucial. New Zealand's universal pension, indexed to wage growth and restricted only by residency, is the most progressive and simple sort of old-age guarantee considered in this chapter. It covers all retirees, does not create disincentives to save through means testing, and its fiscal costs are straightforward. In Australia, the means-tested public pension appears likely to be able to serve as an adequate safety net with few disincentives to save—once a significant proportion of the workforce has participated in the Superannuation Guarantee system for another few decades. The situation would be greatly helped if some level of SG annuitization were required to eliminate the incentive to spend those funds in order to qualify for a public pension.

Conversely, the experience of Chile shows that a low means-tested basic pension in conjunction with a participation-based minimum pension leaves portions of the population uncovered by any form of public old-age income security. Although the minimum pension was supposed to serve as a safety net, its original structure failed to cover a significant proportion of those who needed it.

The U.K. system as it exists now is also deeply flawed by a basic public pension whose value continues to drop as a proportion of preretirement income because it is indexed to inflation rather than wage growth. The complex, means-tested Pension Credit really only serves to mask the poor formulation of the Basic State Pension, and the growing proportion of British workers who would have to rely on it emphasizes the point. While the coming personal accounts system and a return of the Basic State Pension to wage indexing will improve the situation, more work remains to be done.

Encouraging Annuitization

A retirement savings system is only really successful if it allows participants to build enough savings to provide lifetime retirement income. The United Kingdom requires the annuitization of at least 75 percent of a worker's pool of retirement savings, while Chile requires either annuitization or a phased-withdrawal system. Neither Australia nor New Zealand has any such requirement, and efforts by Australia to encourage annuitization through favorable tax treatment have been less than satisfactory. New Zealand's program is too new to have any retirees as yet, but the country's existing pension system features minimal use of annuities.

Annuities pool longevity risk to insure annuitants against running out of resources before death. Otherwise, with increasing longevity, there is a very real risk that a growing number of retirees will run out of assets and end up living in poverty. This issue is a key concern in the United States, where 80 percent of defined contribution plans do not offer an annuity (see chapter 6). However, establishing mandatory annuitization such as in the United Kingdom requires the same political consensus that a mandatory saving program does, and that is not easily achieved. Additionally, for many lower-income retirees in the United States, an annuity may not be the optimal choice given income security provided by Social Security.

Instead, it would be better to consider some form of system based on behavioral economics that guides retirees to annuitization but does not require it. While there is early work on such an approach, it does not exist in practice. As a result, there is also no guarantee that behavioral approaches in pensions' spending stage operate as they have in the accumulation stage. In the interim while these policies are being developed, one avenue that should be encouraged is the type of annuity comparison mechanism available in Chile and the United Kingdom, where consumers can see the available income choices and costs of each. This at least allows consumers to make an educated choice.

The worst approach to the spending stage is to assume that the retirees are able to make appropriate decisions on their own. While the United States may not be ready for mandatory annuitization, it does not have the option of ducking a decision on some form of annuitization policy.

Is a National Retirement Savings System Needed?

The United States simply cannot afford to have about half of its workforce unable to take advantage of a simple, low-cost system of retirement saving.

Most workers cannot afford to live in retirement on just Social Security benefits, and that program's coming fiscal problems make it very unlikely that benefits will increase. If younger workers are to have the same retirement security as their parents and grandparents, they must save for retirement from the time they first enter the workforce until they reach retirement age.

This does not imply that the United States should adopt one of the systems studied in this chapter. Each system developed according to the specific culture and political realities of its home country, and each is a mixture of features that may make sense only for that country. However, each of the four national systems offers positive and negative lessons that are relevant to U.S. policymakers. A U.S. system needs to reflect American political and financial realities, but it can adopt certain components that have worked elsewhere.

The U.S. system does not have to have a centralized mechanism styled after KiwiSaver or the coming U.K. personal accounts system, nor does it have to be mandatory like Chile's or Australia's. Automatic enrollment seems to offer a better solution for the United States than does a mandatory system. If automatic enrollment proves ineffective over time or if certain ethnic, gender, or income groups end up being underserved, the United States could later consider moving to a mandatory system.

Similarly, a decentralized system combined with some form of online component that could match employers with a financial services provider interested in their business may be more efficient and faster to implement. However, if some segments of the market are underserved and cannot get access to a cost-effective retirement savings product, then some more formal and centralized system of providing accounts will have to be created. Somewhat similar problems resulted in Australia's new clearinghouse.

Regardless of what system is chosen, it must operate in tandem with the existing employer-sponsored system and not as an alternative to it. Companies that offer their employees 401(k)-type plans or traditional defined benefit pension plans should not be required to replace them with a new system. Instead, any additional system should apply only to companies that do not offer any type of retirement savings plan or pension and to the self-employed. That is not to say that 401(k)-type plans are perfect. The results of the current economic downturn show otherwise. However, nothing to date indicates that those workers would be better off in a different system.

Each of the four countries surveyed here recognizes that increased retirement saving is essential to improving retirement security and reducing the potential cost of a taxpayer-financed pension system. None of their systems are perfect, but all of them have positive features. As U.S. policymakers seek to increase the proportion of workers who save for retirement, they can learn a great deal from exploring overseas systems.

Notes

1. The World Bank recommends a three-pillar approach: public, mandatory private, and voluntary private. World Bank, "Averting the Old Age Crisis" (Oxford University Press, 1994).

2. Social Security Administration, "Fast Facts and Figures about Social Security 2008," www.ssa.gov/policy/docs/chartbooks/fast_facts/2008/.

3. Dennis Jacobe, "Fewer Americans Expect a Comfortable Retirement" (Washington: Gallup, 2008).

4. The United Kingdom was one of two OECD countries (along with Hungary) to see an increase rather than reduction. OECD (Organization for Economic Cooperation and Development), "Pensions at a Glance: Public Policies across OECD Countries" (Paris: 2007).

5. Mandatory contributions are applied to about $2,427 in earnings per month. A 2006 study found that less than 5 percent of AFP contributors earned over this ceiling. Alberto Arenas de Mesa and others, "The Chilean Pension Reform Turns 25: Lessons from the Social Protection Survey," Working Paper 2006-9 (University of Pennsylvania, Wharton School, Pension Research Council, 2006).

6. Carmelo Mesa-Lago, "Assessing the World Bank Report *Keeping the Promise*," *International Social Security Review* 58, no. 2-3 (2005), pp. 97–100.

7. Barbara E. Kritzer, "Chile's Next Generation of Pension Reform," *Social Security Bulletin* 68, no. 2 (2008), pp. 69-84.

8. Sylvester J. Schieber and John B. Shoven, "Social Security Reform: Around the World in 80 Ways," *American Economic Review,* 86, no. 2 (1996), pp. 373–77.

9. Arenas de Mesa and others, "The Chilean Pension Reform Turns 25."

10. Superintendencia Seguridad Social, Departmento Actuarial, "Variables Previsionales Relevantes; Vigentes al mes de Noviembre de 2007." www.suseso.cl/common/asp/pag AtachadorVisualizador.asp?argCryptedData=GP1TkTXdhRJAS2Wp3v88hMBrze0pOMpr &argModo=inline&argOrigen=BD&argFlagYaGrabados=&argArchivoId=5352.

11. Kritzer, "Chile's Next Generation of Pension Reform."

12. Mesa-Lago, "Assessing the World Bank Report *Keeping the Promise*." The 1981 participation rate was significantly lower than that in the 1970s.

13. Solange Berstein, "The Chilean Pension System: Facts and Challenges," Superintendent of AFP, presentation for the OECD (Santiago: 2006).

14. Kritzer, "Chile's Next Generation of Pension Reform."

15. Solange Berstein, Guillermo Larrain, and Francisco Pino, "Chilean Pension Reform: Coverage Facts and Policy Alternatives," *Journal of Latin American and Caribbean Economic Association* 6, no. 2 (2006), pp. 227–79, as cited in Kritzer, "Chile's Next Generation of Pension Reform."

16. Kritzer, "Chile's Next Generation of Pension Reform."

17. Marcel Commission, Consejo Asesor Presidencial para la Reforma Previsional, "El derecho a una vida digna en la vejez: Hacia un contrato social con la prevision en Chile" (2006), www.consejoreformaprevisional.cl.

18. Kritzer, "Chile's Next Generation of Pension Reform."

19. Alberto Arenas de Mesa and Carmelo Mesa-Lago, "The Structural Pension Reform in Chile: Effects, Comparisons with Other Latin American Reforms, and Lessons," *Oxford Review of Economic Policy* 22, no. 1 (2006), pp. 149–67. A 2002 law created the four different types of funds that exist today and made it possible for contributors to have two accounts. Still, the three largest funds make up 80 percent of the market.

20. Kritzer, "Chile's Next Generation of Pension Reform." Both Argentina and Peru had higher fees as measured by a percentage of the mandatory contribution. However, Chile's fees were not significantly above the 12+ percent charged in Colombia, El Salvador, Mexico, and Uruguay.

21. Berstein, Larrain and Pino, "Chilean Pension Reform: Coverage Facts and Policy Alternatives."

22. Arenas de Mesa and others, "The Chilean Pension Reform Turns 25."

23. Kritzer, "Chile's Next Generation of Pension Reform."

24. E. James and X. Song, "Annuities Markets around the World: Money's Worth and Risk Intermediation," Working Paper (Washington: World Bank, 2001).

25. Stephen J. Kay and Barbara E. Kritzer, "Social Security in Latin America: Recent Reforms and Challenges," *Economic Review* (Federal Reserve Bank of Atlanta) 86, no. 1(2001), pp. 41–52.

26. Berstein, Larrain and Pino, "Chilean Pension Reform: Coverage Facts and Policy Alternatives."

27. Hazel Bateman and John Piggott, "Australia's Mandatory Retirement Saving Policy: A View from the New Millennium," Research Paper 19 (Sydney: Australia School of Business, Retirements Economics Group, 2000).

28. G. Dunsford and M. Rice, "Retirement Incomes Integration: Superannuation, Social Security and Taxation" (Sydney: Institute of Actuaries of Australia, 2004); Ann Harding and Simon Kelly, "Funding the Retirement of Baby Boomers," *Agenda* 11, no. 2 (2004), pp. 99–112.

29. Garry Barrett and Ye-Ping Tseng, "Retirement Saving in Australia," Social and Economic Dimensions of an Aging Population Research Paper 177 (McMaster University, 2007).

30. Gerry Gallery and Natalie Gallery, "Paradox of Choice in a Mandatory Pension Savings System: Challenges for Australian Retirement Income," *Policy and Politics* 33, no. 3 (2005), pp. 519–32.

31. Special residence requirements apply to widowed workers and certain other groups.

32. http://www.centrelink.gov.au/internet/internet.nsf/payments/age_rates.htm.

33. For homeowners, the value of a home is not included in the assets test. OECD, "Pensions at a Glance."

34. Ibid.

35. Barrett and Tseng, "Retirement Saving in Australia."

36. AFG Global Funds Management Index, www.smh.com.au/news/Business/Australia-tops-in-managed-funds/2006/01/23/1137864849431.html

37. Bateman and Piggott, "Australia's Mandatory Retirement Saving Policy," World Bank Pensions Primer (Washington: 2001).

38. *Sydney Morning Herald,* "Super Crunch Wipes out 3 Years of Gains," January 22, 2009.

39. In a country of only 21 million people with a workforce of 14 million in 2008. See Minister of Superannuation and Corporate Law, media release and discussion paper on "Superannuation Clearing House and the Lost Members Framework, Part B," released on November 14, 2008 (www.treasurer.gov.au).

40. The study models saving as a function of income, wealth, and the degree of financial deregulation as measured by the ratio of household debt to income, in addition to a dummy for the introduction of the SG. Ellis Connolly and Marion Kohler, 2004, "The Impact of Superannuation on Household Saving," Research Discussion Paper 2004–01 (Sydney: Reserve Bank of Australia, 2004).

41. www.fido.asic.gov.au/fido/fido.nsf/byheadline/Long-term+performance+figures+for+typical+super+fund+investment+options?openDocument.

42. Katrina Ellis, Alan Tobin, and Belinda Tracey, "Investment Performance, Asset Allocation, and Expenses of Large Superannuation Funds," Working Paper (Sydney: Australian Prudential Regulatory Authority, 2008).The remainder of the funds are in very small Australian Prudential Regulatory Authority accounts.

43. Ibid.

44. Rachel Alembakis, "Super System Needs Reform for Future," *Global Pension,* February 17, 2009.

45. Australia and New Zealand Banking Group, Ltd., "Adult Financial Literacy, Personal Debt and Financial Difficulty in Australia: Summary Report" (2005), www.anz.com/aus/aboutanz/Community/Programs/pdf/ANZ_SumReport_FA. Pdf.

46. Minister of Superannuation and Corporate Law, media release and discussion paper.

47. According to the government, 90 percent of all Australian employers have fewer than twenty employees.

48. The retirement age for women is scheduled to increase to 65 by 2014.

49. Bateman and Piggott, "Australia's Mandatory Retirement Saving Policy."

50. www.australiansuper.com/resources.ashx/formsandpublications/408/File/93064DC27AE22A50D3D2CF4C56A8AC9F/Accessing_your_super_Nov07R.pdf.

51. The Age Pension is set at 25 percent of average earnings and benefits are tax-free. Ross Clare, "Retirement Savings Update" (Sydney: Association of Superannuation Funds of Australia, 2008).

52. Calculated as 100 minus the ratio of the pension Gini index to the earnings Gini index. OECD, "Pensions at a Glance."

53. Bateman and Piggott, "Australia's Mandatory Retirement Saving Policy."

54. Harding and Kelly, "Funding the Retirement of Baby Boomers."

55. Alembakis, "Super System Needs Reform for Future."

56. Retirement Commission, "Review of Retirement Income Policy" (Wellington: 2007).

57. Barbara E. Kritzer, "KiwiSaver: New Zealand's New Subsidized Retirement Savings Plans," *Social Security Bulletin* 67, no. 4 (2007).

58. The government elected in November 2008 froze the required employer match at 2 percent of income.

59. Retirement Commission, "Review of Retirement Income Policy."

60. Kritzer, "KiwiSaver: New Zealand's New Subsidized Retirement Savings Plans."

61. www.ird.govt.nz/news-updates/like-to-know-april-2009-kiwisaver-changes.html.

62. www.treasury.govt.nz/publications/informationreleases/kiwisaver/background/ks-assumptions-note.pdf.

63. www.kiwisaver.govt.nz/media/ks-media-mr-2008-03-25.html.

64. John Gibson and Trinh Le, "How Much New Saving Will KiwiSaver Produce," Working Paper 03/08 (University of Waikato, 2008), estimate that each dollar of KiwiSaver assets represents only $0.09 – $0.19 of new saving. They show that homeowners are 45–88 percent less likely to fund KiwiSaver contributions with reduced spending than are renters with otherwise similar characteristics. Similar results are seen in the United States, where contributors without housing assets have a higher fraction of new saving than reshuffled saving; see D. J. Benjamin, "Does 401(k) Eligibility Increase Saving? Evidence from Propensity Score Subclassification," *Journal of Public Economics* 87, no. 5 (2003), pp. 1259–90.

65. These numbers assume 50 percent take-up of private accounts by 2016. A 65 percent take-up would increase costs over the projection by one-third. New Zealand Retirement Commission, "Review of Retirement Income Policy."

66. www.fundsource.co.nz/FindAFund.asp?uta=zu011&sShow=25&sort=8.

67. www.sorted.org.nz/.

68. OECD, "Pensions at a Glance."

69. Trinh Le, Grant M. Scobie, and John Gibson, "The Accumulation of Retirement Wealth: Evidence for New Zealand," paper presented at the Fifteenth Colloquium of Superannuation Researchers (University of South Wales, 2007).

70. New Zealand Retirement Commission, "Review of Retirement Income Policy."

71. Le, Scobie, and Gibson, "The Accumulation of Retirement Wealth."

72. National Insurance contributions are roughly similar to U.S. Social Security payroll taxes. In 2009 employees pay 11 percent on earnings between 90 and 770 pounds per week and 1 percent on amounts above 770 pounds per week.

73. The approximate annual value of the basic pension in March 2009 was $6,540 for individuals and $10,630 for couples.

74. Gemma Tetlow, "Pension Policy in the UK: Recent Developments," PowerPoint presentation, London, Institute for Fiscal Studies, December 8, 2008.

75. OECD, "Pensions at a Glance."

76. DWP (U.K. Department for Work and Pensions), "A Detailed Guide to State Pensions for Advisers and Others" (London: 2008).

77. For details, see www.scottishlife.co.uk/scotlife/Web/Site/Adviser/TechnicalCentral Area/InformationGuidance/General/TheStateSecondPensionExplainedPage.asp.

78. Nearly 65 percent of workers were enrolled in their employer's plan in 1979. DWP, "Security in Retirement: Towards a New Pensions System: Summary" (May: 2006).

79. An individual can have more than one stakeholder pension.

80. This amount and the upper-limit amount will be indexed to average earnings.

81. These rates will be phased in over three years beginning in 2012. The 1 percent government contribution comes from all employee contributions to personal accounts being tax-free. DWP, "Personal Accounts: A New Way to Save: Summary" (2006).

82. Respondents were asked to rate how likely they were to stay in or opt out of their employer's plan. Twenty-four percent said they would definitely stay in and 45 percent said they would probably stay in. Only 11 percent said they would definitely opt out. DWP, "Personal Accounts: A New Way to Save."

83. DWP, "Personal Accounts: A New Way to Save."

84. DWP, *Pensions Bill: Impact Assessment,* ch. 2 (2008).

85. Data from BMRB International, reported in DWP, *Pensions Bill: Impact Assessment,* ch. 2.

86. Estimates from the Pension Policy Institute in London show that returns in personal accounts with low costs could be up to 5.9 percent, 2 percentage points higher than in stakeholder accounts. Pensions Policy Institute, "Written Evidence on the Pensions Bill 2007-8" (London: 2007).

87. Pensions Commission, "A New Pension Settlement for the Twenty-First Century: Executive Summary" (London: 2004).

88. OECD, "Pensions at a Glance"

89. Individuals who are at the mean of earnings in 2007–08. DWP, "A Detailed Guide to State Pensions for Advisers and Others" (2008); Office of National Statistics, "Household Pensions Resources," in *Pension Trends,* ch. 12 (2008), www.statistics.gov.uk/cci/nugget. asp?id=2044.

90. H.M. Treasury, "The Annuities Market" (London: 2006).

91. Bank of Scotland Annuity Service, "Pension Annuity Search Service" (Edinburgh: 2007).

92. Social Security Administration, "The 2009 Annual Report of the Board of Trustees of the Federal Old-Age and Survivors and the Federal Disability Insurance Trust Funds" (May 2009).

93. David Rajnes, "An Evolving Pension System: Defined Benefit and Defined Contribution Plans," Issue Brief (Washington: Employee Benefit Research Institute, 2002). The reforms in 2001 increased limits on contributions to qualifying 401(k) and IRA plans, increased the deductibility of employer contributions to plans, and enabled IRA participants to choose whether to treat contributions as traditional or Roth IRA contributions.

94. AARP, "Retirement Security of Insecurity? The Experience of Workers Aged 45 and Older" (Washington: 2008).

95. Employee Benefit Research Institute, "The U.S. Retirement Income System" (Washington: 2005). The Revenue Act of 1978 established deferred compensation 401(k) plans.

96. William G. Gale, J. Mark Iwry, and Peter R. Orszag, "The Automatic 401(k): A Simple Way to Strengthen Retirement Savings." Policy Brief 2005-1 (Washington: Retirement Security Project, 2005).

97. Brigitte C. Madrian and Dennis F. Shea, "The Power of Suggestion: Inertia in 401(k) Participation and Savings Behavior," *Quarterly Journal of Economics* 116, no. 4 (2001), pp. 1149–86.

98. Bureau of Labor Statistics, "National Compensation Survey: Employee Benefits in Private Industry in the United States, March 2003" (U.S. Labor Department, 2006).

99. www.tsp.gov/rates/tsp-expense-ratio.pdf.

PART II

Taking the Money Out

6

Increasing Annuitization in 401(k) Plans with Automatic Trial Income

WILLIAM G. GALE, J. MARK IWRY, DAVID C. JOHN, AND LINA WALKER

Over the next two decades, an estimated 75 million Americans who were born during the postwar years will retire. While much attention has been focused on whether retirees will have saved enough, less attention until very recently was paid to the distribution stage of the retirement planning process and whether retirees will manage their retirement resources to ensure that they last throughout retirement.

A major challenge for retirees at the distribution stage is deciding how to allocate their resources when they do not know exactly how long they will live. If they live longer than expected, they face the dire prospect of running out of funds late in life. Alternatively, and perhaps equally unfortunately, they may be too conservative when drawing down their resources and may forgo consumption earlier in their retirement, which would have made them better off.

Lifetime-income products solve this planning problem. Consumers exchange a portion of their retirement saving for guaranteed periodic lifetime payments from a provider and are assured of never running out of resources. Thus, these products have the potential to make consumers better off because they mitigate

We thank Jeff Brown, Tom Davidoff, Doug Elmendorf, Jason Furman, Pascal Noel, Karl Scholz, Paige Shevlin, Tim Taylor, and industry experts for helpful comments at various stages of writing this chapter. Industry experts include Jodi Strakosh and colleagues at Metlife, Tom Boardman and colleagues at Prudential, PLC, Chris O'Flynn from the ELM Income Groups, and Walter Welsh and Jim Szostek from ACLI. Catherine Lee provided outstanding research assistance.

the risk of consuming too much too soon or consuming too little over time. Although the provider assumes the risk that the consumer may live longer than expected (which would require longer-than-expected payments), the provider is able to diversify and therefore spread this risk across a large pool of consumers with different survival probabilities.

Despite the potential benefits, few retirees purchase lifetime-income products through the private market.[1] Among current retirees, private annuities account for less than 2 percent of total household income (table 6-1).[2] One possible reason for this, supported by a growing body of evidence, is that markets for lifetime income function poorly. For example, lifetime-income products are priced to reflect the higher-than-average survival of current buyers (adverse selection), which makes these products more expensive for the average consumer than they would be if there were a much larger and more diversified group of buyers.[3] A second example is that consumers are unfamiliar with these products, often have misperceptions or biases against them, or may be unwilling or unable to make the effort required to make sensible choices.[4] These findings imply that demand would increase and workers would be better off if market function improved and behavioral obstacles were circumvented or mitigated. These problems of pricing and demand will loom ever larger as fewer retirees derive lifetime income from defined benefit (DB) pension plans.

The question that policymakers face is whether and how to respond to the issues created by the decline in the share of retirement resources that is annuitized among a growing number of retirees in the next few decades. The private market is responding by developing new lifetime-income products that attempt to address some behavioral obstacles in the hopes that demand may increase. However, a market solution alone may be insufficient; these products will have varying success at matching consumers' preferences and needs, and they may reach only a select group of consumers. A particular challenge is to ensure that any proposal is flexible enough to accommodate retirees who have varying needs for additional annuitization through private markets because some may already have sufficient protection against outliving their resources through alternative sources such as Social Security, Medicare, and arrangements within their families.

This paper proposes a strategy that "threads the needle" between these concerns. We propose establishing a default trial-income arrangement within 401(k)-type retirement plans. Workers would have a substantial portion of their retirement assets directed into this default, unless they affirmatively choose to opt out. Under the default, each retiree would receive twenty-four consecutive monthly payments, after which the retiree could opt for any distribution option under the plan. However, if the retiree made no affirmative decision at the end

Table 6-1. *Share of Income from Different Sources*[a]
Percent

Item	Employer-sponsored pensions	Private annuities	Social Security	Earnings and business income	Asset income	Government assistance	Other
All	17	1	50	11	9	4	7
Gender							
Male	18	1	45	15	9	3	9
Female	16	1	55	8	10	4	7
Household income							
Bottom quintile	5	0	80	1	3	8	1
Second quintile	14	1	68	6	6	2	3
Third quintile	22	1	51	9	9	3	6
Fourth quintile	24	2	36	16	11	2	9
Top quintile	19	2	18	25	19	2	16

Source: Richard Johnson, Leonard Burman, and Deborah Kobes, "Annuitized Wealth at Older Ages: Evidence from the Health and Retirement Study" (Washington: Urban Institute, 2004).
a. Rows may not sum to 100 due to rounding.

of the trial period, the temporary payments would automatically convert to a permanent income-payment program. Plan sponsors would be encouraged to offer the trial-income program and would have discretion over some of its structure and implementation.

Several benefits of the plan are worth highlighting. First, adding "automatic" (default) features to 401(k)s allows inertia to work in favor of lifetime income, as it has done in increasing 401(k) participation rates and contribution levels.[5] Second, the trial-income arrangement would provide valuable information to consumers about income solutions, giving them a tool to appropriately evaluate their distribution options to ensure a more secure retirement. Third, launching a trial-income program through 401(k)-type plans, which have millions of participants, has the potential to mitigate the adverse selection problem in lifetime-income contracts and to lower prices. Fourth, the trial program initially would provide income for a limited time, and workers who preferred to direct their own retirement assets or take distributions in other forms could opt out if they so chose.

For such a strategy to work and be sustainable, certain issues would have to be resolved and certain structures established; they are discussed later in this chapter. Many of the questions we raise do not yet have clear solutions, and some of these processes may evolve gradually. The aim of this chapter is to lay out the issues and begin a dialogue that ultimately would lead to a strategy that provides improved retirement outcomes for workers.

The Role of Lifetime-Income Products

Lifetime-income products operate by pooling the resources of many individuals with different survival probabilities. Payments to surviving annuitants each period are made from the pool. As individuals age, the number of surviving annuitants gets smaller and the pool is spread over a smaller and longer-lived group.[6] Those who survive a long time, therefore, may receive more in total payments than they contributed to the pool. This is one of the primary benefits of these products—they provide insurance against living longer than expected. An additional benefit is that these products remove the need to actively manage one's retirement resources, which reduces the possibility of over- or underspending.

A conversation has begun within policy circles about whether lifetime-income products should play a more prominent role in retirees' overall retirement planning strategy. This discussion has been motivated, in part, by the decline in lifetime pensions through employer-sponsored retirement plans. DB pensions were previously the primary form of employer-sponsored retirement coverage, and these plans traditionally paid lifetime pensions to their workers. Among current retirees, DB pensions represent a sizable portion of total household retirement resources, accounting for around 20 percent for many retired households (table 6-2). The majority of workers today, however, are covered by defined contribution (DC) plans, and nearly 80 percent of these plans do not offer the option to annuitize assets when workers retire. (In addition, many remaining DB plans have been converted to cash-balance or other hybrid formats that offer annuities but commonly pay lump sums.) Thus, workers who retire in the next twenty years and later and who have been primarily covered by DC plans would have a significantly lower portion of their retirement assets annuitized than would current retirees.

Whether retirees should use some portion of these assets to purchase lifetime-income products through the private market largely depends on whether households are sufficiently annuitized through Social Security—which pays inflation-indexed lifetime benefits—and other sources.[7] Social Security benefits replace 56 percent of preretirement income for lower-income households.[8] With more than half of their retirement resources in the form of lifetime income through Social Security, these households potentially have little need for additional annuitization through private sources.[9] Medium- and higher-income households, conversely, have lower Social Security replacement rates and are less likely to be overannuitized through Social Security. These households are also more likely to be covered by 401(k)-type plans and would rely on assets in these and other saving accounts to maintain their preretirement living standards.

Millions of workers with a 401(k)-type plan would have contributed and accumulated investment returns in these accounts for many years. They are

Table 6-2. *Social Security and Defined Benefit Plans as Share of Wealth*
In 2000 dollars, unless noted

Item	Total wealth deciles									
	1 (lowest)	*2*	*3*	*4*	*5*	*6*	*7*	*8*	*9*	*10 (highest)*
Couples										
Retirement wealth	153,364	244,224	309,309	337,310	402,198	443,513	470,932	497,493	643,843	819,387
Social Security	142,111	209,310	227,351	251,752	260,138	272,463	261,455	270,474	296,868	301,920
DB pensions	10,203	28,973	75,548	77,523	129,641	160,455	187,735	205,334	303,128	394,919
DC pensions	1,050	5,971	6,410	14,895	12,419	10,595	21,742	21,685	43,847	122,548
Net nonretirement financial wealth	2,547	17,870	33,327	61,868	77,461	103,869	178,362	275,926	365,292	852,772
Property	27,981	49,910	72,096	92,295	104,334	140,692	154,831	185,561	215,589	568,069
Total wealth	183,892	312,004	414,732	491,473	583,993	688,074	804,125	958,980	1,224,724	2,240,227
As percent of total wealth										
Social Security	77	67	55	51	45	40	33	28	24	13
DB pensions	6	9	18	16	22	23	23	21	25	18
Social Security + DB pensions	83	76	73	67	67	63	56	49	49	31
Number of observations	180	158	158	144	140	139	128	126	131	114
With DB	44	78	118	96	120	117	103	101	107	74
Singles										
Retirement wealth	48,858	80,297	99,083	122,992	156,425	152,342	190,968	218,778	286,574	376,370
Social Security	48,255	76,283	88,380	112,529	105,517	101,489	120,855	124,787	125,908	136,255
DB pensions	597	3,724	10,136	8,847	46,983	48,726	62,951	90,020	155,121	216,720
DC pensions	6	290	567	1,616	3,925	2,127	7,162	3,971	5,545	23,395
Net nonretirement financial wealth	40	1,149	7,096	7,977	7,150	42,444	41,725	92,725	163,253	352,784
Property	1,124	8,190	14,145	22,445	33,826	56,117	80,399	90,144	119,975	299,845
Total wealth	50,022	89,636	120,324	153,415	197,401	250,903	313,092	401,647	569,802	1,028,999
As percent of total wealth										
Social Security	96	85	73	73	53	40	39	31	22	13
DB pensions	1	4	8	6	24	19	20	22	27	21
Social Security + DB pensions	97	89	81	79	77	59	59	53	49	34
Number of observations	69	60	53	60	52	47	46	49	51	33
With DB	4	11	12	16	33	29	37	37	41	24

Source: Irena Dushi and Anthony Webb, "Household Annuitization Decisions: Simulations and Empirical Analyses," *Journal of Pension Economics and Finance* 3, no. 2 (2004): 109–43, using data from the Health and Retirement Study.

expected to retire with a large store of wealth in these accounts. One study projects that the average DC balance will be in the range of $348,000 to $575,000 (table 6-3) for retirees in 2040.[10] This is at least thirteen times higher than the level held by an average retiree today. DC balances, therefore, will be a far more significant source of retirement funding in the future, and households will have to manage these balances to achieve their desired consumption path.

Managing assets over an uncertain horizon is complicated, and the stakes are high if one makes a mistake. Table 6-4 illustrates this point. A 65-year-old man can expect to live to age 82, on average, but has a 19 percent chance of living to age 90 or beyond. Similarly, a 65-year-old woman can expect to live to age 85 on average but has a 31 percent chance of living to age 90 or beyond. Given this uncertainty, workers in medium- and higher-income groups generally could gain from annuitizing at least some portion of their defined contribution balances, although the benefit of annuitization will vary across households. (Those with longer life expectancy and less access to resource sharing through family members will benefit more.)[11]

Despite these potential gains, however, absent any intervention, demand for lifetime-income products among medium- and higher-income workers is expected to be low, just as it has been for current and previous generations of workers.

One oft-cited anecdotal reason for low demand is that lifetime-income products are inflexible and expensive. Until recently, this has largely been true. These contracts, which often paid fixed, nominal returns, typically were irreversible. Prices were high for the average consumer, at least in part because these products were priced to reflect the expected payout obligations to a small and select pool of buyers who tended to have longer-than-average life expectancy (adverse selection). Also, prices are high in part because providers cannot completely hedge against aggregate longevity risks and must pass on some of the costs to consumers.[12] Although the market has evolved and new products offer more flexibility, many consumers still are not responding.

A growing body of evidence points to behavioral biases as an important reason for the limited use of lifetime-income products in retirement planning, and these biases seem unlikely to be resolved on their own. For instance, a recent study found that consumers' valuation of lifetime-income products is strongly influenced by the way the attributes of these products are presented.[13] When they were presented in a consumption frame (providing lifetime-consumption possibilities), consumers preferred lifetime-income products to savings accounts. When lifetime-income products were presented in an investment frame, however, which is the way most lifetime-income products are typically presented, consumers preferred savings accounts.

Finally, lifetime-income products are complicated, and there is strong evidence that consumers do not respond optimally when choices are complicated.

Table 6-3. *Projected 401(k) and Social Security Assets for Workers Retiring in 2040, by Earnings Groups*
In 2000 dollars, unless noted

	Lifetime earnings deciles										
Item	1 (lowest)	2	3	4	5	6	7	8	9	10	All (highest)
Historical equity rate of return											
401(k)	3,688	50,857	128,600	274,958	489,558	644,261	822,220	947,474	1,134,979	1,242,580	575,117
Social Security wealth (SSW) + 401(k)	74,877	148,754	239,065	414,172	668,388	838,892	1,048,759	1,191,540	1,394,752	1,521,485	756,946
Ratio: 401(k)/SSW+401(k)	0.05	0.34	0.54	0.66	0.73	0.77	0.78	0.80	0.81	0.82	0.76
Historical equity rate of return less 300 basis points											
401(k)	2,072	31,625	81,916	172,671	292,902	382,988	484,933	560,366	680,937	785,150	348,284
Social Security wealth (SSW) + 401(k)	73,261	129,522	192,381	311,885	471,732	577,619	711,472	804,432	940,710	1,064,055	530,113
Ratio: 401(k)/SSW+ 401(k)	0.03	0.24	0.43	0.55	0.62	0.66	0.68	0.70	0.72	0.74	0.66

Source: James Poterba, Steven Venti, and David Wise, "New Estimates of the Future Path of 401(k) Assets," Working Paper 13083 (Cambridge, Mass.: National Bureau of Economic Research) (May 2007).

Table 6-4. *Life Expectancy and Probability of Survival at Age 65*

Item	Men	Women
Remaining life expectancy	17.0	19.7
Probability of surviving to age		
70	0.895	0.928
75	0.757	0.827
80	0.588	0.692
85	0.391	0.517
90	0.193	0.309
95	0.062	0.128
100	0.011	0.032

Source: Felicitie Bell and Michael Miller, "Life Tables for the United States Social Security Area 1900–2100." Actuarial Study 120 (Social Security Administration, 2005).

The experience of companies that adopted automatic features in their 401(k)-type retirement plans provides a powerful illustration of this behavior. During the saving phase in most 401(k) plans, individuals must make explicit choices about whether to participate in the retirement plan, how much to contribute, and where to invest contributions. These decisions are not always easy and have deterred many from participating in the plan or have caused others to make imprudent investment choices. The result has been that workers, particularly workers who would have benefited most from 401(k) saving, tended to stay with the status quo, which in 401(k) saving was not to participate. However, when the decision was simplified for workers (by changing the default option) and they were automatically enrolled unless they specifically opted out, or contributions were automatically tied to annual salary increases, enrollment and contribution rates increased significantly and remained high over time.[14]

Buying a lifetime-income product under the current 401(k) framework is more complicated than making 401(k) saving decisions, likely deterring many participants. Most 401(k) plans do not offer a lifetime-income option, so retirees would first have to withdraw their assets from their retirement account and then purchase an income product through the private market. The effort needed to evaluate providers, compare product features, and compare prices may be an insurmountable hurdle for many consumers, who may opt to forgo annuitization rather than incur the effort. Even when workers are given the option to purchase income products through their plan sponsors, they have to evaluate the value of income plans relative to options that are very different and for which there are no readily available comparison tools. These other options (lump-sum and installment payments) are more familiar to workers and easier to understand, which may make them more appealing—though potentially imprudent—alternatives.[15]

This empirical and observational evidence implies that market imperfections, adverse selection, and behavioral biases inhibit demand for lifetime-income products by lowering the actual and perceived value of these products. Therefore, consumers could be made better off if they could buy lifetime income at a better price, or if there were some way to overcome their behavioral obstacles so that they could annuitize a higher portion of their retirement assets.

To some extent, insurance companies have responded by offering or beginning to offer lifetime-income products that provide more flexibility and address some of these behavioral obstacles. In addition to deferred as well as immediate annuities and variable annuities offering equity returns (all of which have been available for years), newer features have included the option of downside investment protection or guarantees combined with upside potential; the ability to lock in investment gains and convert them to annuity income at a later time; the option to unwind or cash out contracts; death benefits and guaranteed payouts, either through a minimum number of payment periods (such as life and twenty years certain) or a minimum guaranteed amount; and more favorable pricing.

Financial institutions that are not annuity carriers have responded by offering a competing product: an actively managed investment account that is targeted to provide specified payments for a prespecified period of years. Although this type of phased or recalculated withdrawal product does not offer longevity insurance and the associated mortality credits, its professional management does provide some assurance against consuming too much too soon or too little over time.[16] In light of these market innovations, one approach to increasing annuitization may be to allow the market to evolve unimpeded. Over time, there may be a better match between what is demanded and what is supplied as a result.

There are, however, a number of drawbacks that make it prudent to consider alternatives. First, although these new product features directly resolve certain behavioral obstacles (for example, the annuity death benefits and ability to cash out of, or unwind, the contract), many consumers may not be aware of these innovations and may continue to perceive lifetime-income products as a poor fit. As noted earlier, until recently these products offered limited features and tended to be quite expensive. Many consumers probably would not learn about these innovations because few would have any experience or familiarity with these products in the course of their preretirement planning. Consequently, the pace of adoption is expected to be slow. It may take time for information about and confidence in these innovations to replace prior notions.

Second, prices will continue to reflect a great deal of adverse selection, and hence the products will not be as good a value for the average consumer until the pool of lifetime-income buyers increases. Unless value improves, however, the average consumer will tend to be reluctant to purchase the products. Disentangling this gridlock may take a while under a market-only approach.

Third, although the newer versions of lifetime-income products offer consumers more choice and flexibility, they are also more complicated. The increased complexity makes pricing even less transparent than it has been. We noted earlier that consumers vary in the degree to which they are able to manage their resources or will need additional annuitization (if any) over their existing sources.

Consequently, not all products are equally suitable for all consumers. Some financially knowledgeable consumers may appreciate the additional options and be able to appropriately value these products, but, with increased complexity, less-experienced consumers may well accept or reject the lifetime-income options contracts without fully understanding their costs or evaluating their benefits and might therefore be worse off.

The aim of policy in this area should not be to promote annuitization per se or to manage the risk of outliving one's assets to the exclusion of all other risks or concerns pertaining to retirement security. Rather, the goal should be to promote reasonably sensible payout strategies that maximize retirement security and minimize any unintended harm. We take seriously each of the obstacles to annuitization discussed here and develop a process that weaves a thread through these issues. As a general matter, we think that an approach that is likely to be effective while minimizing the risk of doing harm is to give consumers the tools they need so that they are better positioned to evaluate their retirement distribution options. For a particular individual, the best course of action might or might not include additional annuitization. However, recognizing that many are unable or prefer not to make these complicated evaluations, and that the benefits of lifetime income are often underappreciated, our proposed strategy would provide simple and effortless access to lifetime income.

The Proposal: Trial-Income Payments

Many behavioral obstacles to annuitization stem from either misperceptions or limited understanding of lifetime-income products. Consumers may be reluctant to give up a lump sum for a stream of payments because they do not sufficiently grasp the terms of the trade.[17] Furthermore—since these products are complicated, consumers are unfamiliar with them, and there are no simple or common benchmarks with which to evaluate them—consumers are apt to avoid or mistrust these products, particularly when their peers are doing so.[18]

The way 401(k) benefits are presented does not facilitate the take-up of income payments at retirement. Account balances in 401(k) plans are presented as a lump sum. Consumers internalize this information and view the lump sum as the status quo. There is ample evidence that consumers tend to remain with the status quo, especially when the choices are complex. This "status quo bias" could very likely explain, to some degree, why only 6 percent of 401(k) participants choose to take distributions as an annuity when given the option.[19]

Therefore, a strategy that allows consumers to learn about these products and reframes the status quo would go a long way toward correcting misperceptions, reducing mistrust, conveying the benefits of income options, and therefore increasing take-up of income options.

The usual method of providing information, however—through written materials, on paper or online, and by means of oral explanation—is unlikely to be enough, and may be more likely to benefit those who already have the financial acumen to understand the risk-pooling value of these products. Also, many will lack the time, ability, or desire to assimilate this kind of information, evaluate options, and formulate a distribution program when they retire. For these workers, new information about lifetime-income products would be useful but may not translate into action.

Because many people learn best by doing, giving consumers a chance to experience monthly income may be a more effective means of conveying some of the benefits of lifetime income to a wider audience than written or oral presentations alone. Those who become "exposed" to regular income payments may become accustomed to them, better able to resist some of the behavioral biases described earlier, and therefore more open to choosing lifetime-income products.

Currently, however, no process is in place that allows consumers to "test drive" an income product. It would be costly for consumers to set up a trial program for themselves by purchasing either a lifetime-income contract or a phased withdrawal plan in the individual market and potentially withdrawing from the contract or plan after a short time. Thus, an opportunity to experience "trial" income payments for a limited time, evaluate these monthly payments relative to monthly consumption needs, and update any prior perceptions of income products, all at a relatively low cost, would be a valuable planning tool for retirees.

An additional advantage of a trial period with income payments is that consumers may change their frame of reference after they start receiving regular monthly payments. The hope is that they may begin to perceive monthly payments—rather than the lump sum—as the norm or the status quo. If so, discontinuing these monthly payments would be perceived as a "loss," and, as a result, participants may be more inclined to remain with the income option even after the trial period ends.

For those who decide against a permanent lifetime-income option, a third advantage of a trial arrangement is that it is temporary. As noted, workers vary in the degree to which they would benefit from annuitization in addition to

Social Security (because the Social Security annuity replaces a higher percentage of preretirement income for low-income workers). Given consumers' varying needs, a permanent one-size-fits-all approach runs the risk of doing more harm than good. With a trial approach, however, income payments end after a limited trial period. If workers decide against additional annuitization, they can readily choose a different option at the end of the trial period (or even before the period starts).

Building on the Automatic 401(k)

The experience of automatic (default) features in 401(k) plans has demonstrated that a process that enlists the power of inertia can be used to improve outcomes significantly without restricting individuals' choices. Firms that have implemented automatic features in their 401(k) plans are enjoying striking success in expanding participation and improving the investment behavior of those who participate.[20] The automatic approach has the potential to apply to distribution choices as well. Building on the success of the automatic approach in the enrollment and investment phases, automatic features could also be used to facilitate the learning process and final distribution choices in 401(k)-type plans. Funds could be automatically directed into a trial program that pays benefits monthly. This would put inertia to work on behalf of the income stream rather than on behalf of the lump sum. The automatic feature would not bind workers to a particular option—those who prefer to direct and manage their assets could opt out of the default and choose their desired manner of distribution—but those who are unable or prefer not to make active decisions would not be required to do so.

A strategy that accesses the universe of employer-sponsored retirement plans should also significantly reduce the adverse selection pricing problem for lifetime-income products and make them a better value to a larger population. As noted earlier, millions of 401(k)-type plan participants are expected to retire with substantial account balances. Defaulting more participants, with varying life expectancies, into a lifetime-income plan would increase the diversity of the lifetime-income pool. It is expected that some participants may choose to opt out of the program; these participants would tend to be financially savvy individuals or those who prefer to manage their resources on their own.[21] However, because the cost of remaining in the trial program is relatively low, it is expected that many would remain with the default, and the larger pool would reduce adverse selection and lower prices. Thus 401(k)-type accounts provide a natural platform from which to implement a strategy of encouraging broader consideration of lifetime income.

An Automatic Trial-Period Income Strategy

We propose a strategy that includes automatic annuitization of assets in 401(k) plans. This strategy also builds in the opportunity for participants to "test-drive" income products. Specifically, we propose the following:

—A substantial portion of assets in 401(k)-type accounts would be automatically directed into an income program for a two-year trial period (the default trial arrangement), unless workers affirmatively elect a different form of payout permitted under the retirement plan.[22]

—There would be trial income of twenty-four consecutive monthly payments.

—After the trial period, participants would regain the ability to opt for alternative forms of payment. Those who made no affirmative choice within a specified period would continue to receive income payments because the program would convert automatically from trial-period income to permanent income.

Triggering the Default

The automatic (that is, default) trial-period income option would be designed to avoid precipitating the depletion of retirement assets any earlier than would otherwise occur and to avoid interfering with portability of retirement savings through pre-retirement-age rollovers. Accordingly, it would not apply to participants below a specified age (perhaps 55) and in any event would not apply unless the participant has requested a distribution exceeding some threshold amount. Thus, for example, unless participants explicitly made an affirmative election to decline it, the automatic trial-period option would be triggered when cumulative voluntary withdrawals from 401(k)-type plans reached a certain threshold, such as $10,000 or 10 percent of the account balance, whichever is greater. A participant who requested a lump-sum distribution triggering the trial-period default option would be informed that the trial-period income would be paid unless the participant affirmatively opted out of it in favor of the lump sum, another payout alternative, or no distribution at all. Under such an approach, an individual with an account balance of $500,000 could withdraw, cumulatively, up to $50,000 before automatic trial-period distributions applied. However, as discussed below, the automatic option would not apply to participants with account balances below a specified threshold.

Automatic payments would begin within a specified time period (a few months) after they were triggered. Flexibility would be built into the plan so that participants who wanted to begin taking trial monthly payments sooner could elect to do so even before reaching the withdrawal trigger thresholds.

Accounts Subject to the Trial-Income Default

The plan sponsor could decide to apply the automatic trial-income option only to accounts that exceeded a specified amount. The plan sponsor might conclude that participants whose account balances are sufficiently small (less than $100,000, for example) should maintain the entire balance as a contingency fund to give them the flexibility to meet emergencies or pay irregular expenses (such as health care expenses) during retirement. In addition, at some point the annual amount of an annuity might be small enough to raise questions for some plan sponsors about whether it justifies the administrative cost of providing it. For an account smaller than $30,000, for example, if half were defaulted into an annuity, the annuity payment might be less than $100 a month.

Selecting the Default Program

Plan sponsors could choose to administer the payout of the income program or could arrange for an outside provider to offer it. Plan sponsors would also be given the flexibility to offer as a default either a two-year lifetime-income contract or a managed income payout plan rather than a formal annuity. Because costs and specifics can vary tremendously, and in an attempt to minimize any inappropriate or perverse incentives, plan sponsors would be encouraged to compare across different but equivalent default plans and select a provider and terms of the arrangement (including cost, risk exposure, and terms on potential exit by the participant after the trial period) that satisfied applicable fiduciary standards.[23]

Alternatively, plan sponsors could choose from a list of qualified low-cost and low-risk default income options. Qualified providers and qualified income plans would meet federally specified standards relating to costs and risk exposure. The advantage of and incentive to choose a qualified default income option would be that plan sponsors offering these options would receive some measure of protection against fiduciary liability for any negative investment consequences resulting from their default income option. This arrangement would be somewhat similar to the qualified default investment alternative approach that applies to automatic investments in 401(k) and similar plans, where plan sponsors are allowed a measure of fiduciary relief when they use certain types of default investments.

Although plan sponsors could, in principle, choose any default trial-income program, they may be limited in the type of program they could offer given the temporary nature of the trial—at least with the current product selection. Because individuals would be able to opt out completely after two years, any income contract purchased for the default would have to accommodate contract termination after two years. While some providers already offer products that are appropriately structured for a temporary trial plan (such as a recalculated withdrawal plan), others may have to develop new products to accommodate the temporary nature of a default trial-income plan.[24]

It is important to note that the permanent program would not face the same limitations. Furthermore, the trial plan is limited only as long as the product space is limited. As providers develop new and creative ways of financing their product and as new products are developed that are more cost-effective within the trial period, plan sponsors may have more options from which to select a trial-income solution.

Plan Sponsors' Role

Plan sponsors that adopt the default trial program would have some discretion over how to structure and implement it and the permanent default income options that would follow, subject to a limited number of regulatory standards. Plan sponsors could determine the portion of the account balance that would be subject to the default trial-income option, within regulatory limits specifying the permissible upper (for example, 75 percent) and lower bounds (for example, 33 percent). Sponsors also would choose the provider or providers and type of default trial income and permanent income products, subject to regulatory guidelines. This would allow them to select products that may have particular appeal to participants because they provide the flexibility and other innovative features that participants seek.

These products could include annuity contracts that provide death benefits—whether by returning the annuitant's remaining unpaid premiums to the decedent's heirs or guaranteeing payments for a minimum fixed period of years even if the annuitant dies during that period—that give the owner the flexibility to make withdrawals under certain conditions; that guarantee a floor level of monthly income; that provide inflation protection (or that increase at a fixed percentage over time); and that provide upside potential by increasing monthly payments based on the highest market value that the account attained on any anniversary of its purchase. Some such features may be effective in inducing participants to choose lifetime income; at the same time, the same features can dilute the longevity risk protection, risk pooling, and mortality credits that give annuities much of their special value.

Postdefault Distribution Option

The plan sponsor or provider administering the default trial income would be required, before the end of the trial period, to give participants an explanation of the terms of the automatic continuation of the trial payments and the other distribution options. After the end of the trial period, participants who were receiving regular monthly income would continue to do so automatically with respect to the same portion of their account balance, unless they affirmatively opted for an alternative form of payout. If the trial-income plan were payable as a recalculated withdrawal program, the plan sponsor could either continue payouts in the same form under its permanent income program, or change the income program to a lifetime-income contract, with the default being a joint-and-survivor annuity for married participants or a single-life annuity for unmarried participants.

Permitted Exemptions

After retirees reach age 70 1/2, the existing required minimum distribution rules generally require them to recognize income on a minimum amount of their aggregate tax-favored retirement accumulations each year. Although the rules do not require actually taking the funds out of saving (as opposed to simply removing them from the tax-favored retirement account), many if not most retirees over age 70 1/2 probably interpret the rules as a "signal," and in any event find it easiest to comply with the rules by withdrawing the funds from their savings. The minimum distributions are based on an annual recalculation of account balance divided by life expectancy, which is similar to a recalculated life expectancy income program and in keeping with the spirit and intent of the default trial-income program. Therefore, the default trial-period income program would not apply to retirees who take distributions from their retirement plan through managed payouts that follow the pattern of the minimum required distributions.[25]

The proposal would also allow consumers who wished to purchase a lifetime-income contract from the outset of the trial period to do so. The aim of the trial-income program is to help level the playing field for income options; without that trial program, consumers tend to undervalue them. Thus, participants who have already chosen an income option for the long term would be deemed to have complied with the trial-period default.

Additional Benefits for Consumers

In addition to the benefits described previously, making monthly income the mode through the trial plan may suggest to employees that it is the payout form implicitly recommended by the plan sponsor or by financial experts, constituting an "endorsement effect" that might be persuasive to at least some employees. This should help change the way consumers view their retirement resources by framing them as an income stream rather than as a lump sum. Consumers accustomed to receiving account statements showing the accumulated balance in their retirement accounts tend to develop a sense of ownership over the lump sum. Research has shown that people can be powerfully motivated by a desire to avoid losing something they own. This may partly explain the high propensity to choose the lump-sum distribution option in 401(k) plans and other plans that present accumulated benefits as an account balance.

An automatic trial period of monthly income based on a substantial portion of their assets could accustom individuals to the consistency, security, and simplicity of receiving regular monthly payments and help reframe the way they view their retirement resources. The regular income stream (or "pension paycheck"), rather than the lump sum, may come to be seen as the status quo or presumptive form of benefit.

Additional Benefits for Providers

Insofar as the default proposal applied to a substantial portion of all retirement assets, it could generate substantial new volumes of business for firms providing income products. Total 401(k) assets were approximately 38 percent of GDP in 2005. By some estimates, total 401(k) assets are projected to reach between 98 percent and 155 percent of GDP in 2040.[26] This expected growth provides strong financial incentives for firms to participate in both the default trial- and permanent-income market. If greater fiduciary protection could be afforded to plan sponsors that offered qualified trial-income programs, income providers would have an added incentive to offer products that are competitively priced and comply with federal standards.

Increased sales of lifetime-income products, in turn, could generate incentives and opportunities for insurers to develop and engage in more cost-effective capital and risk-management strategies.[27] For instance, anticipated growth in the income market spurred by the default proposal could provide the necessary impetus to develop new options for hedging aggregate longevity risks.[28]

Over time, improved capital and risk management and an increased retiree pool should further reduce the price of lifetime-income contracts, further lowering another obstacle that has inhibited demand. In today's market, annuity contracts are often perceived as a poor value for the average person. However, as the pool of retirees purchasing annuities increases, it is likely to reduce insurers' capital and risk-management costs, ultimately reducing annuity prices. While these changes may take place gradually, over time the combination of new volume and responses on the supply side should substantially increase the value, and hence the appeal and utilization, of lifetime-income products.

Other Significant Issues

The proposal outlined above offers an opportunity to provide greater retirement security to a large number of retirees. However, several key issues need to be addressed before such a proposal can be effectively implemented and sustained over time. Some are implementation issues, such as whether and how existing 401(k) and other qualified plan rules might need to be modified to accommodate lifetime-income solutions, and whether special annuity selection safe harbors, such as giving plan sponsors added protection from exposure to fiduciary liability for selecting annuity providers, or other incentives would be appropriate to encourage plan sponsors to adopt the trial-income option. Two important broader questions are whether further measures would be advisable, first, to protect participants (and plan sponsors) from products with excessive costs or costs that are not sufficiently transparent—especially because the annuity would be a default option—and, second, to guarantee the security of potentially billions of dollars of additional assets invested in lifetime-income products. Some of these issues do not have immediately obvious solutions. These issues (and the form of the default trial program), however, would benefit from a dialogue with plan sponsors and other interested participants as to their merits and challenges, as well as further evaluation and (possibly) testing.

What Regulatory Modifications or Employer Incentives Are Needed?

What regulatory modifications or employer incentives might be necessary and appropriate to promote a trial program and expand the use of income options in 401(k) and other similar plans? First, one concrete step would be to modify the current minimum required distribution rules to the extent necessary to accommodate lifetime-income options, particularly longevity insurance and, to the extent necessary, the proposed automatic trial-income program. Current federal law requires most participants in tax-qualified retirement plans, including 401(k) plans, and IRAs to start taking minimum "distributions" (for tax purposes) from their retirement accounts by April 1 following the year they reach age 70 1/2 (or, if later, the year they retire in the case of a qualified plan). These rules do not require actual distribution or consumption of assets, but do require assets to be taxed as if they were distributed in order to prevent the use of the pension tax preference for estate planning instead of retirement security. The minimum distribution rules could constrain plans' ability to offer longevity insurance and other deferred withdrawal schedules. A possible accommodation of these rules to a strategy of encouraging annuitization is discussed in chapter 7.

Second, the possible application of the 10 percent early withdrawal penalty would need to be addressed. If trial-period income began before age 55, or before age 59 1/2 for a participant still employed by the plan sponsor, a 10 percent early withdrawal penalty could apply unless the participant continued the life annuity or life expectancy payouts after the trial period. One possible approach would be to set 55 as the earliest age at which the trial-income default arrangement would be triggered, thereby avoiding the early withdrawal penalty in the typical case where the participant's employment has terminated. In the smaller number of cases where an active employee between 55 and 59 1/2 could withdraw certain 401(k) balances, consideration could be given to amending the law to exempt default trial income from the penalty regardless of whether the individual annuitized after the trial period. In addition, these participants might be warned that, if they did not continue an annuity after the trial period and were then still under age 59 1/2, the penalty would apply to any further withdrawals (which would be another incentive to annuitize).

Third, Congress recently relaxed, to some degree, the standards applicable to 401(k) plan sponsors in selecting an annuity provider. However, rules regarding plan sponsors' fiduciary responsibilities in the selection of income providers, the pricing of income products for married couples, and the application of the joint-and-survivor spousal protections to new income solutions may still add a measure of complexity and uncertainty to the administration of income solutions within 401(k)s.[29] This is one reason why only one of five defined contribution plans offers the option to annuitize account balances.[30] These rules—including how the spousal survivor protections would apply to the automatic trial-period income option—need to be reviewed and clarified to minimize uncertainty and complexity and thus accommodate trial-period income, longevity insurance, and other deferred and immediate annuities.

In addition, it is worth considering whether special incentives should be provided to encourage 401(k) plan sponsors to adopt the trial-income option and, more generally, to offer income options. One direction that might be explored is whether safe harbors relating to the selection of annuity providers would be feasible, appropriate, and consistent with the goal of protecting plan participants through operation of the pension fiduciary standards. Another possibility that might be explored would be a possible exemption of non–highly compensated employees from the application of the minimum required distribution rules in plans that offer a trial-period option.

How to Safeguard Assets in Income Plans?

To have a robust annuity market, consumers must have faith that the benefits from their annuity contracts will be paid. However, in any system where private sector companies provide annuities, sooner or later one or more of those companies will fail. Such a failure could result in the loss or significant reduction of benefits for retirees, shaking consumer confidence in annuities, and making it even harder to encourage them to consider appropriate lifetime-income products. This is true not only in connection with efforts to promote the use of lifetime-income options in 401(k)-type plans but also with efforts to maintain or expand annuitization (as opposed to lump-sum payouts) in defined benefit pension plans. Under current law, if a DB plan provides benefits through the purchase of commercial annuities, the individuals entitled to those benefits must thereafter look solely to the insurance carrier that provides the annuities, rather than to the plan or the federal Pension Benefit Guaranty Corporation. The Pension Benefit Guaranty Corporation ceases to insure pension benefits once an annuity provider assumes the obligation to provide them.

Currently, state guarantee funds provide coverage for contracts issued by insurance companies in their state. The adequacy of the current arrangements is unclear, however, and coverage limits vary across states. If a major annuity provider were to fail, it is uncertain how effective the state guarantee funds would be in protecting annuitants. Moreover, retirees would have different coverage protection in different states even if they purchased identical contracts. Nonuniform state coverage results in unequal protection of retirees.

A federal insurance agency patterned on the Federal Deposit Insurance Corporation (FDIC) could provide uniform insurance coverage and establish uniform financial standards and safeguards for consumers, regardless of the state in which they purchased their contract. As long experience in the banking industry has shown, consumer confidence can be very fragile but can also be restored through a federal guarantee. A previous bank run in the United States (Hartford Federal Savings and Loan, 1982) and the most recent bank run in the United Kingdom (Northern Rock, 2007) both promptly ended once a government guarantee of deposits was announced. However, such a guarantee should be more than a paper promise. As with the FDIC, lifetime-income providers could pay an appropriate annual premium for this protection and be subject to regular reporting and examinations to ensure that they maintain appropriate assets and investments underlying the contracts, adequate management procedures, and appropriate consumer protections. Such federal oversight could both reduce the potential for provider failure and establish appropriate guidelines for their investment and other practices.

Thus, one approach might propose establishing federal insurance for lifetime-income contracts, similar to federal deposit insurance provided through the FDIC. Federal annuity insurance could guarantee lifetime-income payments, up to, for example, $500,000 in present value terms per contract holder if an insurance company failed or the contract outlived the insurer. Lifetime-income contracts from different providers could be insured separately and up to the limit. Thus, a retiree with two contracts from two different insurers might be insured for as much as $1 million in annuity payments. An alternative approach would be for the federal insurer to guarantee up to a certain amount of monthly income in much the same manner as today's Pension Benefit Guaranty Corporation does for DB pension plans.

In return for the ability to display a seal similar to that of the FDIC, providers could be required to meet federally specified minimum financial and management standards. These could include minimum reserve ratios, probably a requirement that an appropriate portion of the firm's assets be held in very long bonds or other appropriate investments, and the payment of a risk-based insurance fee. The standards could provide some safeguards for consumers against excessive risk taking by providers.

One of the concerns such a proposal raises, however, is that federal insurance for lifetime-income contracts might weaken the market discipline that contract holders might normally impose on insurers. While regular call reports and examinations have served as a substitute for this market discipline in banks, similar procedures do not yet exist for annuity providers, and would have to be developed. Consumers whose benefits are guaranteed against potential losses might become relatively indifferent to the risks taken by lifetime-income providers. This indifference, in turn, could make providers less cautious about taking risks.

There are also concerns that a federal entity would not have the political will or the incentive to set appropriate prices for risks, resulting in a possible mismatch between the premium and the risks that this federal insurance agency would face. Concerns have also been raised about the risk that surplus reserve funds from the insurance agency would be tapped to fund other more pressing or more politically sensitive programs, without appropriate regard to the long-run viability of the fund. The experience of the Pension Benefit Guaranty Corporation highlights some of the potential issues that might arise if a federal insurance program for lifetime-income products were not carefully thought out in advance and closely monitored.[31]

While these concerns are valid, other federal insurance agencies, such as the FDIC, have operated relatively successfully.[32] It may also be possible (although not without potential political opposition) to adopt additional safeguards that give these federal insurance agencies greater autonomy in risk assessment, such as giving the federal insurance agency flexibility to establish risk categories based on variables that are relevant to an insurer's risk of failure and examiner risk rating.

How to Change the Conversation about Lifetime Income

Moving the retirement market toward a more appropriate investment in lifetime income will involve a fundamental change in the way most American households think about providing for their retirement. The account-balance, lump-sum mind-set that has become so prevalent is reinforced by the behavioral tendencies noted earlier and has been promoted by the promotion and expansion of lump-sum options in DB and 401(k) plans. Adjusting this mind-set will be a challenge.

A national conversation is already under way regarding saving for retirement and other long-term needs. This includes campaigns to encourage households to plan and save for retirement and active discussions in the media and within and among consumer groups, policymakers, industry participants, and other interested parties. This discussion has recently turned to the potential role of lifetime-income options in providing for a more secure retirement. It is, however, still at the early stages; it may be necessary to educate not only consumers but also plan sponsors and financial providers to be more open to directing at least a portion of retirement saving into lifetime-income options.

Many financial advisers and intermediaries have traditionally steered consumers away from lifetime-income products in part because they were less profitable to these advisers than other investment options. Increased consumer awareness and demand for these products may motivate some financial advisers to offer or recommend income products, but this may not be enough to motivate others absent new financial incentives. Income products such as variable annuities and recalculated phased-withdrawal income plans differ from fixed lifetime-income contracts in that they require more active management of assets and therefore tend to charge maintenance fees. On the one hand, higher maintenance fees render these products more profitable, making it more likely that financial advisers will promote them to consumers; on the other hand, if consumers do not fully understand the products they are buying, they may incur more harm than good in purchasing these products.

At the consumer level, lifetime-income products would have a better chance of being seriously considered and adopted if their advantages could be translated more simply and effectively for the average saver and retiree. The case needs to be made—giving fair attention to drawbacks as well as advantages—in terms that most consumers can readily understand. In addition to making the point that people need to consider how to manage the risk of outliving their assets, an education campaign might usefully incorporate a different way to think about retirement planning. This could include the following points, among others:

—Frame lifetime income in payout terms, such as a regular pension paycheck similar in form to Social Security and as a supplement to fill the gap between Social Security income and monthly income needs in retirement.

—Remind consumers and plan sponsors that purchasing lifetime-income products is not an all-or-nothing proposition. These products can play a supporting role in an individual's retirement security strategy through investment of only a portion of available assets.

—Point out that guaranteed income simplifies the mechanics of retirement payout. It is an easy "set it and forget it" way to convert one's assets to regular income and spares retirees the need to engage in active management of their assets.

Points such as these could usefully be developed and refined—and debated—through an open collective process to increase the level of awareness and thoughtfulness regarding lifetime income and, by increasing discussion and consumer demand, to help make inroads on entrenched resistance by those with contrary financial interests.

A concrete step to anchor the expanded awareness and discussion of lifetime-income options would be to reframe 401(k) and IRA account statements. To help reinforce a sense of ownership of the income stream rather than of only the lump sum, DC plan sponsors and IRA providers should be required to present the participant's benefits as a stream of monthly or annual lifetime payments in regular statements and in summary plan descriptions, in addition to presenting the benefits as an account balance in accordance with current practice. It may be possible to develop an industrywide method of computing and presenting the stream of payments, with appropriate disclaimers.[33]

Over time, this change may help encourage account owners to become accustomed to thinking of their retirement resources as monthly income. Taking the distribution as monthly payments would seem natural—that is, it would be equivalent to maintaining the status quo. The intent is to reposition their frame of reference so that consumers do not feel a "loss" when they receive an income stream rather than a lump sum. Portraying the payments from an annuity as a consumption stream has been found to be a useful and more illuminating way of presenting the benefits of annuities, and consumers appear to respond positively to this new frame.[34]

Should an Optional Federal Insurance Regulator Exist?

Most existing annuity products are sold by insurance companies. However, the current state-based insurance regulatory system could hamper the development of innovative annuities by that industry. Thus, in addition to federal annuity insurance, a broader initiative that could facilitate the provision of annuities by insurance companies would be the creation of an optional federal insurance charter. This would allow an insurance company to opt for being regulated by one federal regulator rather than by a host of individual state insurance commissioners. While proposals relating to insurance generally are beyond the scope of this paper, because they implicate a host of issues apart from the provision of retirement annuities, several substantial arguments in favor of an optional federal insurance charter relate specifically to the annuity line of business.

One federal agency, rather than fifty state agencies, would result in more uniform standards for licensure and regulatory compliance and should increase efficiency. Currently, these standards vary across states and product lines. Today, annuity providers that sell insurance contracts in multiple states must comply with the standards of each state. In particular, providers that sell contracts with an investment component, such as variable annuities, are governed by state regulators as well as by federal securities law. Regulation by multiple agencies can result in gaps in protection, as evidenced by the inconsistent treatment across states with respect to whether variable annuities are considered securities. Moreover, while other types of financial organizations will increasingly offer annuity-type products, those entities already have the option of a single federal regulator. An insurance company that opted for a federal charter could sell uniform annuity products in every state, an arrangement that could be well suited to service the needs of a mobile workforce that may be employed in several states during the course of a career.

Conclusions

Future retirees are expected to retire with larger retirement assets, live longer than current retirees, and have fewer sources of longevity-income protection. These developments increase their risk of outliving their resources. This paper presents a strategy to increase retirement security for future retirees by reframing the way individuals view their retirement choices, providing them with more information and time to decide (which should help them better evaluate their choices), and incorporating automatic features in 401(k)-type plans to facilitate the selection of lifetime-income solutions.

Several important questions need to be resolved before this strategy can be implemented, and this paper does not attempt to answer all of these questions. Rather, it highlights the issues and maps out the first of several steps toward increasing the use of annuity-like products in 401(k)-type plans. Because existing consumer attitudes are so biased against lifetime-income products, increasing their acceptance and use will be gradual. The strategy in this paper is designed to highlight the benefits of guaranteed retirement income, to give consumers the tools to evaluate the options, and ultimately to increase the selection of lifetime-income and improve retirement security.

Notes

1. A large literature has developed that seeks to explain this "annuity puzzle." Early seminal work includes Douglas Bernheim, "The Economic Effects of Social Security: Toward a Reconciliation of Theory and Measurement," *Journal of Public Economics* 33, no. 3 (1987),

pp. 273–304; Benjamin M. Friedman and Mark J. Warshawsky, "The Cost of Annuities: Implications for Saving Behavior and Bequests," *Quarterly Journal of Economics* 105, no. 1 (1990), pp. 135–54; Laurence Kotlikoff and Avia Spivak, "The Family as an Incomplete Annuities Market," *Journal of Political Economy* 89, no. 2 (1981), pp. 372–91; Olivia Mitchell and others, "New Evidence on the Money's Worth of Individual Annuities," *American Economic Review* 89, no. 5 (1999), pp. 1299–1318; and Menahem Yaari, "Uncertain Lifetime, Life Insurance, and the Theory of the Consumer," *Review of Economic Studies* 32, no. 2 (1965), pp. 137–50.

2. The data are from the Health and Retirement Study and the sample includes adults aged sixty-five and older in 1999. For more details, see Richard Johnson, Leonard Burman, and Deborah Kobes, "Annuitized Wealth at Older Ages: Evidence from the Health and Retirement Study" (Washington: Urban Institute, 2004).

3. Mitchell and others, "New Evidence on the Money's Worth of Individual Annuities."

4. Wei-Yin Hu and Jason Scott, "Behavioral Obstacles to the Annuity Market," Working Paper PRC-WP2007-10 (University of Pennsylvania, Wharton School, Pension Research Council, 2007).

5. Brigitte C. Madrian and Dennis F. Shea, "The Power of Suggestion: Inertia in 401(k) Participation and Savings Behavior," *Quarterly Journal of Economics* 116, no. 4 (2001), pp. 1149–87; Richard Thaler and Shlomo Benartzi, "Save More Tomorrow: Using Behavioral Economics to Increase Saving," *Journal of Political Economy* 112, no. S1 (2004), pp. S164–87.

6. Essentially, those who survive the longest are financed by those who predecease them. This is sometimes referred to as the "mortality credit." The mortality credits from annuities increase with age as fewer survivors share the pooled resources.

7. Partial, rather than complete, annuitization may be optimal because consumers may desire to leave bequests or to hold liquidity for uncertain medical expenses. On bequests, see Thomas Davidoff, Jeffrey Brown, and Peter Diamond, "Annuities and Individual Welfare," *American Economic Review* 95, no. 5 (2005), pp. 1573–90; on uncertain medical expenses, see Sven Sinclair and Kent Smerters, "Health Shocks and the Demand for Annuities," Working Paper 2004-9 (Congressional Budget Office, 2004); and Casso Turra and Olivia Mitchell, "The Impact of Health Status and Out-of-Pocket Medical Expenses on Annuity Valuation," in *Recalibrating Retirement Spending and Saving*, edited by John Ameriks and Olivia S. Mitchell (Oxford University Press, 2008). For both reasons, see Karen Dynan, Jonathan Skinner, and Stephen P. Zeldes, "The Importance of Bequests and Life-Cycle Saving in Capital Accumulation: A New Answer," *American Economic Review* 92, no. 2 (2002), pp. 274–78. In addition, family members may share risk and pool resources—through marriage, for instance—which provides an additional hedge against the risk of outliving their resources (Kotlikoff and Spivak, "The Family as an Incomplete Annuities Market").

8. Social Security Administration, "The 2007 Annual Report of the Board of Trustees of the Federal Old-Age and Survivors Insurance and Federal Disability Insurance Trust Funds" (Washington: 2007). Replacement rates were computed for scaled low, medium, high, and steady maximum earners. Estimated replacement rates are for workers retiring at the normal retirement age under intermediate demographic and economic assumptions; they are 56 percent, 42 percent, 35 percent, and 29 percent, respectively.

9. Davidoff, Brown, and Diamond, "Annuities and Individual Welfare."

10. James Poterba, Steven Venti, and David Wise, "New Estimates of the Future Path of 401(k) Assets," Working Paper 13083 (Cambridge, Mass.: National Bureau of Economics Research, 2007).

11. Households with shorter life expectancy, who tend to be lower-income, would benefit less from lifetime-income products. Brown, however, finds that even those with shorter life spans could benefit from annuitization; Jeffrey R. Brown, "Redistribution and Insurance: Mandatory Annuitization with Mortality Heterogeneity," *Journal of Risk and Insurance*, 70, no. 1 (2003), pp. 17–41.

12. Aggregate longevity risk is the risk that life expectancy of workers born around the same time will either improve or decline. This is a concern for providers because unexpected increases in aggregate life expectancy would increase their payout obligations. Providers who are unable to hedge completely against this risk will transfer some of the increased risk to consumers through higher premiums. This paper does not address this issue directly. See Jeffrey Brown and Peter Orszag, "The Political Economy of Government-Issued Longevity Bonds," *Journal of Risk and Insurance* 73, no. 4 (2006), pp. 611–31.

13. Jeffrey Kling and others, "Why Don't People Insure Late Life Consumption? A Framing Explanation of the Under-Annuitization Puzzle," *American Economic Review* 98, no. 2 (*Papers and Proceedings*, 2008).

14. Esther Duflo and others, "Saving Incentives for Low- and Middle-Income Families: Evidence from a Field Experiment with H&R Block," *Quarterly Journal of Economics* 121, no. 4 (2006), pp. 1131–46; Madrian and Shea, "The Power of Suggestion"; Thaler and Benartzi, "Save More Tomorrow."

15. Other behavioral biases have been inferred from the choices made by consumers. Consumers appear to worry overly about dying soon after buying an annuity and, for that reason, prefer products that guarantee payments for a certain time. About 73 percent of all immediate life annuities sold in the United States have guaranteed payments and a similar proportion of TIAA-CREF annuitants purchase a guarantee; see John Ameriks, "Recent Trends in the Selection of Retirement Income Streams among TIAA-CREF Participants," Research Dialogue 74 (New York: TIAA-CREF Policy Institute, 2002). In the United Kingdom, an overwhelming majority of annuitants also purchase an annuity with a five- or ten-year guarantee period; see Liran Einav, Amy Finkelstein, and Paul Schrimpf, "The Welfare Cost of Asymmetric Information: Evidence from the U.K. Annuity Market," Working Paper 13228 (Cambridge, Mass.: National Bureau of Economic Research, 2007).

16. Longevity insurance is guaranteed protection against living longer than expected by pooling longevity risk.

17. Richard Thaler, "Towards a Positive Theory of Consumer Choice," *Journal of Economic Behavior and Organization* 1, no. 1 (1980), pp. 39–60.

18. For more discussion about the tendency to make decisions relative to some benchmark, see Daniel Kahneman and Amos Tversky, "Prospect Theory: An Analysis of Decision under Risk," *Econometrica* 47, no. 2 (1979), pp. 263–91.

19. Hewitt Associates, "Survey Findings: Trends and Experiences in 401(k) Plans" (Lincolnshire, Ill.: 2005)

20. For additional details, see William G. Gale and J. Mark Iwry, "Automatic Investment: Improving 401 (k) Portfolio Investment Choices," Policy Brief 2005-4 (Washington: Retirement Security Project, 2005); William G. Gale, J. Mark Iwry, and Peter R. Orszag, "The Automatic 401(k): A Simple Way to Strengthen Retirement Saving." Policy Brief 2005-1 (Washington: Retirement Security Project, 2005); and J. Mark Iwry, "Promoting 401(k) Security" (Washington: Tax Policy Center, 2003). Another major direction in which automatic strategies can expand retirement security is outside the 401(k)—through IRAs—which would benefit the 78 million working Americans who have no access to an employer

plan; see chapter 4. For more information on these topics and proposals, see www.retirement securityproject.org.

21. An example of the former category are individuals with poorer health who expect to have shorter-than-average life expectancy and who are able to compute the benefits of the lifetime-income product relative to an alternative investment option.

22. The two-year trial default is part of a more general strategy of using defaults to encourage people to choose income solutions. Automatic features to promote the expanded use of guaranteed income could apply directly to the benefit payout decisions plan sponsors and individuals confront in the distribution phase of the plan or indirectly through plan sponsors' and participants' investment decisions toward the end of their careers. The two-year default explores the use of automatic strategies directly in the distribution phase. (The indirect use of automatic strategies in the investment phase to improve distribution decisions is explored in chapter 7.)

23. The requirement of an apples-to-apples comparison may generate demand for a third party that collects, maintains, and disseminates (perhaps at a cost) information on prices and features. The Financial Services Authority in the United Kingdom maintains an annuity pricing Web site: www.fsa.gov.uk/tables. There is at least one similar comparative tool in the United States, and it is maintained by a private firm for retirement plans that subscribe to that service. Although a clearinghouse established for this purpose would likely charge a fee and might be accessible only to plans rather than to consumers, as the market grows equivalent services would likely develop specifically for consumers.

24. Providers that offer lifetime-income contracts would have to accommodate two-year cash-outs. For some, this option may be costly to provide. One option around this issue may be to offer a "blended" product, which is a withdrawal plan in the first twenty-four months and a lifetime-income contract (with longevity protection) when the default trial transitions to a permanent plan.

25. The default program would apply to those who request lump-sum distributions or partial lump sums that significantly exceed the minimum required distributions.

26. Poterba, Venti, and Wise, "New Estimates of the Future Path of 401(k) Assets."

27. For a discussion of possible strategies, see Alex Cowley and J. David Cummins, "Securitization of Life Insurance Assets and Liabilities," *Journal of Risk and Insurance* 72, no. 2 (2005), pp. 193–226.

28. For instance, insurers could look to reinsurers or capital markets for new ways to hedge against aggregate longevity risks. At least in the U.K. annuity market, some reinsurers are currently reluctant to reinsure lifetime-income contracts because these contracts are opaque and the risks are difficult to evaluate. For more discussion about the pension annuity market in the United Kingdom, see Association of British Insurers, "The Pension Annuity Market: Further Research into Supply and Constraints" (London: February 2005).

29. For instance, plan sponsors must comply with qualified plan rules on what type of annuity to offer (joint and survivor for married participants, with spousal consent to an election of a single-life annuity) and how to price annuities (unisex mortality tables); sponsors also must evaluate the soundness and claims-paying ability of lifetime-income providers. See chapter 7 and Jeffrey R. Brown and others, "Taxing Retirement Income: Nonqualified Annuities and Distributions from Qualified Accounts," *National Tax Journal* 53, no. 3 (1999), pp. 563–92.

30. Brown and others, "Taxing Retirement Income."

31. Jeffrey R. Brown, "Guaranteed Trouble: The Economic Effects of the Pension Benefit Guaranty Corporation," *Journal of Economic Perspectives* 22, no. 1 (2008), pp. 177–98.

32. The FDIC, in principle, assesses risk-based premiums; however, in practice, most financial institutions are assessed zero premiums because their reserves qualify them for an exemption.

33. If the sponsor were one of those that choose to add projections of potential future benefits that would likely accumulate if the participant continued contributions at an assumed rate for an assumed period, the projection could also be stated as an income stream in addition to an account balance.

34. Kling and others, "Why Don't People Insure Late Life Consumption?"

7

Automatic Annuitization:
New Behavioral Strategies for
Expanding Lifetime Income in 401(k)s

J. MARK IWRY AND JOHN A. TURNER

W orkers contemplating retirement face significant financial risks. Inflation, an uncertain rate of return on investments, the insolvency of a
former employer or financial provider—all these external factors can deplete
retirees' assets and income. Personal risks such as unemployment, illness, disability, and even life span can lower earning capacity or raise financial need.

A long life, a blessing in so many ways, is especially hard to manage. Some
underestimate how long they will live or neglect to plan for the possibility of
many years in retirement. Many find it difficult to devise and adhere to a plan
for managing retirement assets over an uncertain, and potentially long, time
horizon.

Americans' financial prospects for retirement naturally depend on how much
money they have saved during their working years. Equally important, but often
an afterthought, is how they use it.

Traditionally, the most complete solution to this problem has been to protect retirees from outliving their assets through the use of guaranteed lifetime
income, such as an annuity. Annuities and other lifetime-income arrangements
undertake to make predictable payments for as long as annuitants are alive.

The authors would like to thank Bill Gale, David John, and Lina Walker for helpful discussions and comments at various stages of the paper.

Yet in recent years annuitization rates have fallen. Defined benefit pension plans at the workplace, a traditional source of low-cost annuity income, have increasingly offered and made lump-sum (single cash) payments, either by adding a lump-sum option to the plan's array of payout options or by converting the entire plan to a different, lump-sum-oriented format known as a hybrid. "Cash-balance" plans are the most common kind of hybrid. Many other employers have replaced their defined benefit plans with 401(k) plans, whose accumulated wealth is typically returned to workers upon retirement as a lump sum rather than as monthly payments for the duration of retirement. Only about 2 percent of 401(k) participants choose to convert their savings into annuities upon retirement.

Despite these trends, the need for stable and assured income has increased along with longer life expectancies and retirement periods. The choice between an annuity and a lump-sum distribution may be one of the most important financial decisions a person ever makes. Why more people do not choose annuities has been something of a puzzle within the economics literature and for policy analysts. There are three broad classes of explanations:

—Annuities may not inspire confidence because they are not sufficiently transparent or simple to understand. Consumers find themselves mystified by annuities' complex provisions and worry (based partly on warnings in the personal finance and consumer protection literature) that insurance companies are pricing their products unfairly. Comparison shopping between annuities, let alone between annuities and lump-sum options, can be a lot more complicated than contrasting a Toyota to a Ford in an automobile showroom.

—Annuities may appear to be a risky, high-stakes gamble with insurance companies about how long the retiree will live. Retirees who die young are deprived not only of years of their life but also of years of annuity payments.

—Annuities may preclude important alternative uses of retirement savings.

An Automatic Strategy to Enhance the Appeal of Annuities

To encourage more retirees to put at least some of their retirement savings into lifetime income, it would be natural to consider the use of automatic (default) strategies. The intelligent use of automatic features in 401(k) plans has enjoyed striking success in expanding plan participation and improving investment behavior.[1] There is ample reason to think that the behaviorally inspired strategies that have worked so well to improve participation in 401(k) plans should be extended, as has long been intended, to 401(k) payouts as well.[2]

Currently the most common option in most 401(k) plans is the lump sum; retirees typically receive their savings in the form of a single check. For many retirees, this may not be the best choice. One way to promote a better choice is to make an annuity the default option at decision time. In the saving phase of financing retirement, as made clear in chapters 2 and 3, automatic enrollment in workplace 401(k) plans has greatly increased desired behavior—in this case, saving for retirement. We believe the same principle can be put to work in the payout phase of retirement saving: deciding what to do with the accumulated savings. The authors of chapter 6 put forward a single proposal providing that when retirees cash out their 401(k) plans, the accounts would automatically be used to support an annuity unless the retirees explicitly said they wanted a lump sum. After receiving twenty-four monthly checks, retirees would be able to switch out and take the remaining value of their retirement savings in the form of a lump sum. Presumably, many would not do so.

Given the success of 401(k) automatic enrollment, would making an annuity the default option at retirement similarly increase the percentage of pension participants taking annuities? The evidence suggests it would not. Although a useful element in a strategy to encourage the selection of annuities, the default approach by itself would be far from sufficient. For example, every cash-balance pension plan is required by law to make a lifetime annuity the default method of payment, but the vast majority of participants in these plans opt out of the annuity in favor of a lump sum. In these plans, the benefit is framed as an account balance or lump sum; and even in traditional defined benefit plans, where the benefit tends to be framed as an annuity, participants often, though not as frequently, opt for a lump sum if it is available as an option.

The evidence suggests that when an annuity is the default and a lump sum is the alternative, most participants opt out of the default in favor of the lump sum, at least where the annuity-versus-lump-sum decision is presented as a momentous, all-or-nothing, irreversible decision affecting retirees' entire account balance. The force of inertia that gives the automatic or default strategy its power appears to be weak in these circumstances, and even weaker when the plan has framed the presumptive form of benefit as a lump sum. Could arrangements be designed to enhance the effectiveness of an automatic or default annuity and make participants more likely to accept it? We believe so.

Chapter 6 discusses the factors limiting demand for annuities and outlines a promising proposal to increase demand for and participation in 401(k) plans: automatic trial income. Under this approach, which seeks to use inertia to overcome misconceptions about annuities, a 401(k) plan sponsor could tell retiring participants that half (or some other specified portion) of their account balance was tentatively earmarked for annuitization. The annuitization would begin with regular monthly payments for two years, unless the retiree opted out. At the end of the two-year trial period, retirees could elect an alternative distribution option; but if they did nothing, regular monthly payments would automatically continue for life. The underlying assumption is that once workers had an opportunity to "test-drive" an annuity for a limited period of time and become accustomed to its advantages, they would be more likely at the end to accept it permanently. The regular income stream (or "pension paycheck"), rather than the lump sum, might come to be seen as the status quo or presumptive form of benefit.

We believe this automatic trial-income approach would go a long way toward addressing many of the obstacles to broader use of lifetime income in 401(k)s. However, it would not address all of them, and it would address some only to a limited degree, in part because it would apply mainly at the point of retirement (the start of the plan's payout phase). Accordingly, it may be that the use of lifetime income would be expanded through a complementary approach that could be used in conjunction with the trial-income approach (or that could be offered to plan sponsors as another alternative, reflecting a similar behavioral strategy).

The complementary approach we have in mind would involve the phased or incremental acquisition of deferred annuities during the plan's accumulation phase. Like the trial-income approach, this strategy is designed to eliminate or mitigate significant obstacles to the expanded use of lifetime income, without purporting to remove all of the obstacles. Even as innovative product designs have recently come onto the market, each approach would help address an over-lapping set of concerns. In combination, the approaches outlined in chapter 6 and here are designed to overcome, in a mutually reinforcing manner, much of what currently limits 401(k) participants' demand for lifetime income.

Phased or Incremental Acquisition of Deferred Annuities

Based on our analysis of the factors inhibiting demand for lifetime income, a strategy that would make the automatic (default) approach a more powerful tool to promote lifetime income should incorporate three simple but important elements.

—*Avoid all-or-nothing decisions.* Instead of requiring retirees to use all, or none, of their savings to buy lifetime-income instruments, the new approach could allow them to use only a portion of their balance to purchase an annuity. New retirees could take possession of the balance of their retirement savings as a lump sum. The relative amounts of savings devoted to provide regular income and to fund a lump-sum payment would presumably vary from one household to the next depending on circumstances.

—*Avoid now-or-never decisions.* Plan participants could be allowed to choose incremental annuitization over time, rather than being confronted with a single moment of truth when the decision of whether or not to take an annuity is thrust upon them. The stress that accompanies making such a decision is not only unpleasant but also an incubator of bad decisionmaking. We would divide the decision not only in amount (through partial annuitization) but in time (through incremental annuitization).

—*Avoid never-or-forever decisions.* Today's practice generally forbids retirees to reverse any or all of an annuity purchase, at least for a while. This compounds the stress related to the initial decision; retirees who get it wrong do not have another crack at it.

These three elements effectively lower the stakes so that someone who passively accepts the default has almost nothing to lose. On any given day, the incremental cost of postponing an active decision and going along with the default is de minimis.

We would give effect to these three principles in a system in which a specified portion of worker and employer contributions to 401(k) accounts would be invested in units of deferred annuity. This portion would grow with time and with additional contributions. (This would not be the traditional deferred annuity that has often been used only as an investment vehicle, without ultimately being paid out in regular installments over the owner's lifetime. Instead, it would be designed mainly to provide lifetime guaranteed income beginning after retirement.)

Instead of making a single purchase decision at retirement, the employee would acquire an annuity incrementally, beginning either in mid-career (at age 45 or 50, for example,) or earlier, and continuing until retirement distributions began.[3] The employee could opt out of the arrangement entirely (although the default would be renewed from time to time, requiring an employee who was not interested in acquiring annuity-income units to opt out periodically). Alternatively, the employee could choose to dedicate a different percentage of current contributions to the incremental acquisitions.

Annuities' Advantages

Incremental purchases through regular, small contributions over a period of years should promote a fundamental reframing of the way 401(k) benefits are presented to participants. They would come to see the benefits not as a lump sum in a single account but as an income stream. They would regard each payment to them as a pension paycheck—deferred compensation for work done. The reframing could be accomplished in two ways: through regular benefit statements, and by accumulation. The benefit statement approach, which could apply in 401(k) plans and other defined contribution plans as well as to individual retirement accounts (IRAs), cash-balance plans, and other hybrid plans that present benefits as an account balance, is described in chapter 6.

The gradual acquisition of annuity-income units would also circumvent the wealth illusion or "sticker shock" that tends to discourage individuals from paying a "large" amount to an insurance company in exchange for an ostensibly "small" regular monthly payment. This is true for many of the same reasons that 401(k) payroll deduction contributions tend to work effectively as a saving mechanism: Participants would not see a large sum being transferred out of their account to an insurance company. Instead, they would pay small amounts over time, which should inflict little or no psychological pain. Incremental annuitization would avoid sticker shock not only because it is gradual but because it takes place years before the annuity is fully acquired, meaning that smaller contributions can be set aside to acquire the annuity given the additional time for tax-free investment earnings.[4]

Whether or not incremental accumulation of annuity-income units began by default, it would continue without requiring the participant to take any initiative or make any decision.[5]

Individuals confronted with the initial decision of whether to opt out of the gradual use of a portion of their contributions to acquire deferred annuity units would find the stakes at that moment to be low. It should be easier for individuals to accept the default with respect to any given contribution because it represents only a small amount. For example, whether to opt out of having 20 percent of current contributions automatically placed in a relatively stable investment for the next few pay periods should not present itself as a momentous decision. (The plan might provide that, over the next five or ten years, the percentage would gradually, but automatically, increase to 30 or 40 percent.) Procrastination would be easy because the decision would be reversible. One could always decide to opt out later, before very much had been invested in the annuity units.

In addition, incremental acquisition could include an "unwind," or cash-surrender, option permitting the participant to opt out retroactively subject to a surrender charge. Such an unwind arrangement should be designed to encourage participants to engage in or accept incremental acquisition, because it is not irreversible, but should be set at a level that would discourage most participants from actually using it.

The incremental acquisition of annuity units would mitigate the interest rate risk associated with a point-in-time acquisition. Because individuals would face different interest rates throughout the purchase period, the rate in any single period would be averaged over time with other rates (much like an investment using dollar cost averaging).

For some participants, accepting the annuity-income default would mean postponing receipt of much (for example, half) of their lump-sum distribution for two years. They might not be willing to defer gratification in this way. In fact, the evidence shows that the vast majority of retiring or terminating cash-balance plan participants override the default annuity in favor of a lump-sum payment. By contrast, participants in the accumulation phase might not perceive the incremental acquisition of annuity income as imposing a similar sharp trade-off or as requiring deferral of gratification.

Many plan participants may be drawn to the annuity option as a "safe" and stable investment, especially when markets are turbulent. While investors generally are warned not to act on emotion or attempt to time the market, many— especially those close to retirement—worry understandably during times of market volatility about the risk associated with equity investments. These individuals might welcome an investment strategy that is not centered on money market or stable-value funds (neither of which is a perfect solution). Investment in fixed annuities or in variable annuities with sufficient payout guarantees or floors could be part of the response to a potential and actual "flight to safety" in 401(k) plans.

Incremental acquisition of annuity income during the accumulation phase might be particularly responsive to these concerns. Fixed annuities or variable annuities with guarantees could serve as a "safe" investment composing a portion of a balanced, diversified portfolio. This particular advantage—the stability of a fixed or guaranteed annuity as an investment during periods of market volatility—is more likely to be demonstrated to participants over a decade or several decades of accumulation (spanning at least one market cycle, including at least one period of depressed or volatile market values) than at a particular point in time.

Holding Costs Down

For several reasons, the gradual acquisition of deferred annuities through an employer plan should also help reduce cost.

—Group annuities (or annuities purchased through a group purchase) are less costly than those purchased on the individual market because the group (through the plan sponsor) has greater bargaining power and can bring a greater degree of knowledge (including the help of an outside consultant) to the negotiating table.

—Group purchase should be less expensive insofar as it is less subject to adverse selection (although individuals with shorter life expectancies could be expected to opt out of the lifetime income approach and be underrepresented in the pool). But retirement annuities purchased earlier in life, when people have less information about their health status at retirement, might entail less adverse selection than purchase decisions at retirement and to that extent should be less expensive than annuities purchased at retirement.

—The deferral period should also reduce the perceived cost. A lengthy interval between purchase and payment means that the annuity value should have time to build up with investment earnings so that the annuity provider could offer a larger nominal monthly payment for each dollar of contributions.[6]

More generally, strategies such as the one outlined here—which could be used in conjunction with, or as an alternative to, the trial-income approach described in chapter 6—have the potential to expand the market sufficiently to make lifetime income a staple within the 401(k) universe. This should lead to a better-functioning market, with greater opportunities for standardization, transparency, and, ultimately, lower costs.

Implementing Incremental Acquisition

Typically 401(k) plans entail a strong framing of the benefit as a lump sum; indeed, the account balance itself can be and is viewed as a presumptive lump-sum benefit. To compete with this deep-seated framing and strong participant bias in favor of lump sums, 401(k) plans could be required (as noted earlier) to regularly report accumulating benefits as an annuity equivalent, in addition to an account balance. (A similar approach might be considered for IRAs.) In fact, it might be especially useful to show the annuity equivalent at three alternative annuity starting ages, such as 62, 65, and 70. (This approach might encourage some workers to postpone retirement, depending in part on how they interpret the relative value of the higher annuity dollar amounts beginning at the later ages.)

In the specific context of 401(k) plans, two particularly promising vehicles could encourage participants to accumulate deferred lifetime income over the latter part of their working lives. We suggest these as alternatives, each of which may appeal to a different subset of plan sponsors.

Tapping the Employer Match

Most 401(k) plans provide employer matching contributions. A plan sponsor could make phased acquisition of annuity-income units more likely to occur (or ensure that it would occur) by dedicating its employer matching contributions to this purpose. A plan sponsor could choose to make such an investment mandatory or could make it the default, allowing participants to opt for a different investment. Either approach would be permissible under current law. The sponsor could even begin by using only a portion of the employer match to purchase annuities, gradually increasing to all of the match over time. The logic of a "bright line" segregation of employer matching contributions used to accumulate an annuity from other contributions invested in other ways should reinforce the "framing" of participant expectations that a portion of their account balance would be used to provide lifetime income.

We see three main potential advantages of using employer contributions in this way. First, the notion that the employer matching contribution is directed to a particular investment, either by dictate or by default, is a familiar one in the 401(k) universe. Traditionally, the prospect of obtaining Employee Stock Ownership Plan tax advantages, saving employer cash flow, enhancing worker incentives and productivity, and fending off hostile takeovers led many 401(k) plan sponsors to make employer contributions in the form of employer stock (or to provide for them to be invested in employer stock), subject, in many cases, to participants' ability to elect otherwise. Now that Congress has limited employers' ability to force investment of matching contributions in employer stock, there is an opportunity to use a similarly assertive approach with respect to the investment of employer contributions in the interest of expanding lifetime income.[7]

Second, participants who are skeptical about turning their assets over to an insurance carrier may be more accepting of "employer money" being invested in annuity income.[8] The difference between employers, as opposed to employees, bearing the cost of funding the benefits exists in employee and even employer perceptions, if not reality. (This chapter does not explore the issues relating to the actual differences between employee and employer contributions, which are beyond the scope of this discussion.) Because employees and employers perceive an important distinction between employee and employer contributions, employees may feel that their employer is entitled to decide how "its own contributions" are used. This should be even more true in the case of employer nonmatching ("nonelective") contributions.

Third, this use of employer contributions avoids presenting the employee with an all-or-nothing choice and spares the employee the need to decide exactly what portion of his or her contributions to invest in deferred annuity units. Employer matching contributions often account for about a third of the account balance (or slightly less). To many employees, this might feel like a reasonable or acceptable portion to devote to lifetime income.

The accumulated annuity-income units acquired with employer matching contributions could be used as an alternative to the two-year trial annuity proposed in chapter 6. Alternatively, plan sponsors might choose to use both approaches as default strategies. Plan participants who declined the investment of employer matching contributions in incremental annuity units might be willing to accept an automatic two-year trial annuity for a portion of their account balance at retirement, in part because of the earlier framing of a portion of benefits as a potential annuity. (However, for participants who accepted the investment of the employer match in annuity units, a two-year trial annuity is less likely to be necessary or appropriate; and plan sponsors purchasing annuity income for participants long before retirement may get a better price from annuity providers than those purchasing trial-income annuities.)

The employer contribution strategy may have special appeal to two types of plan sponsors. The first are companies that have previously made or invested employer contributions in employer stock and are now interested in reducing participants' (and the plan fiduciaries') exposure by reducing the amount of employer stock in the plan.[9] The second are those that have recently frozen, terminated, or otherwise reduced a defined benefit plan. Such sponsors often try to mitigate the expected loss to employees of an employer-funded defined benefit by making certain improvements in their 401(k) plans. To partially compensate employees for losing the advantages of the defined benefit, the sponsor might, for example, increase the employer match in the 401(k), add a nonmatching employer profit-sharing type of contribution to the 401(k), or introduce automatic enrollment and automatic increases in employee contributions. Using employer 401(k) contributions to buy annuity-income units would have the advantage of replacing some of the expected retirement income that was lost when the company reduced its defined benefit plan.

Embedding Lifetime Income in a Life-Cycle Fund or Another QDIA

As an alternative to dedicating the 401(k) employer matching contributions to the phased purchase of lifetime-income units, plan sponsors and financial providers might consider incorporating the phased purchase of deferred annuity units into a qualified default investment alternative, or QDIA, specified by the Department of Labor. In regulations interpreting the 2006 Pension Protection Act, the Labor Department has specified several types of default investments that 401(k) and similar plans could offer without losing the degree of protection from fiduciary liability that results from allowing participants to select among certain investment options defined by the plan. Typically in conjunction with automatic enrollment, the 401(k) market has been moving briskly to incorporate these automatic or QDIA default investments.

Probably the most prevalent form of QDIA currently available is the target-date maturity fund, also known as the life-cycle fund. Often structured as a composite "fund of funds," the life-cycle fund generally holds a mix of asset classes, largely diversified equities, and fixed-income investments. A life-cycle fund for people who are decades away from retirement typically invests a majority of its assets in diversified stocks. As individuals approach their assumed target retirement date, the asset mix shifts gradually away from the potentially higher-return but higher-risk equities to a higher percentages of less volatile or more conservative investments such as bonds or other fixed-income investments (this process is often referred to as a "glide path"). Thus far, these target-date or life-cycle funds generally have been well accepted by employees as a means of achieving asset allocation and diversification that reflects a fairly broad consensus within the expert financial advisory community.[10]

The phased purchase of annuities would fit neatly into the life-cycle-fund rubric; and a new kind of life-cycle default fund could facilitate the phased purchase of annuities. The steadily growing fixed-income component of the life-cycle fund might be composed of fixed annuity-income units that accumulate over time and that would be paid out as an annuity at retirement. Thus, fixed deferred annuity units could substitute for the bond component of the life-cycle fund, either entirely or in part. (Whereas variable annuities are invested in equities, fixed annuities tend to be backed up, at least indirectly, by insurance company investments in bonds.) As a result, the percentage of 401(k) contributions being used to purchase deferred annuity-income units would grow as employees approached their expected retirement date. These new life-cycle or target-date funds would go beyond the funds currently offered insofar as they would not only serve as an investment but would also help participants manage the postretirement spend-down of their 401(k) assets.

If 401(k) plan sponsors chose to offer such funds, they would enlist inertia in the cause of persuading employees to allow a portion of their account balance to be invested in deferred annuities. Employees would have the usual ability to opt out of the default life-cycle investment fund. However, there is reason to expect that the current pattern with respect to conventional life-cycle QDIAs—a high rate of employee acceptance, as opposed to opt-outs—might well hold in the case of such new QDIAs. For most employees, the nonequity components of the default life-cycle fund are largely a "black box." Employees are unlikely to be highly sensitive to differences in the composition of the conservative portion of the asset mix, absent a meaningful reduction in expected return, a perception that the new type of investment was risky, or an increase in expenses. (This paper does not investigate potential expenses to plan sponsors or employees associated with the use of deferred annuities in standard QDIA investments.)

We obviously are not suggesting that annuities "stow away" in the currently popular life-cycle default funds without full and effective advance disclosure to participants. However, some of the same employees who might resist purchasing an annuity at retirement with their entire 401(k) account balance may be far more willing to accept partial deferred annuitization purchased incrementally— far more willing to accept the incremental choices involved in not opting out of a default life-cycle fund that includes deferred annuity units as its fixed-income component. Such a plan also would help them manage their assets after retirement and spread the risk that low interest rates at the time of purchase would reduce the amount of annuity that could be purchased with a given dollar of contributions.

Plans using this new kind of life-cycle fund as a QDIA could, of course, also offer other investment options including more conventional life-cycle funds that use fixed-income investments instead of annuity-income units. Conversely, the phased acquisition of deferred annuity units could be incorporated in any of the three principal QDIAs—not only the target-maturity or life-cycle fund but also balanced funds that do not change their asset mix over time, and managed accounts.

Complementary Approaches

The automatic phased or incremental annuity acquisition strategy could serve as an alternative to, or be used in coordination with, the automatic trial-income approach proposed in chapter 6.

First, viewing the incremental strategy as an alternative or a precursor to the trial-income annuity strategy addresses the fact that not all plan participants are in similar circumstances or are driven by the same considerations or concerns. Each approach might appeal to a different subset of the participant population; if each is effective with a different group, together they might encourage more lifetime income than either alone. In a rough, schematic way, table 7-1 shows the specific concerns inhibiting demand for lifetime income that are intended to be addressed by each of the two incremental purchase strategies described here (employer match and QDIA), by the trial-period income strategy described in chapter 6, and by a combination of these strategies. The table suggests that each of the strategies addresses a wide range of the issues that have been identified as inhibiting demand, and each appears likely to do better than the others in one or more areas. In the aggregate, they offer a range of possible strategies to plan sponsors, some of whom might feel more comfortable with one or another (or a combination) of these approaches.

Second, participants' choice (explicit or by default) to purchase annuity-income units for a period of years before retirement could make the trial-income approach more effective. While regular statements of benefits in annuity, as well as account-balance, form certainly promise to be helpful, they are only descriptive; reinforcing the effect of those statements through the incremental purchase of annuity-income units is experiential (as is the two-year trial of regular income) and thus potentially more powerful. Incremental annuity purchases would likely go far toward reframing participants' expectations regarding their plan benefits as an income stream rather than a presumptive lump-sum payment.

Third, a plan that has an incremental accumulation-phase element in its overall income strategy might, for example, make the actual commencement of

Table 7-1. *How Policy Options Address Concerns Affecting Demand for Lifetime Income*[a]

Concern or obstacle	Trial income	Phased accumulation	Phased accumulation using QDIA or employer match
Many consumers lack confidence in annuities: not sufficiently transparent, simple, or well priced			
Lack of knowledge	✓		
Mistrust	✓✓	✓	✓
Nontransparent costs			
High prices	✓	✓	✓
Ostensibly unfavorable terms of trade		✓✓	✓✓
Loss of sense of ownership	✓	✓✓	✓✓
To some retirees, choosing an annuity seems risky			
Risk of losing to insurance company	✓	✓	✓
All-or-nothing choice	✓	✓✓	✓✓
Irreversibility	✓	✓	✓
Market timing interest rate risk		✓✓	✓✓
Insurance company insolvency	✓	✓	✓
Annuity purchase seems to require giving up important alternatives			
Bequests	✓	✓	✓
Liquidity	✓	✓	✓
Financial flexibility	✓	✓	✓
Loss of equity premium	✓	✓	✓
Loss of investment control	✓	✓	✓✓
Loss of current consumption	✓	✓	✓

Source: Authors' compilation.

a. For a description and discussion of these concerns inhibiting demand as well as factors inhibiting the supply of lifetime income, see Jeffrey Kling and others, "Why Don't People Choose Annuities? A Framing Explanation," Research Brief (Washington: Retirement Security Project, March 2008).

✓ = addresses concern to some degree; ✓✓ = strongly addresses concern; QDIA = qualified default investment alternative.

annuity-income the default, but not mandatory, and combine the incremental option with the two-year trial approach. Participants who have accumulated annuity units might be more likely to go along with the initial default (preceding the two-year period) and experience the two-year trial, especially if the accumulated annuity units were used to provide the two-year trial payments. These participants might also be more likely to go along with the subsequent default (at the end of the two-year period), choosing permanent annuitization, again especially if accumulated annuity units were sufficient to fund some of those annuity benefits. (In fact, such participants might even ultimately annuitize portions of the account balance that do not represent accumulated annuity-income units.)

Fourth, plan sponsors may feel more comfortable actually requiring the two-year trial (rather than merely making it a default option) for annuity-income units that plan participants have purchased over a period of years on the understanding that they will presumptively be annuitized. The sponsor might, for example, allow participants to opt out of annuitization of such long-accumulated annuity-income units after the two-year trial period but may not feel constrained to offer the opt-out choice at the start of the two-year trial as well (assuming, as we do for current purposes, that the plan qualification rules would not require otherwise). As a result, more participants are likely to experience the two-year trial instead of opting out of it.

In addition, as discussed earlier, annuities (whether acquired through trial income or incremental accumulation) may be more attractive to many households in times of economic turmoil, especially because fixed annuities can provide stability of investment returns, assuming the long-term solvency of the provider. Incremental acquisition of annuity income during the accumulation phase may be particularly responsive to these concerns, insofar as the safety and stability of fixed annuities is likely to become more evident to participants over a long period of accumulation than during a two-year trial-income period.

New Product Features Address Some Key Concerns

Many concerns have been or are being addressed to some degree by traditional features or by innovations in annuity products or other competing financial products, although each additional feature inevitably comes at a price. Following are some examples.

—Variable annuities have long provided the option to make equity investments within an annuity and the option for the annuitant to exercise control over the investments (while exposing the annuitant to investment risk).

—Some of these products combine equity exposure with certain kinds of guarantees or floor values, including features that may lock in certain equity gains. The combination provides participants with upside potential together with a measure of protection against the risk of loss.

—Joint-and-survivor annuities that provide lifetime protection to an annuitant's surviving spouse, term-certain and life annuities that promise payments for a fixed number of years even if the annuitant is deceased, and annuities that provide lump-sum death benefits have been long-standing options designed to deal with annuitants' concern that an early death will leave the insurance carrier with most of their money. However, death benefits and cash-surrender options dilute the longevity risk protection by reducing the mortality credit for long-lived annuitants.

—Some annuities offer cash-surrender features that essentially allow annuitants or potential annuitants to change their minds and get much of their purchase price back, at least within a specified time frame, or allow partial ad hoc withdrawals to meet "economic shocks" or for other purposes. (However, annuity providers need to protect themselves against the risk of adverse selection by annuitants who discover their life expectancy has suddenly shortened.)

—Some annuities offer inflation protection for an additional premium. The inflation-protected annuity amount could be indexed to cost-of-living indexes or could increase by predetermined percentages designed to provide rough, partial inflation protection.

—Mutual funds and other financial institutions outside the insurance industry have developed products that provide regular monthly income at a predetermined or variable level, with greater flexibility than many annuity products but without the lifetime guarantee or longevity risk sharing of a life annuity.

Many of these results can be achieved simply by purchasing an annuity with only a portion of one's retirement savings and using the remainder to provide survivor protection, equity investment opportunities, spending flexibility, inflation protection, and the like.

Several insurance companies are offering products to 401(k)s that would permit participants to purchase deferred annuity units on an incremental basis. However, these products have yet to be widely adopted. We believe that strategies such as those described here and in chapter 6 may be needed to spark greater employee demand for lifetime income, including the use of employer matching contributions to fund deferred annuities, QDIAs to incorporate deferred annuities, and a trial-income arrangement to try out annuities. We are encouraged to learn that one provider has gone to market with a product that embeds an annuity in a life-cycle fund, similar to the concept outlined above.

Solving the Portability Problem

The strategy outlined here raises a number of important issues and confronts several key challenges. The most significant challenges are how to

—ensure reasonable portability of the lifetime income arrangement as employees change jobs;

—ensure that the cost of the annuity or other lifetime income is reasonable, given market imperfections;

—manage the risk that the annuity provider will become insolvent or otherwise go out of business during the many decades over which the individual will be relying on the lifetime income promise; and

—protect plan sponsors from undue fiduciary risk, while protecting employees from unduly risky lifetime income providers or arrangements.

We address the first of these issues below because the portability problem is generally unique to the preretirement accumulation strategy outlined here. The other three issues are discussed in chapter 6, because they are also raised by the postretirement trial-income approach outlined there. In addition, using 401(k) plans as a vehicle in the manner described here raises a variety of regulatory and other issues, including unisex pricing of annuities and the application of the survivor protection and spousal consent requirements.[11] We intend to pursue these issues in future work and hope others will do so as well.

The phased or incremental acquisition of deferred annuities presents a significant challenge to pension "portability." Participants in a 401(k) who begin to accumulate a deferred annuity and then leave their job often have no opportunity to continue their 401(k) accumulation. The employee who takes a new job would be unable to add to the annuity-income units unless the new employer offered a 401(k) plan that happened to offer a comparable annuity accumulation opportunity with the same provider—not a high probability—and that was willing to accept a transfer or rollover of the previously accumulated units. If the accumulated amounts were small, either or both the employee and the new employer might question whether it was worth the administrative burden to take them as rollovers and whether expenses would threaten to erode their value over time. Some might argue that the portability concern militates in favor of providing that larger amounts of contributions be defaulted toward incremental purchase of annuity units. However, this would help only to the extent amounts had accumulated over a sufficient period, and it might well reduce participants' willingness to go along with the default. Before we suggest potential solutions, it is worth noting that the magnitude of the portability problem, while considerable, should not be overstated. First, incremental accumulation of lifetime income, as proposed here, generally would not begin until middle age. By that point in a worker's career, the typical frequency of job changes has declined significantly, especially for employees covered by a 401(k) plan.[12] Second, the prospect of receiving lifetime income from several providers, as opposed to a single, consolidated source, is messy but not impossible or necessarily ineffective. Retirees fortunate enough to have accrued benefits under more than one defined benefit plan may be in a similar situation.

Several approaches might mitigate this potential lack of portability:

TOP UP OR TAP OUT. Beginning with arrangements that are currently in effect, some employees could "top up" a deferred annuity account by making an ad hoc transfer of assets from other 401(k) or IRA investments. Topping up might be effective in some circumstances, but many workers will lack other resources that would be available for this purpose. For those who have the resources, counting on them to top up would depart from the "behavioral" assumptions and strategy outlined here by requiring employee initiative to make what may be a difficult decision.

As a last resort, deferred annuity accounts that are deemed unlikely to grow and too small to be worth annuitizing might be converted to other investments. This approach may be similar to accumulating funds in an account for future purchase of annuity units only if and when the account reaches a designated critical mass. Such an approach might be viewed as giving the employee a claim to purchase future annuity income rather than actually purchasing the future income. However, it is unclear how much of a difference there would be between a purchase with a surrender option and a claim with a purchase option. In either case, the funds would need to be appropriately invested in the meanwhile and, to give the employee the benefit of interest-rate averaging, steps would need to be taken to lock in interest rates during the interim period. The degree to which a more tentative or contingent arrangement, short of the actual purchase of annuity units, would be more efficient and worth doing presumably would depend largely on the transaction costs of surrendering and liquidating the small annuity-income accumulation. (This issue is somewhat analogous to the question, discussed in chapter 6, of whether the two-year trial income should constitute the first twenty-four monthly payments of an annuity purchased from an annuity provider and subject to surrender after twenty-four months or is better structured as a twenty-four-month installment paid directly by the 401(k) from the assets held in the individual's account.)

IRA ROLLOVER. Another alternative that can be pursued using arrangements currently in effect is to roll over the original deferred annuity to an IRA (in this case, an individual retirement annuity). The IRA would be sponsored by the same annuity provider that provided the 401(k) accumulation annuity and would offer a similar option to invest in deferred annuity units. Individuals could then continue contributing to build up their deferred annuity. Yet for many people the IRA contributions would "compete" with the opportunity to contribute to a new employer's 401(k) plan. The terms of that competition could be unfavorable to the IRA insofar as

—the employee's 401(k) contributions typically would be matched by the employer up to a specified percentage of pay;

—the employee would be entitled to an exclusion from income or tax-favored Roth treatment for contributions to the 401(k) but might not be eligible for a corresponding IRA deduction or Roth IRA treatment for contributions to the IRA; and

—absent the regular payroll deduction mechanism used in 401(k) plans, the contributions to the IRA would be unlikely to begin or continue automatically and therefore would be less likely to be made.

GREATER STANDARDIZATION. Widespread adoption of similar arrangements in 401(k) plans could mitigate the portability problem. However, this would likely be effective only to the extent that annuity providers were willing to facilitate like-kind exchanges of annuity products that allowed individuals to transfer and consolidate deferred annuities with a single annuity provider in a manner analogous to rollovers to IRAs. This in turn would seem unlikely to be efficient or to minimize transaction costs unless providers offered sufficiently homogeneous products. Standardization would be in tension with competitive innovation and, to some degree, with the offering of annuity features designed to respond to consumers' desire for greater flexibility and risk protection (such as death benefits, surrender options, inflation protection, and the ability to share in potential equity returns).

These obstacles might be addressed through a structured marketplace or platform on which competing income-accumulation products could be offered to plan sponsors. Products would be permitted to compete on the platform on condition that they met specifications assuring uniform features, price transparency, and sufficient transferability among products to achieve reasonable portability. At least one private firm offers a somewhat similar arrangement to plan sponsors, which makes it easier to offer and compare annuities for retiring employees. Ultimately, providers might be encouraged to participate in consolidated, standard industrywide products that would not only facilitate portability but spread insolvency risk among all participating providers. In view of these features, such omnibus multiprovider arrangements might qualify for some form of federal government reinsurance or guarantee that would be more uniform and effective than existing state guaranty funds (see chapter 6).

A multiprovider product that spread insolvency risk could also make plan sponsors more willing to offer lifetime income options by significantly reducing the fiduciary risk they otherwise face when choosing among annuity products offered by competing providers. If implemented on a large scale, such an arrangement would increase manyfold the odds that an employee moving to a new employer could continue accumulating deferred income units.

Conclusion

With increased reliance on 401(k) plans, an important challenge facing the U.S. retirement system is how to help retirees manage the risk of outliving their assets. In the past Americans frequently met this problem using private pensions that guaranteed a particular monthly benefit for life. That approach shifted risk onto employers, many of which reacted by replacing defined benefit pension plans with 401(k) plans, which define a particular contribution, leaving it to the workers to invest that money well and to figure out how to use it to see them through their retirement years.

Each of the "automatic" or default strategies outlined here—including acquiring lifetime income incrementally through the use of employer contributions or embedding a deferred annuity in a QDIA, as well as implementing the automatic trial income proposal described in chapter 6—is designed to draw on experience and insights from behavioral economics to help replicate, within the 401(k), one of the valued features of the traditional defined benefit pension. That feature is guaranteed lifetime income at group rates (combined, in most cases, with professional investment management).

We do not hold the view that annuitization of 401(k) balances is necessarily appropriate for all 401(k) participants. We do believe, however, that biases and other obstacles to lifetime and other long-term income options are responsible for the low annuitization rate. This chapter and the preceding one present a strategy for reducing those obstacles and thereby improving retirement security. Further work is needed to resolve a number of significant issues relating to cost, solvency protection, portability, employer fiduciary responsibility, and other implementation questions.

Notes

1. Brigitte C. Madrian and Dennis F. Shea, "The Power of Suggestion: Inertia in 401(k) Participation and Savings Behavior," *Quarterly Journal of Economics* 116, no. 4 (2001), pp. 1149–87; William G. Gale and others, "Improving 401(k) Investment Performance," Issue Brief 2004-26 (Boston College, Center for Retirement Research, 2004); William G. Gale and J. Mark Iwry, "Automatic Investment: Improving 401(k) Portfolio Investment Choices," Policy Brief 2005-4 (Washington: Retirement Security Project, 2005).

2. A related goal would be to encourage portability through rollovers. This related topic is addressed in chapter 4.

3. Ideally, employees who change employers between age 45 or 50 and retirement would continue their gradual acquisition of annuity-income units, but they generally would find it more cumbersome to do so.

4. A thoughtful experiment by Jeffrey Kling and others, "Why Don't People Choose Annuities: A Framing Explanation," Research Brief (Washington: Retirement Security Project, March 2008), provides some evidence that consumers might respond positively to framing annuity benefits as a consumption stream rather than as an investment. The reframing we propose, especially by embedding the annuity purchase in the life-cycle or balanced default fund (QDIA), presents the annuity both as a secure and convenient income stream and as an attractive investment. There is no need to run away from the investment dimension of a deferred annuity that is assigned its "rightful" place in an asset-allocated portfolio (whether self-constructed or a balanced or life-cycle fund). We believe that the deferred annuity that makes up only a portion—potentially the fixed income portion—of a diversified portfolio

can be effectively presented as such to consumers while also touting its advantages as a secure and predictable income stream after retirement. In addition, framing a deferred annuity as a default incremental purchase opportunity applicable to a portion of current 401(k) contributions should increase the likelihood of acceptance by plan participants. We would welcome further experimentation by Kling and others, building on the excellent work they have done thus far, to test this hypothesis.

5. This approach has similarities to some plans offered through TIAA-CREF (Teachers Insurance and Annuity Association-College Retirement Equities Fund), an insurance company which is a major retirement provider for academics and teachers. In the TIAA plans, workers generally incrementally purchase units of annuities while they are working, rather than making a single annuity purchase at retirement.

6. By the same token, the lengthy deferral period may require protection against inflation (at least unless the deferred annuity is a variable annuity, invested largely in equities, which entails greater risk). The deferred aspect of an annuity purchased gradually with contributions resembles the deferred annuity sometimes known as longevity insurance, which may be purchased at retirement but does not begin payment until an advanced age, such as 85.

7. As a broad generalization, we believe that 401(k) participants on average would be better served by less employer stock and more lifetime income.

8. Economic analysis suggests that, in the long run, most employer contributions and benefits can be expected to come out of the overall employee compensation package, and thus most of the cost might ultimately be borne by employees. The extent and timing of this shift, however, depend on the company's specific circumstances, including the dynamics of the labor market. Labor and management tend to take it for granted that, at least in the short run, there is an important difference between "employee" and "employer" contributions in many situations.

9. For more on the risks of excessive concentration in employer stock, see J. Mark Iwry, "Promoting 401(k) Security," Tax Policy Issues and Options 7 (Washington: Urban-Brookings Tax Policy Center, September 2003); Gale and others, "Improving 401(k) Investment Performance"; and Gale and Iwry, "Automatic Investment: Improving 401(k) Portfolio Investment Choices."

10. Katie Benner, "Life-Cycle Funds Not a Retirement Cure-All," *TheStreet.Com,* Sept. 4, 2006, notes that most of the clients of T. Rowe Price that use automatic enrollment use life-cycle funds as the default investment.

11. Regulatory issues are described in two very thoughtful papers by Robert Toth: "Distributing Annuities from Defined Contribution Plans: The Qualified Plan Distributed Annuity," CCH Pension Plan Guide, Benefit Practice Portfolios (Riverwoods, Ill.: CCH Incorporated, June 2008); and "Annuitizing from 401(a) Defined Contribution Plans: A Technical Overview," ERISA Compliance and Enforcement Strategy Guide (Washington: Bureau of National Affairs, July 2008).

12. Alan L. Gustman and Thomas L. Steinmeier, *Pension Incentives and Job Mobility* (Kalamazoo, Mich.: Upjohn Institute, 1995).

PART **III**

Retirement Saving
for Vulnerable Groups

8

Retirement Security for Latinos: Bolstering Coverage, Savings, and Adequacy

PETER R. ORSZAG AND ERIC RODRIGUEZ

The terms *Latino* and *Hispanic* are used interchangeably by the U.S. Census Bureau and throughout this chapter to identify persons of Mexican, Puerto Rican, Cuban, Central and South American, Dominican, and Spanish descent; they may be of any race. Similarly, the use of the term *white* in this chapter denotes *non-Hispanic white.*

Too many Americans—and too many Latinos in particular—are not saving adequately for retirement. Half of all households nearing retirement have only $10,000 or less in an employer-based 401(k)-type plan or individual retirement account (IRA). Among Hispanics, the figures are even more astonishing: over half of Hispanic households aged 55 to 59 have no accumulated assets in a 401(k) or IRA. A variety of other measures confirm that Latinos are disproportionately likely to be undersaving. Only one in two Hispanics has a basic transaction account, such as a checking or savings account. When surveyed, 43 percent of Hispanic workers described their personal knowledge of investing or saving for retirement as "knowing nothing," compared with 12 percent for all workers.[1]

According to the U.S. Census Bureau, Hispanic Americans are the fastest growing segment of the population at or near retirement. The number of Hispanics

The authors would like to thank Laura Bos, Gordon McDonald, Luisa Grillo-Chope, Beatriz Ibarra, and Cristina Bryan for their assistance with this paper. This chapter has been updated from a previously published Retirement Security Initiative policy brief, July 2005.

aged 65 and over will increase from 1.7 million in 2000 to a projected 15.2 million by 2050. As a share of the retirement age population, Hispanics will increase from 4.9 percent in 2000 to a projected 17.5 percent in 2050.[2]

Although the challenge of undersaving among Latinos may seem substantial, a growing body of empirical evidence points the way to a solution. Three commonsense, empirically supported steps to increase retirement saving include:

—*Making it easier to save.* Work, family, and other more immediate demands often distract workers from the need to save and invest for the future. Those who do take the time to consider their choices find the decisions quite complex: individual financial planning is seldom a simple task. In the face of such difficult choices, many people simply procrastinate and thereby avoid dealing with the issues altogether, dramatically raising the likelihood that they will not save enough for retirement. Disarmingly simple concepts—such as changing the default options in 401(k) plans, and making it easy to save part of an income tax refund—have the potential to cut through this Gordian knot and improve retirement security through a set of commonsense reforms. The evidence described below suggests that such changes may have particular benefit for Latino workers.

—*Increasing the incentives to save.* The federal tax system provides little incentive for middle- and lower-income households' participation in tax-preferred saving plans—the households that most need to save more for retirement and whose contributions would most likely represent an actual increase in savings. Furthermore, the rules governing many means-tested government programs entail steep implicit taxes on saving, further diminishing any incentive for moderate- and low-income households to save. Savings incentives can be strengthened by revamping the Saver's Credit, which helps to correct the upside-down structure of tax incentives for retirement saving, and by reforming the asset tests associated with means-tested programs. These reforms may be especially effective at bolstering incentives for Hispanics to save; Hispanics on average have lower incomes than others and therefore currently receive little or no incentive from the tax code to save, while being more likely to face steep implicit taxes on savings from asset tests. Census data show, for example, that 47 percent of all Hispanic workers reported less than $25,000 in earnings in 2006, but only 22 percent of non-Hispanic whites earned as little.[3]

—*Promoting financial counseling.* Targeted and tailored financial counseling appears to be an effective means to encourage retirement savings and sound investment choices, especially for middle- and lower-income workers. Yet the majority of workers have not even attempted to figure out how much they will need to save for retirement. Possible options to improve financial counseling and education for middle- and lower-income workers include grants to community tax preparation sites to provide opportunities for individual retirement

Table 8-1. *Pension Participation Rates for Wage and Salary Workers, 21–64, 2003*
Percent

Annual earnings	White	Hispanic, native-born	Hispanic, non-native-born	All
Less than $15,000	17	14	6	9
$15,000–$29,999	44	35	21	26
$30,000–$49,999	65	59	41	50
$50,000 or more	75	73	58	66
All	53	41	22	29

Source: Craig Copeland, "Employment-Based Retirement Plan Participation: Geographic Differences and Trends," Issue Brief 274 (Washington: Employee Benefit Research Institute, October 2004).

savings counseling and assistance (perhaps in the form of a tax credit) to employers who provide employees with access to an independent financial counselor once a year.

This paper documents retirement savings and adequacy trends among Latinos. It then explores three key dimensions along which even relatively small steps could potentially translate into substantial improvements in Latino retirement security: making it easier to save, increasing the incentives to do so, and strengthening financial counseling.

Retirement Savings and Adequacy among Latinos

Latinos face particular challenges in preparing for retirement. Only about a quarter of Hispanic workers participated in an employer-provided pension plan in 2001, compared with about half of the overall workforce.[4] This low level of pension participation represents a threat to Latino retirement security.

The lower rate of Hispanic pension participation persists even within earnings, age, and firm-size categories. For example, table 8-1 shows that pension participation in 2003 was significantly lower for Hispanic workers than for white workers within any earnings category. (Note that native-born Hispanics had participation rates that were significantly higher than non-native-born Hispanics. Participation rates for native-born Hispanics were only somewhat lower than those for white workers within the same earnings category.) Similar patterns emerge within age categories and within firm-size categories.

Data on accumulated assets in 401(k)s and IRAs also point to lower retirement savings among Hispanics, including within any given income category. Table 8-2, which is based on data from the 2007 Survey of Consumer Finances, shows the average 401(k) and IRA balance and the median balance for all households and for Hispanic-headed households.[5] Among all households, the median balance held in these types of retirement accounts was $600; the average

Table 8-2. *Assets Held in 401(k)s and IRAs*
Thousands of 2006 dollars

Income class	All households		Hispanic households	
	Average	Median	Average	Median
Less than 10	2,669	0	23	0
10–20	3,425	0	249	0
20–30	16,982	0	1,231	0
30–40	17,187	0	1,848	0
40–50	32,992	1,000	7,807	0
50–75	55,288	11,000	21,257	0
75–100	85,557	30,000	82,198	32,000
100–200	143,235	72,000	105,576	24,000
200–500	438,581	208,000	238,373	230,000
500–1,000	743,178	483,000	*	*
More than 1,000	1,078,743	487,000	709,983	700,000
All	72,141	0	19,076	0

Source: Authors' analysis of Federal Reserve Board, 2007 Survey of Consumer Finances.
* Inadequate sample sizes.

was $72,141. Among Hispanics, the median was zero and the average was $19,076. The table also shows that asset balances for Hispanics are significantly lower in any given income category: among households with incomes between $50,000 and $75,000, for example, the average balance for all households was more than $55,000; among Hispanics, the average was only a little more than $20,000. The very modest account balances held by Latinos underscore the fundamental challenge of boosting retirement savings specifically for Latinos. Even when Latinos are participating in retirement savings vehicles, they do not take advantage of these options to the extent that they could. Making saving easier could increase retirement security for the Latino community.

Part of the explanation for the sharp differences in table 8-2 is the lower rate of participation in 401(k)s and IRAs among Latinos. Even among those with accounts, however, a significant difference generally remains. In other words, Hispanics are less likely to participate in 401(k)s and IRAs, and those Latinos who do participate typically contribute less than other participants. Table 8-3 shows the accumulated account balances for all households and for Hispanics when the analysis is restricted to those with an account. As the table shows, Hispanic households with a 401(k) or IRA tend to have significantly lower accumulated balances than all households with an account. For example, between $40,000 and $50,000 in income, the average balance for all households was more than $36,000; the average for Hispanics was under $25,000.

Table 8-3. *Assets Held in 401(k)s and IRAs for Those with an Account*
Thousands of 2006 dollars

	All households		Hispanic households	
Income class	Average	Median	Average	Median
Less than 10	774	930	*	*
10–20	9,717	1,400	*	*
20–30	35,209	12,000	*	*
30–40	29,319	11,680	*	*
40–50	36,751	17,000	24,789	2,600
50–75	116,854	40,000	136,639	40,000
75–100	90,364	47,000	88,958	34,000
100–200	146,938	94,000	*	*
200–500	799,169	544,000	*	*
500–1,000	531,525	586,000	*	*
More than 1,000	1,505,540	400,000	*	*
All	143,520	45,000	65,504	9,000

Source: Authors' analysis of Federal Reserve Board, 2007 Survey of Consumer Finances.
* Inadequate sample sizes.

Finally, part of the explanation for the differences highlighted in table 8-2 may reflect the age distribution of Hispanics compared with the overall population. Latinos are a younger population comparatively. But even among those aged 55 to 59, and therefore on the verge of retirement, account balances for Latinos are significantly lower than for other households. Small sample sizes do not permit a full presentation of all income categories, but table 8-4 shows the figures for all incomes combined. Among all households in this age range, the median combined 401(k)-IRA balance was $18,500; among Latino households in the same age range, the median was zero. In other words, the majority of Hispanic households aged 55 to 59 and therefore on the verge of retirement had nothing accumulated in either a 401(k) or an IRA. Similarly, among all households in this near-retirement stage, the average combined 401(k)-IRA balance was over $142,000; among Hispanics, it was just over $47,000.

This low level of pension accumulation means that Social Security benefits dominate as a source of income for retired Latinos. According to the Pew Hispanic Center, 76 percent of elderly Hispanics who receive Social Security benefits rely on those benefits for the majority of their income.[6] Perhaps even more astonishingly, Social Security benefits represent the only source of income for two in five (43 percent) of elderly Hispanic beneficiaries.[7] This is twice the percentage for all elderly beneficiaries, 20 percent of whom rely exclusively on Social Security—still too high a share but much lower than among Latino beneficiaries.

Table 8-4. *Assets Held in 401(k)s and IRAs, Households Headed by Person Aged 55–59*
Thousands of 2000 dollars

	All households		Hispanic households	
Income class	Average	Median	Average	Median
All	142,361	18,500	47,489	0

Source: Authors' analysis of Federal Reserve Board, 2007 Survey of Consumer Finances.

Rigorous economic analysis also suggests disproportionate undersaving among Hispanics. For example, Engen, Gale, and Uccello incorporate the implications of uncertain wages into their analysis of retirement savings adequacy.[8] The analysis recognizes that because a household's future income is uncertain, the level of current assets necessary to live comfortably in retirement is also uncertain. They therefore generate a distribution of optimal wealth targets relative to earnings for narrow classifications of households (separated by age, education, pension status, marital status, and current wage). They then compare actual wealth-earnings ratios to the simulated optimal targets, and see what share of households are above the median simulated optimal target. If every household were saving the right amount for retirement, and the Engen-Gale-Uccello model were exactly correct, half of households should have wealth-earnings ratios in excess of the median simulated optimal ratio for their household type. To undertake these comparisons, the authors apply three definitions of wealth. Broad wealth is equal to all net worth other than equity in vehicles.[9] Narrow wealth is broad wealth excluding equity in the household's primary residence. Intermediate wealth is broad wealth excluding one-half of the household's equity in its primary residence.

Table 8-5 shows the Engen-Gale-Uccello results using the 2001 Survey of Consumer Finances for all households and for Latino households. As the table shows, much smaller percentages of Latino households than other households are at or above their median simulated optimal wealth-earnings ratio. For example, using the narrow wealth measure, 52 percent of all households are at or above the median simulated wealth-earnings ratio for their household type. Among Hispanic households, however, fewer than 20 percent are at or above the median. In other words, under this more rigorous analysis, as under the simple asset calculations above, Latinos appear to be disproportionately saving inadequately for retirement.

According to official projections, Hispanics have higher life expectancy than other Americans (table 8-6). At age 22, for example, Hispanics have a life expectancy of 60 years—three years longer than white non-Hispanics and more

Table 8-5. *Percent of Households at or above Median Simulated Wealth-Earnings Ratio*
Percent

Item	All	Hispanics
Narrow wealth	52.3	19.6
Intermediate wealth	61.0	32.3
Broad wealth	68.8	41.0

Source: Engen-Gale-Uccello analysis of 2001 Survey of Consumer Finances and authors' calculations.

than seven years longer than black non-Hispanics. At age 65 Hispanics have a life expectancy of more than 21 years, again significantly longer than non-Hispanics. Such relatively long life expectancies for Latinos reinforce the concerns about their savings adequacy: longer life expectancies, unless offset by later retirements, increase the accumulated assets needed to live comfortably throughout retirement. Studies like that of Engen-Gale-Uccello assume that Latinos have the same life expectancy as other people; to the extent that Latinos actually have longer life expectancies, their retirement saving adequacy is even worse than that presented in table 8-5.

In evaluating the official life expectancy figures, it should be noted that researchers have raised questions about the longer-than-average life expectancies among Latinos. In particular, life expectancy for native-born Hispanics appears to be similar to that of non-Hispanics. The differential shown in table 8-6 appears to arise solely from non-native-born Hispanics, and it is possible that the life expectancy differential for non-native-born Hispanics reflects measurement errors.[10]

The bottom line is that too many Latino families are failing to save adequately for retirement. As a recent issue brief from the National Council of La Raza concluded,

> Policy-makers who purport to have an interest in opening the doors of economic opportunity for Latinos should ensure that the U.S. pension system works for all American workers and take steps to create more avenues for Hispanic workers to participate. . . . With targeted policy interventions these pathways to prosperity can be enhanced for Hispanic workers, and only then will we begin to constructively address the disparity in wealth between Latino and other American families.[11]

Making It Easier to Save

The trend over the past two decades away from the traditional, employer-managed plans and toward savings arrangements directed and managed largely by the

Table 8-6. *Life Expectancy*
Number of years of additional expected life at given age

Age	White, non-Hispanic	Black, non-Hispanic	Hispanic
22	57.0	52.7	60.1
65	18.3	17.1	21.3

Source: U.S. Census Bureau, 2004 Life Tables, from *Projections of the United States by Age, Sex, Race, Hispanic Origin, and Nativity: 1999–2100.*

employees themselves, such as 401(k)s and IRAs, is in many ways a good thing. Workers enjoy more freedom of choice and more control over their own retirement planning. But for too many households, the 401(k) and IRA revolution has fallen short. As the first section of the chapter shows, a significant number of the households left behind are Hispanic.

To address this problem, policymakers and corporate leaders should make it easier for households, including Hispanic households, to save for retirement. Two key steps that would move in this direction involve automating 401(k) plans and allowing part of tax refunds to be directly deposited into IRAs.

Automating the 401(k)

A 401(k)-type plan typically leaves it up to the employee to choose whether to participate, how much to contribute, which of the investment vehicles offered by the employer to invest in, and when to pull the funds out of the plan and in what form (in a lump sum or a series of payments).[12] Workers are thus confronted with a series of financial decisions, each of which involves risk and calls for a certain degree of financial knowledge. Many workers shy away from these burdensome decisions and simply do not choose. Those who do choose often make poor choices. Among those eligible, many do not participate. Among those who participate, many contribute little to their accounts, and others take the money out before reaching retirement age. And workers often do not follow the most basic norms of prudent asset allocation. Many overinvest in their own companies' stock: in plans that allow employer stock as an investment option, 46 percent of participants hold more than 20 percent of their account balance in employer stock.[13] This overconcentration in employer stock means that any financial difficulties experienced by the employer could expose an employee not only to lost wages but also to a substantial erosion of retirement security. The tendency to overinvest in employer stock further indicates the need for targeted financial counseling so that workers better understand the risks involved in investing.

To enroll in a 401(k), an eligible employee usually must complete and sign an enrollment form, designate a level of contribution (typically a percentage of pay to be deducted from the employee's paycheck), and specify how those contributions will be allocated among an array of investment options. Often the employee must choose from among 20 or more different investment funds. An employee who is uncomfortable making all of these decisions may well end up without any plan, because the default arrangement—that which applies when the employee fails to complete, sign, and turn in the form—is nonparticipation.

Heavy reliance on self-direction in 401(k) plans made more sense when such plans were first developed in the early 1980s. At that time, they were mainly supplements to employer-funded defined benefit pension and profit-sharing plans, rather than the worker's primary retirement plan. Because participants were presumed to have their basic needs for secure retirement income met by an employer-funded plan and by Social Security, they were given substantial discretion over their 401(k) choices. Today, despite their increasingly central role in retirement planning, 401(k)s still operate under essentially the same rules and procedures, based on those now-outmoded presumptions. Yet the risk that workers will make poor investment choices looms much larger now that 401(k)s have become the primary retirement savings vehicle.

To improve the design of the 401(k), the power of inertia in human behavior should be recognized and enlisted to promote, rather than hinder, saving. Under an automatic 401(k), each of the key events in the process would be programmed to make contributing and investing easier and more effective.

—*Automatic enrollment:* Employees who fail to sign up for the plan—whether because of simple inertia or procrastination, or perhaps because they are not sufficiently well organized or are daunted by the choices confronting them—would become participants automatically.

—*Automatic escalation:* Employee contributions would automatically increase in a prescribed manner over time, raising the contribution rate as a share of earnings.

—*Automatic investment:* Funds would be automatically invested in balanced, prudently diversified, and low-cost vehicles, whether broad index funds or professionally managed funds, unless the employee makes other choices. Such a strategy would improve asset allocation and investment choices while protecting employers from potential fiduciary liabilities associated with these default choices.

—*Automatic rollover:* When an employee switches jobs, the funds in his or her account would be automatically rolled over into an IRA, 401(k), or other plan offered by the new employer. Currently, many employees receive their accumulated balances as a cash payment upon leaving an employer, and many of them spend part or all of it. Automatic rollovers would reduce such leakage from the tax-preferred retirement savings system. At this stage, too, the

Figure 8-1. *Effect of Automatic Enrollment among Newly Hired Hispanic Employees*

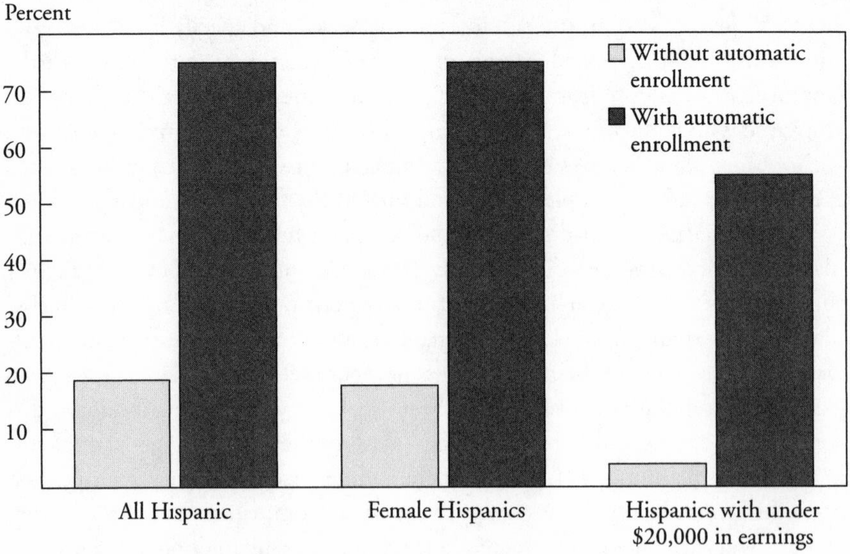

Percent

Source: Calculations by Brigitte Madrian, University of Pennsylvania.

employee would retain the right to override the default option and place the funds elsewhere or take the cash payment.

In each case—automatic enrollment, automatic escalation, automatic investment, and automatic rollover—workers could always choose to override the defaults and opt out of the automatic design. Automatic retirement plans thus would not dictate choices any more than does the current set of default options, which exclude workers from the plan unless they opt to participate. Instead, automatic retirement plans merely point workers in a prosaving direction when they decline to make explicit choices of their own.

These steps have been shown to be remarkably effective. For example, studies indicate that automatic enrollment boosts the rate of plan participation from a national average of about 75 percent of eligible employees to between 85 and 95 percent.[14] The evidence also suggests that automatic enrollment is particularly effective in boosting participation among Hispanics: among new Hispanic employees, automatic enrollment has increased participation from 19 percent to 75 percent (figure 8-1).[15] And even among the lowest-earning Hispanic workers, those with earnings below $20,000, automatic enrollment raised participation from 4 percent to 55 percent. Table 8-7 shows more detail on the effect of automatic enrollment among Hispanics, demonstrating significant increases in participation in each subclassification.

Table 8-7. *Effect of Automatic Enrollment on Newly Hired Hispanic Workers*
Percent

	Participation rate	
Item	*Without automatic enrollment*	*With automatic enrollment*
All Hispanic workers	18.9	75.1
Gender		
Male Hispanics	22.2	75.0
Female Hispanics	17.8	75.2
Age		
Age <20	. . .	75.0
Age 20–29	9.3	72.8
Age 30–39	20.5	76.7
Age 40–49	37.7	77.8
Age 50–59	33.3	72.7
Compensation		
< $20,000	3.5	54.8
$20,000–$29,000	14.7	76.4
$30,000–$39,000	29.4	90.0
$40,000–$49,000	40.0	69.0
$50,000+	53.8	80.9

Source: Calculations by Brigitte Madrian, University of Pennsylvania.

Despite its demonstrated effectiveness in boosting participation, especially for Hispanics, only a small minority of 401(k) plans today have automatic enrollment. According to a recent survey, 8 percent of 401(k) plans (and 24 percent of plans with at least 5,000 participants) have switched from the traditional "opt-in" to an "opt-out" arrangement.[16] Automatic enrollment is a relatively recent development, and even with no further policy changes, it may yet become more widely adopted over time. Recent legislative developments included in the Pension Protection Act (PPA) of 2006 are likely to boost the adoption rate of automatic enrollment among pension administrators (see chapter 2). The PPA also addressed several concerns employers raised about automatic enrollment, including:

—Some firms considering automatic enrollment were concerned that automatic payroll deductions might be prohibited by state antigarnishment laws, which require an employee's explicit written authorization in order to prevent inappropriate and involuntary deductions from employee pay. The PPA provides that federal law preempts such state laws to the extent necessary to allow employers in all fifty states to automatically deduct 401(k) and similar retirement saving contributions from employees' paychecks.

—Another concern of plan administrators was the risk that new, automatically enrolled participants might demand a refund of their automatic contributions, claiming they did not read or understand the advance notice and that 401(k) withdrawal restrictions would prevent the plan from honoring such requests. Moreover, even if refunds were permitted, they would ordinarily be subject to a 10 percent early withdrawal tax. The PPA addressed this concern by providing flexibility through a retroactive "unwind" provision: beginning in 2008, 401(k), 403(b), and 457 plans were allowed to return the full amount of automatic contributions without the 10 percent tax if an employee so requested within ninety days after the contributions begin.

—Plan sponsors are protected to some degree from fiduciary liability for the consequences of investments elected by employees. However, until the PPA, this protection for "self-directed"" investments did not extend to investments that employees "chose" by default (that is, without making an explicit election), as in the case of automatic enrollment. This lack of protection was a concern for many employers considering automatic enrollment. The PPA directed the Department of Labor to issue regulations specifying certain default investments that allow employers the same protection from fiduciary liability that they currently enjoy for employee-elected investments. This fiduciary protection is not total: plan fiduciaries still must be prudent in selecting the investment options on the menu they offer employees, while avoiding conflicts of interest and excessive fees.

—In addition to removing barriers, the PPA attempts to provide a new incentive to use automatic enrollment. By design, 401(k) nondiscrimination standards seek to align management's interests with the interests of average employees and taxpayers who fund tax subsidies for 401(k) plans. These standards link executives' ability to enjoy larger tax-preferred benefits to the employer's success in encouraging or providing greater benefits for the majority of employees.

Legislation supporting automatic enrollment is not yet complete. Congress could establish the federal government as a standard-setter in this arena by incorporating automatic enrollment into the Thrift Savings Plan, the defined contribution retirement savings plan covering federal employees. The Thrift Savings Plan already has a high participation rate, but if automatic enrollment increased participation by even a few percentage points, that would draw in tens of thousands of eligible employees who are not currently contributing. Moreover, the Thrift Savings Plan's adoption of automatic enrollment, along with other elements of the automatic 401(k), would serve as an example and model for other employers.

In sum, a growing body of evidence suggests that the judicious use of default arrangements—arrangements that apply when employees do not make an

explicit choice on their own—holds substantial promise for expanding retirement savings. The effects appear to be particularly promising for Hispanic
households, which often have the greatest need to increase their savings. Recent
efforts to retool America's voluntary, tax-subsidized 401(k) plans to make sound
saving and investment decisions more automatic, while protecting freedom of
choice for those participating, are already producing good results for those with
access but who do not participate or who have low participation rates. Expanding these efforts will make it easier for millions of Hispanic American workers to
save, thereby promising greater retirement security.

The Promise of the Split Refund, and Further Reforms

Most American households—including the majority of Hispanic households—
receive an income tax refund every year.[17] For many, the refund is the largest
single payment they can expect to receive all year. Accordingly, the more than
$200 billion issued annually in individual income tax refunds presents a unique
opportunity to increase personal savings. Census data show that 4.3 million
Hispanic households were eligible for the Earned Income Tax Credit in 2007.[18]
Millions more Hispanic households likely received an income tax refund
because of overwithholding throughout the year.

Recently, the Internal Revenue Service changed its regulations to allow taxpayers to instruct the IRS to deposit their refund in up to three designated
accounts at a financial institution. Because taxpayers often need some of the
refund for immediate expenses, depositing the entire amount in a savings
account is often not a feasible option. Permitting the partial deposit of the tax
refund to a retirement saving account shows a great deal of potential to raise
retirement saving rates.

This policy of allowing taxpayers to split their refund makes saving simpler
and thus more likely, especially if combined with the stronger incentives to save
discussed in the next section of this chapter. Now that the split refund has been
implemented, a key obstacle that might limit participation is the need to have
an IRA to receive the refund. This may be of special concern for Latinos: only
42 percent of Hispanic households even owned an interest-earning account at a
financial institution in 2002.[19] If a household does not already have an IRA, an
IRA must be set up (including choosing a vendor and investment options and
taking any other steps necessary to open the account). These steps may be a significant impediment in some cases. One possibility is to allow taxpayers who do
not have an IRA to direct on their tax return that the government open an IRA
in their name at a designated "default" financial institution that has contracted
with the government to provide low-cost IRAs for this and related purposes.
Another possibility, suggested by Professor Peter Tufano of Harvard Business

School, is to allow tax filers to elect that part of their refund be invested in a government savings bond, which would not require an IRA to be created in their name. Although implementation does raise a variety of administrative issues, none of these issues appears to present an insuperable obstacle.[20]

In summary, allowing households to split their tax refunds and to deposit part of them directly into an IRA is likely to make saving easier and boost saving rates for many taxpayers. Federal individual income tax refunds total more than $200 billion a year, so even a modest increase in the proportion of refunds saved could represent a significant increase in savings.

Increasing Incentives to Save

In addition to making it easier to save, policymakers should increase the incentives for middle- and lower-income households to do so. A ground-breaking study from the Retirement Security Project in collaboration with H&R Block shows that the combination of a clear and understandable match for savings, easily accessible savings vehicles, the opportunity to use part of an income tax refund to save, and professional one-on-one assistance could generate a significant increase in retirement savings participation and contributions, even among middle- and lower-income households.[21] The study found that higher match rates significantly raise IRA participation and contributions. Average IRA contributions among those that offered a 20 percent or 50 percent match were four and eight times higher, respectively, than they were in a control group that received no match.

To improve the financial incentives for households to save, two key steps include strengthening the Saver's Credit and reducing the heavy implicit taxes on savings often imposed through means-tested benefit programs.

Strengthening and Expanding the Saver's Credit

For decades, the U.S. tax code has given preferential tax treatment to employer-provided pensions, 401(k) plans, and IRAs relative to other forms of savings. The effectiveness of this system of subsidies remains a subject of controversy.[22] Despite the accumulation of vast amounts of wealth in pension accounts, concerns persist about the ability of the pension system to raise private and national savings, and in particular to increase savings among those households most in danger of inadequately preparing for retirement.

Many of the major concerns stem, at least in part, from the traditional form of the tax preference for pensions. Pension contributions and earnings on those contributions are treated more favorably for tax purposes than other compensation: they are excludable (or deductible) from income until distributed from the plan, which typically occurs years if not decades after the contribution is made. The value of this favorable tax treatment depends on the taxpayer's marginal tax rate: the subsidies are worth more to households with higher marginal tax rates and less to households with lower marginal rates.[23]

The pension tax subsidies, therefore, are problematic in two important respects. First, they reflect a mismatch between subsidy and need. The tax preferences are worth the least to lower-income families and thus provide minimal incentives to those households that most need to save more to provide for basic needs in retirement. Instead, the tax preferences give the strongest incentives to higher-income households, which, research indicates, are the least likely to need additional savings to achieve an adequate living standard in retirement.

Second, as a strategy for promoting national savings, the subsidies are poorly targeted. Higher-income households are disproportionately likely to respond to the incentives by shifting existing assets from taxable to tax-preferred accounts. To the extent such shifting occurs, the net result is that the pensions serve as a tax shelter, rather than as a vehicle to increase savings, and the loss of government revenue does not correspond to an increase in private savings. In contrast, middle- and lower-income households, if they participate in pensions, are most likely to use the accounts to raise net savings.[24] Because middle-income households are much less likely to have other assets to shift into tax-preferred accounts, any deposits they make to tax-preferred accounts are more likely to represent new savings rather than asset shifting.

The Saver's Credit, enacted in 2001, was designed to address these problems. The Saver's Credit in effect provides a government matching contribution, in the form of a nonrefundable tax credit, for voluntary individual contributions to 401(k) plans, IRAs, and similar retirement savings arrangements. Like traditional pension subsidies, the Saver's Credit currently provides no benefit for households that owe no federal income tax. However, for households that owe income tax, the effective match rate in the Saver's Credit is higher for those with lower income, the opposite of the incentive structure created by traditional pension tax preferences.

The Saver's Credit is the first and so far only major federal legislation directly targeted toward promoting tax-qualified retirement savings for middle- and lower-income workers. It was enacted as part of the Economic Growth and Tax Relief Reconciliation Act of 2001 and made permanent by the Pension Protection Act of 2006. In principle, the credit can be claimed by middle- or lower-income households who make voluntary retirement savings contributions to 401(k) plans, other employer-sponsored plans (including SIMPLE plans), or IRAs. In practice, however, the nonrefundability of the credit means it offers no incentive to save to the millions of lower- and middle-income households with no income tax liability.

Table 8-8. *Saver's Credit*[a]

		Adjusted gross income range for			
Joint filers (dollars)	Singles (dollars)	Credit rate (percent)	Tax credit for $2,000 contribution (dollars)	After-tax cost incurred by individual to create $2,000 account balance (dollars)	Effective after-tax matching rate (percent)
0–30,000	0–15,000	50	1,000	1,000	100
30,001–$32,500	15,001–16,250	20	400	1,600	25
32,501–$50,000	16,251–25,000	10	200	1,800	11

Source: Authors' calculation using the Federal Reserve Board, 2001 Survey of Consumer Finances.

a. Figures in table assume that couple has sufficient income tax liability to benefit from the nonrefundable income tax credit shown; they do not take into account the effects of tax deductions or exclusions that might be associated with the contributions or any employer matching contributions.

The matching rates under the Saver's Credit reflect a progressive structure—that is, the rate of government contributions per dollar of private contributions falls as household income rises. This pattern stands in stark contrast to the way tax deductions and the rest of the pension system subsidize savings. The Saver's Credit is currently a small exception to this general pattern: the Treasury Department estimates that the tax expenditures associated with retirement savings preferences in 2009 will total roughly $120 billion, of which only 0.8 percent ($0.9 billion) is attributable to the Saver's Credit.[25]

The Saver's Credit applies to contributions of up to $2,000 per year per individual. As table 8-8 shows, the credit rate is 50 percent for married taxpayers filing jointly with adjusted gross income (AGI) up to $32,000, 20 percent for joint filers with AGI between $32,001 and $34,500, and 10 percent for joint filers with AGI between $34,501 and $53,000. The same credit rates apply for other filing statuses, but at lower income levels: the AGI thresholds are 50 percent lower for single filers and 25 percent lower for heads of households.

The credit's effect is to correct the inherent bias of tax deductions or exclusions in favor of taxpayers who have high marginal rates. A $100 contribution to a 401(k) by a taxpayer in the 35 percent marginal federal income tax bracket generates a $35 exclusion from income, resulting in a $65 after-tax cost to the taxpayer. In contrast, without the Saver's Credit, a taxpayer in the 15 percent marginal bracket making the same $100 contribution to a 401(k) gets only a $15 exclusion from income, resulting in an $85 after-tax cost. Thus, the tax deduction is worth more to the higher-income household. However, if the lower-income taxpayer qualifies for a 20 percent Saver's Credit, the net after-tax cost is $65 ($100 minus the $15 effect of exclusion minus the $20 Saver's Credit). Thus, the Saver's Credit works to level the playing field by increasing the tax advantage of saving for middle- and lower-income households.

The credit represents an implicit government matching contribution for eligible retirement savings contributions. The implicit matching rate generated by the credit, though, is significantly higher than the credit rate itself. The 50 percent credit rate for gross contributions, for example, is equivalent to having the government match after-tax contributions on a 100 percent basis. Consider a couple earning $30,000 and contributing $2,000 to a 401(k) plan or IRA. The Saver's Credit reduces that couple's federal income tax liability by $1,000 (50 percent of $2,000). The net result is a $2,000 account balance that costs the couple only $1,000 after taxes (the $2,000 contribution minus the $1,000 tax credit). This is the same result that would occur if the net after-tax contribution of $1,000 were matched at a 100 percent rate: the couple and the government each effectively contribute $1,000 to the account. Similarly, the 20 percent and 10 percent credit rates are equivalent to a 25 percent and an 11 percent match, respectively (see table 8-8).

Although it is too soon to obtain a definitive reading of the impact of the Saver's Credit, preliminary estimates and evidence can be useful in identifying some basic themes. The nonrefundability of the credit substantially reduces the number of people eligible for it. Further, the low match rates for middle-income households substantially reduce the number of people eligible to receive a significant incentive. Nonrefundability results in a credit that provides no incentives to tens of millions of low-income filers who qualify on paper for the 50 percent credit rate but who have no income tax liability against which to apply the credit.

In 2005 approximately 59 million tax filers had incomes low enough to qualify for the 50 percent credit.[26] Because the credit is nonrefundable, however, only about one-seventh of them actually could benefit from the credit at all by contributing to an IRA or 401(k).[27] Furthermore, of the 59 million eligible filers, only 43,000—or fewer than one out of every 1,000—could have received the maximum credit ($1,000 per person) if they made the maximum contribution. These are the households that had sufficient tax liability to benefit in full from the Saver's Credit but sufficiently low income to qualify for the highest match rate.

For families with somewhat higher incomes, the nonrefundability of the credit poses much less of a problem, because more of these families have positive income tax liabilities. For these families, however, the credit provides only a modest incentive for saving. For example, a married couple earning $45,000 a year receives only a $200 tax credit for depositing $2,000 into a retirement account. This small credit reflects the modest matching rate at that level of income, which provides less incentive to participate.

IRS data indicate that about 5 million tax filers claimed the Saver's Credit in 2002 and in 2006. Calculations based on the Survey of Consumer Finances suggest that Hispanics represent a share of these 5 million filers in rough proportion to their population share. Because Latinos make up roughly 14 percent of the population (without including residents of Puerto Rico), the implication is that at least 750,000 Latinos are benefiting from the Saver's Credit. Moreover, data from H&R Block suggest that a slightly higher share of Latinos benefit from the Saver's Credit than other H&R Block clients. Tax Policy Center data similarly suggest that over 45 percent of the benefits from the current credit accrue to filers with cash income between $10,000 and $30,000 and that a disproportionate share of Latinos are in this income bracket, making the Saver's Credit of important consequence to the Hispanic community. Households with income below $10,000 receive almost none of the benefits, an outcome that reflects the nonrefundability of the credit.

The results of a study conducted by the Retirement Security Project confirm the basic idea behind the existing Saver's Credit.[28] The study, which involved randomized assignment of different match rates for contributions made to an IRA by tax filers, shows that offering a stronger incentive to save to middle- and lower-income households can encourage them to contribute significantly more to retirement accounts.[29] The study also suggests, however, that the existing Saver's Credit could be made more effective in encouraging additional contributions. Some options to do so are already under active discussion among policymakers:

—First, the credit could be made potentially more salient and effective by redesigning it as a matching contribution that goes into the account, rather than a tax credit. As table 8-8 shows, the current design results in a substantially higher implicit match rate than the credit rate. Instead of the current design in which a tax credit generates cash for a worker, it may be desirable to have matching contributions made directly to a worker's account.

—Second, as noted, tens of millions of lower-income workers are unable to benefit from the existing program because the credit is nonrefundable. The incentives provided by a matching program for retirement contributions should be extended to lower-income working families. Doing so, which would cost perhaps $2 billion to $3 billion a year if based on the current design, would help equalize the tax benefits of saving for higher- and lower-income households, leveling the playing field between those who pay income taxes and workers who pay payroll tax but have no income tax liability. Extending the matching contributions in this manner would significantly benefit lower-income earners, with almost 38 percent of the tax benefit accruing to individuals and families with $20,000 or less in cash income. A disproportionate share of the benefit would likely flow to Hispanic families because many are working in low-paying jobs.

—Finally, another set of possible expansions would extend eligibility to additional middle-income households. The matching contributions could be expanded in this way along three dimensions: changes to the credit rate; changes to the income limit; and changes to the manner in which the credit is phased out. [30]

If reformed in this manner, the Saver's Credit offers the potential to help correct the nation's upside-down tax incentives for retirement savings. The current tax system provides the weakest incentives for participation in tax-preferred savings plans to those who most need to save for retirement and who are more likely to use tax-preferred vehicles to increase net savings than to serve as a shelter from tax. The changes described would further help middle- and lower-income families save for retirement, reduce economic insecurity and poverty rates among the elderly, and raise national savings.

Reducing the Implicit Taxes on Retirement Saving Imposed by Asset Tests

Policymakers have expressed a goal of increasing retirement savings among those with low or moderate incomes. But the asset rules in means-tested benefit programs could penalize any low- and moderate-income families who do save for retirement, by disqualifying them from the means-tested benefit program.[31] The asset tests thus represent a substantial implicit tax on retirement savings—and one that may significantly burden Latino families struggling to save.

Many low-income families rely on means-tested programs at times during their working years—during temporary spells of unemployment or at times when earnings are insufficient to make ends meet. The major means-tested benefit programs, including food stamps, cash welfare assistance, Medicaid, and Supplemental Security Income (SSI), either require or allow the application of asset tests when determining eligibility. The asset tests may in effect force households that rely on these benefits, or might rely on them in the future, to deplete retirement savings before qualifying for benefits, even when doing so would involve a financial penalty. As a result, the asset tests not only penalize low-income savers but may also actually discourage retirement saving in the first place.[32]

Asset tests in means-tested programs, as currently applied, thus constitute a barrier to the development of retirement savings among the low-income population. Modifying or eliminating these asset tests, or even disregarding savings in retirement accounts when applying the tests, would allow low-income families to build retirement savings without having to forgo means-tested benefits at times when their incomes are low during their working years.

Fortunately, substantial progress can be made to mitigate the penalty on saving and to simplify the rules in a number of means-tested programs. Congress could amend the tax code so that retirement accounts that receive preferential tax treatment (such as 401(k) plans and IRAs) are disregarded for purposes of eligibility and benefit determinations in all federal means-tested programs.

There is recent precedent for such legislative action: in the 2008 farm bill, Congress amended food stamp eligibility rules so that savings accumulated in IRAs would no longer count toward a family's assets for the purpose of the asset test for food stamp benefits. Congress also included a similar provision in the 2001 tax cut legislation, with regard to treatment of the child tax credit by means-tested programs. Provisions that exclude certain federally funded Individual Development Accounts from being counted as assets in federal means-tested programs provide another precedent.

Even in the absence of such a cross-program disregard, important recent changes in federal policies have given states the flexibility to craft a more coherent set of rules for exempting more retirement savings from asset tests while simplifying program administration. For example, in Medicaid, the State Children's Health Insurance Program, and programs funded under the Temporary Assistance for Needy Families (TANF) block grant, states have complete discretion over the treatment of assets, including retirement accounts. In 2002, 10.5 million Latinos (26.6 percent) were covered by government health insurance (Medicare and Medicaid); 14.6 percent of all persons covered by government health insurance that year were Latino.[33] It is reasonable to suppose that if asset tests were restructured in the Medicaid program, many Latinos would encounter opportunities to bolster their retirement savings. In the food stamp program, states have the ability to liberalize asset rules within federal parameters. State policymakers could thus begin to move the system in the right direction by taking steps such as:

—Aligning rules regarding retirement accounts in Medicaid (for nonelderly households) and TANF cash assistance to the food stamp program rules, by exempting 401(k) accounts and similar employer-based plans as assets under the Medicaid and TANF programs.

—Disregarding IRAs in Medicaid (for nonelderly households) and TANF cash assistance, so that families with children and people with disabilities who have an IRA, including those who do not have access to an employer-based retirement plan and those who must roll over funds from an employer-based plan into an IRA when they are laid off or change employers, will not have to liquidate retirement savings to obtain means-tested benefits during a period of need.

—Eliminating the Medicaid asset test for families with children, as twenty-two states have already done.

At the same time even if they do not enact a cross-program disregard, federal policymakers should implement specific rule changes within the asset tests applying to the Supplemental Security Income program and also explore a variety of ways in which the implicit tax on retirement savings can be reduced.[34]

Latinos tend to be disproportionately dependent on SSI because their work histories and lower wages may make it harder for them to qualify for Social Security, or they may receive such low benefits from Social Security that they still qualify for SSI. Latino participation rates in the SSI program tend to be higher than those of other groups. Almost one-tenth (8.3 percent) of Hispanic couples over 65 receive SSI, compared with 2.8 percent of black couples over 65 and 1.7 percent of white couples over 65.[35] For unmarried Hispanic women over 65, the results are also striking: 15 percent of unmarried Hispanic women receive SSI, compared with 5 percent of white unmarried women over 65.[36] These high levels of benefit receipt demonstrate perhaps two challenges to Hispanic retirement security. First, Latinos are less likely to have been able to participate in pensions or to receive Social Security. Second, in order to receive SSI, they cannot save much outside of a few income- and asset-exempt items, further compromising Latino retirement security.

Promoting Financial Counseling

A final mechanism for policymakers—as well as employers—to bolster retirement security and savings among Hispanics involves tailored financial counseling strategies.[37] The evidence suggests that disinterested financial counseling is an effective tool in raising savings levels. Households that have planned for retirement tend to save more than other households, even when one controls for income and other characteristics.[38] Employer-provided financial counseling also tends to generate higher savings but should be done in a targeted fashion that responds to their employees' unique concerns. Investments in financial education and counseling are particularly crucial if policymakers and firms fail to take aggressive steps to make it substantially easier to save. Furthermore, implementation of the critical retirement savings opportunities addressed here could prove less effective at addressing wealth-creation opportunities for Latinos if such steps are not combined with a financial counseling effort.

For Hispanics, financial counseling is an especially important subject. Forty-three percent of Hispanic workers described their personal knowledge of investing or saving for retirement as "knowing nothing," compared with 12 percent for all workers.[39] Part of this gap arises because many Hispanics remain disconnected from mainstream financial institutions. Up to one-half of Latinos do not have a transaction account, such as a savings or checking account, which is a basic starting point in financial management and wealth-building for many families. Foreign-born Latinos, in particular, are unlikely to use basic financial services at mainstream institutions. Thus, when these efforts to bolster retirement security for the Latino community are discussed, a tailored financial counseling effort plays a critical role in maximizing opportunities to increase economic security.

According to one study, 77 percent of those with access to retirement education resources in the workplace report using them. Moreover, this study revealed a rise in 401(k) participation with the presence of educational activity. Thus, improvements in financial knowledge can boost pension plan participation.[40] The research also shows that many Latino workers lack access to financial information, which is essential for understanding the importance of investing in employer-sponsored retirement plans. In 2001 one survey found that only 32 percent of Latino workers surveyed were provided with educational materials or had attended seminars about retirement planning from their employer.[41] Thus, a tailored effort to address financial education and counseling is necessary to bolster retirement security.

The research also suggests that individual counseling may produce better results for Latinos than generic financial education targeted to workers. One study showed that workplace financial education, combined with one-on-one financial counseling, affects workers' attitudes and behaviors in a positive way.[42] More specifically, workers with access to financial counselors were more likely to participate in an employer-sponsored retirement plan and to increase contributions to that plan as well. A 2003 survey conducted by the Employee Benefit Research Institute found that 42 percent of Latino workers surveyed reported that investment advice was "very effective." Forty-eight percent of Latino workers reported that individual access to a financial planner was also "very effective." In contrast, videos, online services, brochures, and computer software received low marks among Latino workers.[43]

Because Latinos have specific financial counseling needs and financial choices, a "one-size-fits-all" approach to pension plan counseling is not the best approach to raising their financial knowledge. For example, when targeted to Hispanics, financial education materials often are translated from English to their literal equivalent in Spanish, which may be unintelligible or difficult for the reader to understand. Care must be taken to convey a clear, easy-to-grasp sense in Spanish of what the English text says. Images and idiomatic Spanish phrases can be used, a process known as "transcreation," so that the Spanish-dominant reader learns the same concepts as an English-dominant reader, regardless of how the English original was phrased. Unfortunately, while there are many publications in Spanish, very few have been transcreated from their English original.

Another challenge is that Hispanic workers often hold multiple jobs and are limited to fixed periods of time during the day or week in which to participate in programs. Therefore, in addition to choosing the right curriculum and financial counseling program, Latino-focused financial counseling providers must be mindful of the conditions under which lower-wage Hispanic workers are able to participate at all in such efforts. Providers now often need to make other key decisions before they implement and design a program that affects a working family's ability and willingness to participate, including addressing issues of child care, transportation needs, and program length.

Work-based financial education and counseling could be improved if employers:

—Include access to an independent financial planner for one-on-one counseling.

—Include information that is custom-tailored to address the unique and complex financial challenges that Latinos face, such as immigration status, language barriers, and identification requirements.

—Market or promote pension participation as a way of providing security for one's family, as opposed to emphasizing the direct financial value to the employee.

Policymakers must also do more to support financial education programs in the workplace and enable workers, especially those with lower incomes, access to financial counselors. One option could be to provide financial incentives, perhaps through a tax credit, for employers who provide their employees with access to an independent financial counselor once a year. The Department of Labor could create and maintain a list of certified and approved financial counselors. This effort would require a balance between employers' need to be shielded from liability issues and workers' need to be protected against conflicts of interest and other abuses of the financial advisory role.

Finally, community-based organizations (CBOs) are also major providers of financial education, especially to middle- and lower-income families. Many Latino-serving CBOs are social service providers with connections reaching deeply into the community, and a history of community support and resources are needed to support their financial education efforts. These CBOs could assist in the effort to increase financial counseling.

To increase and improve financial counseling infrastructure at the community level, policymakers could provide grants to community tax preparation sites to expand services to provide individual retirement savings counseling. This way middle- and lower-income workers could discuss a range of investment options for their income tax refunds and their plans for retirement savings, including using their tax refunds to save.

Conclusion

Too many Hispanics are currently undersaving for retirement, but empirical evidence points the way toward addressing the problem. The commonsense reforms described in this paper—making it easier to save, increasing the incentives to do so, and promoting financial counseling—could substantially improve retirement security for the Hispanic community.

Notes

1. Brenda Muniz and others, "Financial Education in Latino Communities: An Analysis of Programs, Products and Results/Effects" (Washington: National Council of La Raza, 2004).

2. Karen Humes, "Demographic Portrait of America's Older Racial and Ethnic Populations," a presentation at the Population Resource Center, May 13, 2005, Washington.

3. U.S. Census Bureau, Current Population Survey, March 2006, table 11.1 (http://www.census.gov/population/www/socdemo/hispanic/cps2006.html).

4. Eric Rodriguez and Deirdre Martinez, "Pension Coverage: A Missing Step in the Wealth-Building Ladder for Latinos," Issue Brief 11 (Washington: National Council of La Raza, March 2004), p. 2.

5. Throughout this chapter, the statistics provided use the most recently available data. In some circumstances, statistics are based on calculations derived from earlier papers and cannot be adjusted using more recent data.

6. Richard Fry and others, "Hispanics and the Social Security Debate" (Washington: Pew Hispanic Center, March 2005), figure 4. The Pew Hispanic Center is a project of the Pew Research Center, which is supported by the Pew Charitable Trusts' Information Cluster.

7. Social Security Administration, *Income of the Population 55 or Older, 2006* (2005), table 9.A3.

8. Eric M. Engen, William G. Gale, and Cori Uccello, "The Adequacy of Household Saving," *Brookings Papers on Economic Activity 1999:2*, pp. 65–165; and Eric M. Engen, William G. Gale, and Cori Uccello, "Effects of Stock Market Fluctuations on the Adequacy of Retirement Wealth Accumulation," *Review of Income and Wealth* (September 2005), pp. 397–418.

9. Broad wealth is thus the sum of equity in the primary residence, other real estate equity, equity in businesses, and net financial assets (which itself is equal to balances in defined contribution plans, 401(k) plans, IRAs, and Keogh plans, as well as non-tax-advantaged financial assets, minus consumer debt).

10. See, for example, Alberto Palloni, "Paradox Lost: Explaining the Hispanic Adult Mortality Advantage," *Demography* 41 (August 2004), pp. 385–415.

11. Eric Rodriguez and Deirdre Martinez, "Pension Coverage: A Missing Step in the Wealth-Building Ladder for Latinos."

12. This section draws upon William G. Gale, J. Mark Iwry, and Peter R. Orszag, "The Automatic 401(k): A Simple Way to Strengthen Retirement Savings," Policy Brief 2005-1 (Washington: Retirement Security Project, March 2005).

13. Jack VanDerhei, "Retirement Security and Defined Contribution Pension Plans: The Role of Company Stock in 401(k) Plans," testimony before the Senate Committee on Finance, February 27, 2002.

14. Brigitte C. Madrian and Dennis F. Shea, "The Power of Suggestion: Inertia in 401(k) Participation and Savings Behavior," *Quarterly Journal of Economics* 116 (November 2001): 1149-87; and James Choi and others, "Defined Contribution Pensions: Plan Rules, Participant Decisions, and the Path of Least Resistance," in *Tax Policy and the Economy*, vol. 16, edited by James Poterba, 67–113 (MIT Press, 2002).

15. "New employees" are defined as those with between three and fifteen months tenure at their current job. The data and technique are the same as those in Madrian and Shea, "The Power of Suggestion," with the sample limited only to Hispanic workers.

16. Profit Sharing/401k Council of America, "47th Annual Survey of Profit Sharing and 401(k) Plans" (Chicago: 2004).

17. J. Mark Irwy, "Using Tax Refunds to Increase Savings and Retirement Security" (Washington: Retirement Security Project, January 2006).

18. U.S. Census Bureau, Current Population Survey, Annual Social and Economic Supplement, table 1, Income Distribution Measures, by Definition of Income: 2002 (Revised) (Households with a Hispanic Origin Householder), March 2003 (http://pubdb3.census.gov/macro/032003/rdcall/1_016.htm).

19. Rakesh Kochhar, "The Wealth of Hispanic Households: 1996 to 2002" (Washington: Pew Hispanic Center, October 2004).

20. See discussion in Iwry, "Using Tax Refunds to Increase Savings and Retirement Security."

21. Esther Duflo and others, "Saving Incentives for Low- and Middle-Income Families: Evidence from a Field Experiment with H&R Block," Discussion Paper 2005-5 (Washington: Retirement Security Project, May 2005).

22. This section draws upon William G. Gale, J. Mark Iwry, and Peter R. Orszag, "The Saver's Credit: Expanding Retirement Savings for Middle- and Lower-Income Americans," Policy Brief 2005-2 (Washington: Retirement Security Project, March 2005).

23. Technically, the lifetime subsidy from such accounts comes from two sources: the difference (if any) between the tax rate at the time of contribution and that at the time of withdrawal, and the tax-free accumulation of funds. See Leonard E. Burman, William G. Gale, and David Weiner, "The Taxation of Retirement Saving: Choosing between Front-Loaded and Back-Loaded Options," *National Tax Journal* 54 (September 2001); and Eric M. Engen, John Karl Scholz, and William G. Gale, "Do Saving Incentives Work?" *Brookings Papers on Economic Activity 1994:1*, pp. 85–151. In practice, however, these items are often correlated with the tax rate at the time of the contribution, and casual evidence suggests that the upfront deductibility of most of these plans, such as 401(k)s and traditional IRAs, which provide the tax advantage at the time of contribution rather than distribution, is an important determinant of whether people make contributions.

24. See, for example, Eric M. Engen and William G. Gale, "The Effects of 401(k) Plans on Household Wealth: Differences across Earnings Groups," Working Paper 8032 (Cambridge, Mass.: National Bureau of Economic Research, December 2000); and Daniel Benjamin, "Does 401(k) Eligibility Increase Saving? Evidence from Propensity Score Subclassification," *Journal of Public Economics* 87, no. 5-6 (2003), pp. 1259–90.

25. Office of Management and Budget, *Fiscal Year 2009 Analytical Perspectives*, table 19.1.

26. These estimates were generated by the Urban-Brookings Tax Policy Center microsimulation model.

27. Some households that can benefit from the Saver's Credit do not have positive income tax liability, but do have positive income tax liability before taking into account the Earned Income Tax Credit (EITC). For these households, the EITC refund is increased to the extent that the Saver's Credit reduces their pre-EITC tax liability.

28. Duflo and others, "Saving Incentives for Low- and Middle-Income Families."

29. Although this study did not put forth a Latino breakdown, it demonstrates that many lower-income households will save for retirement if given a clear incentive to do so. Muniz

and others, "Financial Education in Latino Communities," also note one study in which three in five (62 percent) Latino nonsavers said they could set aside $20 per week, compared with 54 percent for all similar U.S. workers. Clearly, there is a desire to save in the Latino community that could be enhanced by offering matching contributions of a type similar to those outlined in Duflo and others, "Saving Incentives for Low- and Middle-Income Families."

30. These options are explored in Gale, Iwry, and Orszag, "The Saver's Credit: Expanding Retirement Savings for Middle- and Lower-Income Americans."

31. For more detail on these proposals, see Zoë Neuberger, Robert Greenstein, and Eileen Sweeney, "Protecting Low-Income Families' Retirement Savings: How Retirement Accounts Are Treated in Means-Tested Programs and Steps to Remove Barriers to Retirement Saving," Policy Brief (Washington: Retirement Security Project, June 2005).

32. For a more in-depth discussion of research on the relationship between asset tests and saving rates, see Gordon McDonald, Peter R. Orszag, and Gina Russell, "The Effect of Asset Tests on Saving" (Washington: Retirement Security Project, June 2005).

33. U.S. Census Bureau, Current Population Survey, March Supplement 2003.

34. For more detail on these proposals, see Neuberger, Greenstein, and Sweeney, "Protecting Low-Income Families' Retirement Savings."

35. Social Security Administration, *Income of the Population 55 or Older, 2002* (Washington: 2005), table 1.3.

36. Ibid.

37. Muniz and others, "Financial Education in Latino Communities."

38. B. Douglas Bernheim, Daniel M. Garrett, and Dean M. Maki, "Education and Saving: The Long-Term Effects of High School Financial Curriculum Mandates," Working Paper 6085 (Cambridge, Mass.: National Bureau of Economic Research, July 1997); B. Douglas Bernheim and Daniel Garrett, "The Determinants and Consequences of Financial Education in the Workplace: Evidence from a Survey of Households," Working Paper 5667 (Cambridge, Mass.: National Bureau of Economic Research, 1996); Patrick J. Bayer, B. Douglas Bernheim, and John Karl Scholz, "The Effects of Financial Education in the Workplace: Evidence from a Survey of Employers," Working Paper 5655 (Cambridge, Mass.: National Bureau of Economic Research, July 1996); Annamaria Lusardi, "Explaining Why So Many People Do Not Save," Working Paper 2001-05 (Boston College, Center for Retirement Research, September 2001).

39. Employee Benefit Research Institute, "2003 Minority Retirement Confidence Survey" (Washington: May 2003).

40. Muniz and others, "Financial Education in Latino Communities."

41. Employee Benefit Research Institute, "2001 Minority Confidence Survey" (Washington: February 2001).

42. Jinhee Kim, "The Effectiveness of Individual Financial Counseling Advice," in *Proceedings of the 2001 Annual Conference of the Association for Financial Counseling and Planning Education*, ed. Jeanne M. Hogarth (Columbus, Ohio: 2001).

43. Employee Benefit Research Institute, "2003 Minority Confidence Survey."

9

Retirement Security for Women: Progress to Date and Policies for Tomorrow

LESLIE E. PAPKE, LINA WALKER, AND MICHAEL DWORSKY

As the baby boomers approach retirement, hardly a day passes without reference—in media outlets, policy discussions, and research circles—to concerns about whether households are saving enough to finance adequate living standards in retirement.[1] Most of this discussion, however, focuses on the generation as a whole. In this chapter, we explore financial prospects and problems for women, together with policies that could materially improve their financial security in retirement.

The last several decades have seen major shifts in the economic opportunities and challenges facing women. These shifts imply that women face a number of issues that are often not addressed sufficiently in retirement policy debates.

First, as has been frequently noted and justly celebrated, women's education, earnings, and employment have risen substantially over time. Nevertheless, because of the demands of childbirth, child rearing, adult care, and other factors, women still tend to experience shorter and more interrupted careers than men do and are more likely to work either part-time or in low-paying occupations. The resulting work patterns adversely affect women's ability to save for

We thank William G. Gale, Melissa Green, Benjamin Harris, J. Mark Iwry, and David John for very helpful comments. Andrew Gisselquist, Catherine Lee, Gina Russell, and Spencer Walters provided outstanding research assistance. We are grateful to Mark Doms, Karen Holden, Ethan Lewis, and Cathleen Zick for sharing their data.

retirement and to accumulate pension rights. Because of these differences in work and retirement patterns, the shift in the structure of pensions from defined benefit (DB) to defined contribution plans (DC)—has differentially affected the ability of men and women to prepare for retirement. Defined contribution plans tend to have faster vesting schedules, and they also place less emphasis on long job tenures than defined benefit plans—these attributes help women save given their employment patterns. The loss of life annuities through DB plans, however, hurts women more than men because women tend to live longer and benefit more from the protection that guaranteed lifetime income provides against outliving their resources.

Second, marriage patterns and living arrangements have been changing in ways that adversely affect women's economic outcomes. Marriage rates have been falling, and in recent years most of that decline has been among women with lower educational attainment. Single motherhood has also increased dramatically over the same period. Marital status and economic status are closely linked for women. The decline in marriage rates, particularly among households with lower educational attainment, and the rise in single motherhood increase the likelihood that these families will be ill prepared for retirement.

Third, women are likely to experience longer retirement periods than men because they tend to live longer than men and to stop working at earlier ages so that they can retire at the same time as their typically older husbands. Not only do elderly women have to fund a longer retirement period, they also face the prospect of falling into poverty when their husband dies, in part because of expenses incurred at his death and, in part, because of the loss of his income. As a result, women have a greater need for retirement saving and for forms of wealth that protect against outliving their assets.

This chapter describes the underlying reasons for the differences between men's and women's retirement preparedness and the challenges for women from lower-income families. It then delineates a series of specific policies that could materially improve the economic status of women in retirement. These policies include:

—Allowing caregivers to contribute to an individual retirement account (IRA) and providing Social Security credit for episodes of caregiving, so that people who interrupt market work to care for family members are not penalized in terms of retirement saving

—Establishing automatic 401(k) plans and Automatic IRAs, so that almost all workers would be enrolled in a plan where the default is set so that they would participate unless they actively chose to withdraw

—Expanding, rationalizing, and making refundable the Saver's Credit, so that moderate- and low-income workers would face clear and rewarding incentives to accumulate retirement wealth

Figure 9-1. *Labor Force Participation Rates, by Gender*

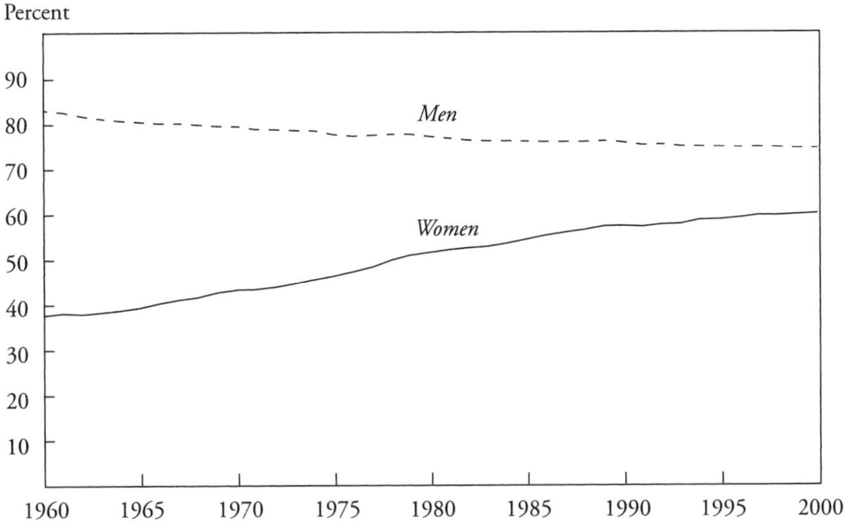

Percent

Source: Robert Szafran, "Age-Adjusted Labor Force Participation Rates, 1960–2045," *Monthly Labor Review* (September 2002): 25–38.

—Reforming the asset tests that accompany federal means-tested benefit programs, so that single mothers are not penalized for accumulating retirement saving

—Making tax filers and preparers aware that individual income tax refunds may be directly deposited by the IRS into multiple accounts, so that tax filers have an easy and simple way of saving some portion of their refund

The final section of the chapter highlights a number of other areas where more research and policies are needed, including increased ability to annuitize retirement resources, to access housing equity for retirement consumption purposes, and to pay for long-term care.

The Changing Economic Landscape for Women

Women have experienced substantial gains in the labor market over the last several decades. The share of women in the labor force has grown from under 38 percent in 1960 to almost 60 percent in 2000 (figure 9-1). Women have also made concomitant gains in educational attainment levels and wage rates. Today a higher proportion of women than men graduate from college (figure 9-2), and women's earnings are approaching the level of men's. These gains have been driven in part by institutional changes that created employment opportunities

Figure 9-2. *Percentage of 25–29-Year-Olds with a Bachelor's Degree or Higher, by Gender*

Percent

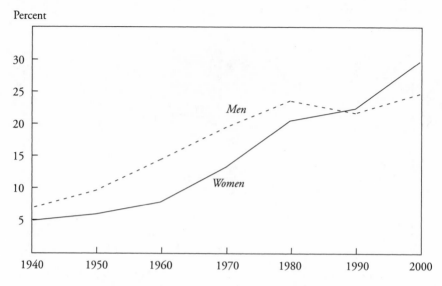

Source: Census Bureau, *A Half-Century of Learning: Historical Statistics on Educational Attainment in the United States, 1940 to 2000* (2000), PHC-T-41.

for women and in part by changes in social norms that transformed the perception of women's work from a "job" to "career" and galvanized women's participation in the labor force.[2]

Despite the improvements in women's employment outcomes, gender differences in employment persist in several key aspects. First, women are more likely to choose jobs that are part-time, to have shorter careers in the paid job market, and to experience shorter job tenure at any given point in time than men.[3] Second, even though many women have entered highly skilled and highly paid occupations (figure 9-3), the majority of women still work in occupations or industries with lower wages.[4] Women continue to account for a higher proportion of workers in service, sales, and office occupations, which tend to have lower earnings relative to other occupations. Even among professional workers, women are more likely to be employed in professions with lower relative earnings, such as education, training, and library occupations, rather than in computer and mathematical occupations (figure 9-4).

These gender differences in employment patterns partly explain women's lower earnings relative to men.[5] Women's wages remain 20 percent lower than men's even among full-time workers with comparable educational attainment and age. Between 1979 and 2005, the difference between men's and women's

Figure 9-3. *Women's Employment and Change in Employment Share, 1975–95, by Occupation*[a]

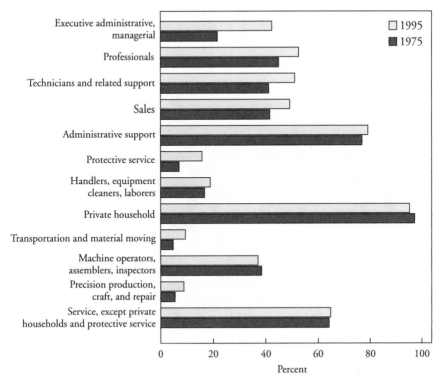

Source: Barbara Wootton, "Gender Differences in Occupational Employment," *Monthly Labor Review* (April 1997): 15–24.

a. Data for 1995 are not directly comparable with data for 1975 because they reflect a major redesign of the Current Population Survey (CPS) and incorporate 1990 census-based population controls, adjusted for the estimated undercount. For additional information, see "Revisions in the Current Population Survey Effective January 1994," Employment and Earnings (Bureau of Labor Statistics, February 1994). Change in women's share of employment by occupation between 1975 and 1995.

hourly wages (the gender wage gap) shrank by almost half. Most of the decline occurred during the 1980s (figure 9-5). The shrinking wage gap in the 1980s is largely attributable to women's increasing labor force attachment and market skills gained from education and experience.[6]

Retirement Plans

These gender differences in employment and wages lead to lower overall retirement saving for women than for men. During the past thirty years employer-

Figure 9-4. *Female Median Weekly Wages, across and within Occupation Groups*[a]

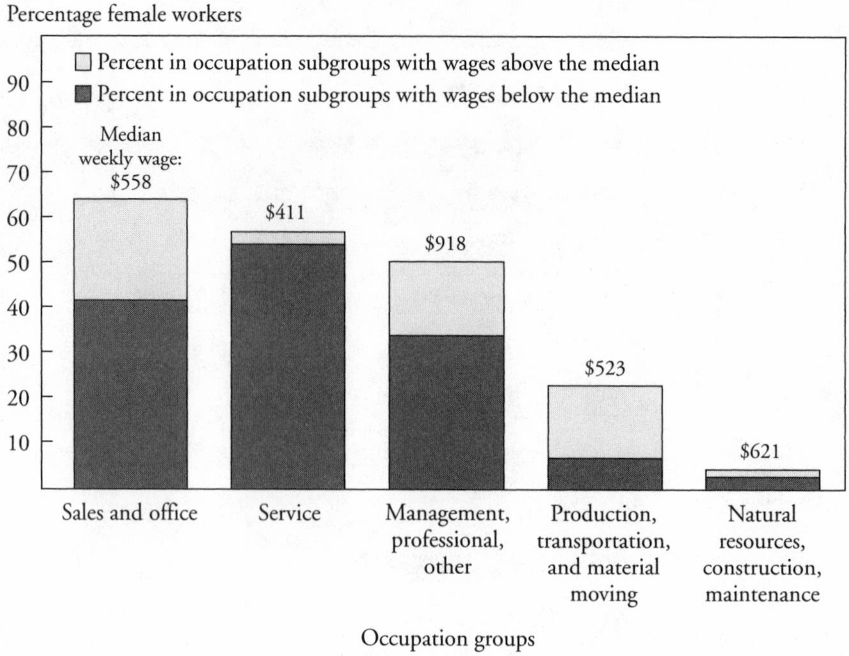

Percentage female workers

Occupation groups

Source: U.S. Department of Labor, *Women in the Labor Force: A Databook* (2005).

provided retirement coverage has shifted from defined benefit to defined contri-bution plans. In a DC plan, which emphasizes accumulating assets, women are able to save less than men because they have shorter careers and lower wages. Women near retirement are five percentage points less likely than men to have a pension or a retirement plan, such as a 401(k) or IRA. Women also have lower retirement assets than their male counterparts: the median female worker near retirement held $34,000 in a 401(k) plan or IRA, whereas her male counterpart held $70,000 (table 9-1).[7]

Accounting for differences in employment patterns removes much of the gender difference in men's and women's saving pattern. Not only do women have comparable participation and contribution rates to men at each earnings level, female wage and salary workers are slightly more likely to participate in a pension or retirement plan than male workers and the difference is largest among workers in the middle- and lower-income ranges.[8] For instance, in 2005, 58.2 percent of female wage and salary workers participated in an employer plan, compared with 55.4 percent of male wage and salary workers, and among

Figure 9-5. *Male-Female Wage Gap among Full-Time Workers*

Percent

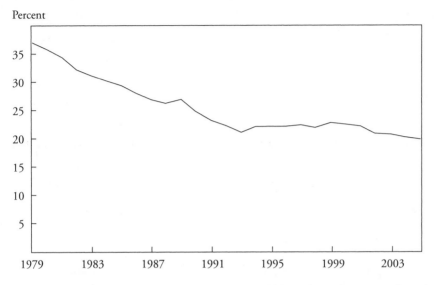

Source: Mark Doms and Ethan Lewis, "The Narrowing of the Male-Female Wage Gap," *FRBSF Economic Letters,* February 2008), using data from the Current Population Survey and controlling for education and age.

employed workers ages 18 to 62, women contributed 7.2 percent of their salary to a defined contribution plan while men contributed 7.5 percent.

Differences in retirement balance may also be attributable to differences between men and women in investment patterns. Participation in 401(k) plans requires management of investment accounts. If women are more likely to invest in less risky assets than men, they will experience lower returns on their 401(k) investments, which lead to lower 401(k) balances over time. Although some studies have found gender differences in risk-taking behavior, the evidence is mixed and inconclusive.[9]

The shift from DB plans to DC plans has affected more than just women's retirement balance sheets, and these other changes have both helped and hurt prospects for women in retirement. Compared with DB plans, 401(k) plans offer greater portability, faster vesting, and faster accrual of benefits, all of which are better suited to women's interrupted work history and shorter job tenure. Pension benefits in a DB plan typically increase with earnings and years of service with a firm. As a result, they penalize those with short job tenure, because benefits at a particular job accrue at rates that are proportional to job tenure and because benefits "start over" in a new job. In addition, DB benefits vest more

Table 9-1. *Retirement Accounts and Balances, by Age Group and Gender*

| | Percentage with a pension or retirement plan[a] | | | | Retirement account balance (in thousands of dollars) | | |
Age group	DB only	DC plan and/or IRA only	DB and DC/IRA both	Total DB/DC/ IRA	Mean balance	Mean	Median
Women							
25–34	7.6	34.7	4.1	46.3	6.1	15.7	5.4
35–44	10.5	47.8	4.2	62.5	19.8	38.1	18.0
45–54	13.4	50.5	5.8	69.7	30.3	53.8	25.0
55–64	10.1	57.8	5.2	73.2	57.8	91.7	34.0
Men							
25–34	7.1	41.1	4.4	52.6	12.7	28.0	14.0
35–44	7.8	48.3	7.3	63.4	37.1	66.7	30.0
45–54	12.0	46.2	10.0	68.2	83.8	149.1	70.0
55–64	8.9	58.1	10.8	77.7	151.2	219.5	70.0

Source: Authors' tabulation using Federal Reserve Board, 2004 Survey of Consumer Finances.

a. The groups with coverage through defined benefit (DB) only, defined contribution (DC) and/or IRA only, and both DB and DC/IRA are mutually exclusive. The final row sums across these three groups. Sample includes workers who currently work for pay.

slowly than 401(k) balances. In a 401(k) plan, employees' contributions are vested immediately and employers' contributions under DC plans tend to be vested earlier than under DB plans.[10]

The major disadvantage for women of the shift away from defined benefit plans and toward 401(k) plans is the loss of the automatic life annuity through an employer-based retirement plan. DB plans must offer (as a default) the option of benefits in the form of a life annuity and often pay benefits in that form. In contrast, 401(k) plans generally provide a lump-sum distribution at retirement (in 2005, only 20 percent of employers with 401(k) plans offered an annuity payout option).[11] Because women tend to live longer than men, a life annuity, which insures against outliving one's resources, is more valuable to women than to men (figure 9-6).[12] Although one could use the lump-sum distribution to purchase a private annuity, markets for individual annuities are poorly developed and feature high expenses, making such investments unattractive (see chapter 6). Private annuity contracts are a particularly bad deal for women because their longer life spans mean they face relatively higher prices for an annuity that pays a fixed amount per year for life.[13] This type of disparity does not exist under a DB system where men and women receive similar benefits over their lifetime if they have similar employment histories.

Figure 9-6. *Life Expectancy at Birth, by Gender and Race*

Age in years

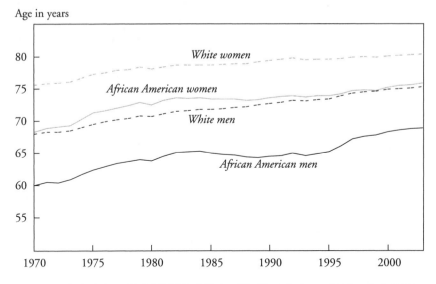

Source: Elizabeth Arias, "U.S. Life Tables," *National Vital Statistics Reports* (2006, revised 2007).

An additional disadvantage of DC plans for women is that generally spousal consent is not required when the retired worker makes distribution choices at the distribution date.[14] Under traditional DB pension plans, benefits to married workers are automatically paid as a lifetime annuity with survivor benefits for the spouse unless the spouse consents to waive the survivor benefits. By contrast, DC plans typically have no default distribution option, and a worker may choose to take distributions as a lump sum or in installments without the spouse's consent. Men and women, however, will likely have different preferences regarding the form of the distribution because of differences in the length of their retirement period. Requiring spousal consent when the worker makes distribution choices could potentially increase the proportion of workers taking distributions in the form of a life annuity with survivor protection. Evidence indicates that when the default option in DB plans for married couples was changed to a joint annuity in which survivors continue to receive a half benefit after the primary beneficiary dies (that is, joint-and-survivor annuity) unless the spouse consented to an alternative option, the selection of survivor annuities by married male pension plan participants increased from 48 to 64 percent.[15]

As 401(k) plans have become increasingly electronic, they have increased the potential to reduce administrative costs. Spousal consent proposals, by calling for a spouse's signature that is notarized or witnessed by a plan representative, generally have been viewed as precluding electronic administration in this phase of 401(k) plan operations. Accordingly, plan sponsor representatives have expressed concerns that expanding 401(k) plan spousal consent requirements could increase administrative complexity and costs. This issue has been the subject of considerable discussion and controversy for years. It would be useful to continue this discussion and explore approaches that could balance the legitimate interests in protecting spouses, promoting lifetime guaranteed income, and minimizing 401(k) costs and administrative requirements.

Marriage, Living Arrangements, and Widowhood

Marriage patterns and living arrangements have changed considerably over the past half century. Fewer adults are married; more are choosing to divorce, remain single, or live in cohabiting households. Marriage rates fell from 77 per 1,000 unmarried women in 1970 to 41 in 2005.[16] In recent years, most of the decline in marriage rates has occurred among households with lower educational attainment.[17] The rise in single motherhood is also notable. The percent of all births to unmarried women has increased dramatically, rising from 5 percent in 1960 to 37 percent in 2005 (figure 9-7).[18]

Marital patterns vary by race. The share of currently married white women declined from 67 percent in 1960 to 54 percent in 2006. The decline in the proportion of African American women currently married was even steeper, falling by nearly half from 60 percent to 34 percent. There are also large racial differences in the percentage of births to unmarried women. In 2005, 69 percent of births to African American women and 48 percent of births to Latino women were outside of marriage, whereas only 25 percent of births to white non-Hispanic women were outside of marriage.[19]

The decline in marriage rates creates concerns for women's retirement security because of the close link between marital status and economic status for women. Unmarried women, on average, have fewer economic resources than married women. Newly or nearly retired unmarried women are three times more likely to be poor and to have lower household income and net worth than similarly aged married couples (table 9-2).[20] Even compared with unmarried men in the same age group, unmarried women are financially worse off. Unmarried women from minority groups have even lower economic resources: nearly 30 percent of unmarried African American and Latino women are living in poverty, and they have between 1 and 25 percent of the net worth of unmarried white women (table 9-3).

Single mothers are particularly more vulnerable to living in poverty than other types of households with children. In 2006, 37 percent of female-headed households with children under age 18 had income below the poverty line,

Figure 9-7. *Births to Unmarried Mothers, by Race*

Percent

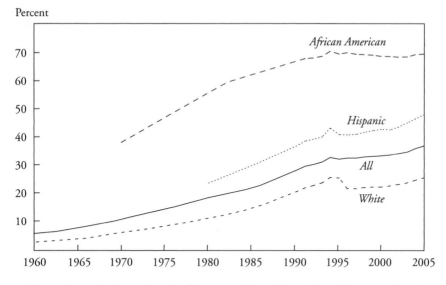

Source: Centers for Disease Control and Prevention, National Center for Health Statistics (2000).

compared with 18 percent of male-headed households and 6 percent of married couples.[21]

The importance of marital patterns and living arrangements for economic welfare persists into the retirement years. Elderly widows are three times as likely to be poor as elderly married couples.[22] In part, that is because widows are more likely to have incurred large out-of-pocket medical expenses from their husband's illness. Additionally, households in which a husband dies at a relatively young age may have lower resources even before widowhood than households in which both spouses survive.[23] One study found that 44 percent of the difference in economic status between widow(er)s and married elderly persons was attributable to disparities in economic status that existed before widowhood.[24]

In addition to facing higher expenses, new widows also face a reduction in household income when the husband dies. Social Security and, potentially, pension benefits are reduced by one-third to one-half at the husband's death. The reduction in Social Security and pension benefits are meant to reflect the household's smaller size and needs. Evidence suggests, however, that the reduction in benefits is greater than the reduction in needs of the widowed household.[25] Relative to couples that stay intact, the income-to-needs ratio of widowed households falls by almost 33 percent at the time of the spouse's death (figure 9-8).[26]

The loss of Social Security benefits at the husband's death likely has a larger effect on poverty transitions among lower-income households than among

Table 9-2. *Economic Characteristics of Nearly or Newly Retired Individuals, by Marital Status*

		Unmarried			
	Married			Never	
Characteristic	All	All	Divorced	married	Widowed
Women					
Population share (percent)	60.6	39.4	17.5	5.0	16.9
Poverty rate (percent)	5.3	17.8	17.7	22.6	16.4
Median income (thousands)	54.4	19.3	19.0	19.3	19.3
Median net worth (thousands)	288.0	67.5	57.9	65.0	76.3
Men					
Population share (percent)	78.3	21.8	12.7	5.0	4.0
Poverty rate	5.7	15.8	16.9	17.1	10.5
Median income (thousands)	64.1	28.8	29.3	24.5	31.6
Median net worth (thousands)	267.0	113.0	93.1	121.0	143.5

Source: Authors' tabulation of population shares and poverty rates using the 2006 March Current Population Survey, ages 62–67; authors' tabulation of household income and net worth using the 2004 Health and Retirement Study database, ages 60–67.

higher-income households. Lower-income elderly households, represented by households with lower education attainment, rely mostly on Social Security income (figure 9-9). The loss of the husband's Social Security benefits would represent a proportionately larger decline in total household income for lower-income households than higher-income households.

Specific Proposals to Improve Women's Retirement Prospects

For the reasons discussed above, many women will reach retirement age without having prepared adequately for their future. A number of options are available to policymakers to rectify these problems. Many of these options would also have the salutary effect of improving preparation for retirement among males as well. An important component of a strategy to improve women's retirement preparedness would be to improve labor market opportunities and outcomes for women. These options could include incentives that enable women to continue working while providing care, by allowing more flexible work arrangements through job sharing or telecommuting, or by shifting caregiving responsibilities to a third party through direct or indirect subsidies for caregiving.

After decades of improvement, women's advances in earnings and entry into traditionally male-dominated industries appear to have slowed substantially in the 1990s.[27] Furthermore, social norms and customs that affect women's

Table 9-3. *Economic Characteristics of Nearly or Newly Retired Women, by Race*
Percent unless otherwise noted

	White		African American		Latino	
Category	Married	Unmarried	Married	Unmarried	Married	Unmarried
Population share	64.1	35.9	36.5	63.5	53.8	46.2
Poverty rate	3.9	14.2	13.3	29.1	10.1	30.5
Median income (thousands of dollars)	57.6	23.4	40.5	14.0	31.2	10.6
Median net worth (thousands of dollars)	336.0	105.1	93.0	25.0	123.0	12.0
Distribution of income sources						
Social Security income	27.3	31.7	31.6	30.6	39.5	33.5
Pension and other retirement income	19.1	13.0	15.8	14.4	12.3	11.7
Current earnings	40.8	40.7	45.4	36.7	42.9	30.8
All public assistance	0.8	4.8	3.3	13.6	2.2	17.3
Asset and other income	12.1	9.7	3.9	4.7	3.1	6.7

Source: Authors' tabulation of population shares and poverty rates using the 2006 March Current Population Survey, ages 62–67; authors' tabulation of household income, net worth, and income sources using the 2004 Health and Retirement Study database, ages 60–67.

employment choices (such as being the primary caregiver) may prove difficult to change.[28] In the absence of further policy changes, the current gap, or at least a significant gap, in male-female employment patterns will likely persist in the future. Hence, while we do not wish to downplay the importance of continued labor market improvement for women, we focus our discussion here on ways to make it easier for women to prepare for retirement, even assuming a gender wage gap will continue to exist.

One labor market pattern is worth highlighting, however. As more women claim benefits based on their own work history, the employment choices women make and the age at which they claim benefits will have an increasingly larger impact on their retirement security. Social Security benefits are based on the worker's thirty-five-year average earnings, and the benefits are actuarially adjusted if the worker claims at ages other than the normal retirement age. Benefits are reduced if the worker claims early and increased if the worker claims later.[29]

Given the way benefits are computed, working longer and delaying Social Security claiming is more beneficial to women than for men for a couple of reasons. First, because women live longer than men and will receive Social Security payments for a longer period of time, the value of increased payments from

Figure 9-8. *Income-to-Needs Ratio during Months Surrounding Widowhood*

Income-to-needs ratio[a]

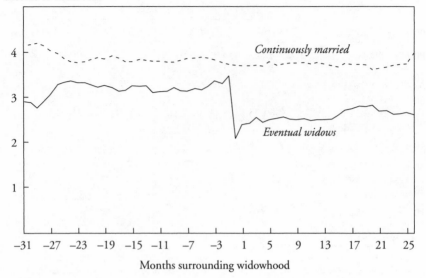

Months surrounding widowhood

Source: Karen Holden and Cathleen Zick, "Insuring against the Consequences of Widowhood in a Reformed Social Security System," in *Framing the Social Security Debate,* edited by R. Douglas Arnold, Michael Graetz, and Alicia Munnell (Brookings and the National Academy of Social Insurance, 1998), pp. 165–67.

a. The income-to-needs ratio is the ratio of total family income relative to the poverty line. For married couples, the time period shown is the entire period of the study rather than the months surrounding widowhood.

delayed claiming will be higher for women than for men.[30] Second, working beyond age 62 could increase the worker's thirty-five-year average earnings and increase the base over which her benefits are computed, which would lead to higher overall payments. Higher Social Security receipts could alleviate the probability of widowhood poverty for women because the additional resources through current earnings (or additional retirement saving) could help weather shocks arising from their husband's death, such as large out-of-pocket medical expenses.

Despite the benefits of delayed claiming for women, the most common claiming age for both men and women is 62 (table 9-4). Unmarried women are more likely to work longer than either married women or men. Married women, on the other hand, are more likely than men to claim at the earliest claiming age, partly because married couples usually choose to retire at the same time and women tend to be married to older men.[31] Choosing later retirement ages thus could help women navigate retirement more easily.

Figure 9-9. *Income Sources for Men and Women Ages 70 and Over, by Education*

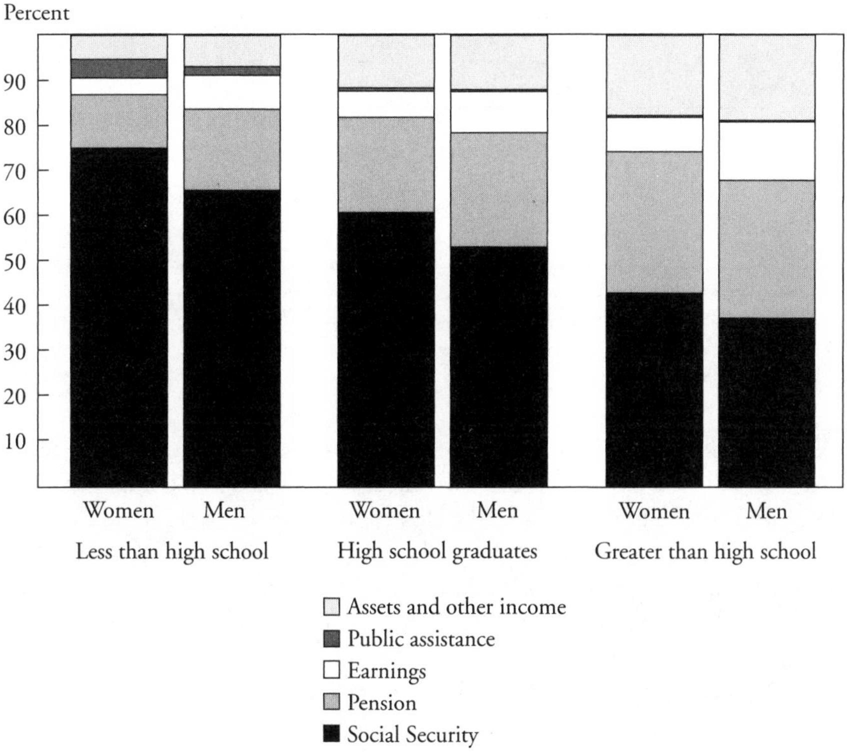

Percent

Source: Authors' tabulation using the data from the 2004 Health and Retirement Study.

Expanding IRA Eligibility to Caregivers

To help workers who interrupt market work to care for a child or adult, we propose modifying the earnings requirement for IRAs so that they have an opportunity to save in a tax-deferred environment even when interrupted employment leads to limited or no earnings. In a typical scenario, a parent (usually the mother) may take time off market work, either completely or partly, to care for children; or a family member (usually an adult child) or friend will interrupt work to care for an elderly person. Under existing rules, caregivers who have limited or no earnings are not allowed to contribute (or are limited in what they can contribute) to an IRA.[32] Our proposal would permit caregivers to contribute to an IRA, up to the qualified contribution limit and to benefit from the preferred tax treatment.[33] The IRA could operate in conjunction with tax or financial incentives that target caregivers or more general incentives that increase retirement saving (such as the Saver's Credit).[34]

Table 9-4. *Age of Initial Claims of Social Security Benefits, 1992–2002*[a]
Percent

	Women		Men	
Age	Married	Single	Married	Single
62	67.1	48.9	58.1	64.1
63	14.5	14.7	11.9	10.4
64	6.6	9.2	9.6	7.1
65	9.8	20.6	15.8	11.7
66 and older	2.0	6.5	4.7	6.7

Source: Alicia H. Munnell and Natalia Zhivan, "Earnings and Women's Retirement Security," Working Papers 2006-12 (Center for Retirement Research at Boston College, revised June 2006), using the 1992–2002 Health and Retirement Study database.
a. Columns sum to 100.

To qualify, caregivers would have to demonstrate that they are providing care to children or adults and that their income had fallen as a result. The qualified contribution limit would be the IRA contribution limit based on the individual's adjusted gross income in the year before becoming a qualified caregiver. In other words, the caregiver would be able to contribute the same amount to her IRA after she becomes a qualified caregiver as she would have if she had not interrupted employment. The individual ceases to be a qualified caregiver when the individual's income returns to at least the level before the caregiving or when the individual stops being a caregiver. At that point, the earnings exemption no longer applies, and the individual must meet the usual IRA requirements.

We also propose modifying the Medicaid asset transfer rules so that qualified transfers from recipients of care to the IRA of qualified caregivers do not prevent the care recipient from qualifying for Medicaid nursing home benefits. Under current Medicaid rules, assets transferred by the Medicaid applicant during a specified window prior to applying for Medicaid nursing home benefits are added back to the applicant's assets and counted for eligibility determination, which could result in either delay or denial of Medicaid nursing home assistance for the care recipient. We propose that the transferred amount, up to the caregiver's qualified contribution limit, be disregarded for eligibility determination under the Medicaid nursing home program.[35]

To ensure that these transfers from care recipients to caregivers remain in the retirement system, the Medicaid asset exclusion would apply only if the transfer were made directly to the caregiver's IRA. The caregiver would receive the IRA tax treatment for the transfer and the care recipient would receive the Medicaid exclusion. If the care recipient instead makes transfers directly to the caregiver, the Medicaid asset exclusion would not apply and the transferred amount would be subject to Medicaid's asset transfer rules. For tax purposes, qualified transfers from care recipients to qualified caregivers' IRAs would be considered to be gifts. This is because the majority of elderly caregiving arrangements are informal (uncompensated) and involve an adult child or family member taking time off work, with a resulting fall in income, to care for an aging relative. (The requirement that individuals demonstrate a fall in income when they become a caregiver would preclude paid in-home aides from being qualified caregivers under this plan.)

Enabling care recipients to reward their caregivers without being penalized for making the transfer has several benefits. First, if informal caregivers are rewarded for their caregiving efforts, they have a greater incentive to provide care and to provide it for a longer period of time. Second, care recipients who prefer to remain in the community, in turn, are more likely to remain in the community longer when there are willing and available caregivers. Finally, extending the informal caregiving arrangement in the community and delaying entry into a nursing home could reduce the reliance on Medicaid nursing home assistance and, over time, reduce Medicaid nursing home expenditures.

The proposed IRA expansion for caregivers could usefully be supplemented by changes to Social Security rules. The spousal-and-survivor benefit formula partly compensates women for their home production (such as caregiving) rather than market work if their earnings are very low relative to their husband's. Similar adjustments, however, are not available to unmarried women and are available only to a limited extent to married women whose earnings are more similar to their husband's (through the survivor benefits). When workers interrupt market work to become a caregiver, the period of low or no earnings could depress future Social Security benefits. The Social Security benefit formula could be adjusted to remove the penalty for caregiving, and proposals to that effect include either disregarding or imputing a wage for the years spent out of the labor force (years with zero or low earnings).[36]

Automatic 401(k) Plans

Currently 401(k)-type plans typically leave it to the employee to decide whether to participate, how much to contribute, which investment option provided by their employer to select, and when and how to withdraw their assets when they retire. Each of these financial decisions is complicated, and many workers who do not have the time or financial knowledge to make these decisions may shy away from them and make no decision at all. Or, when they do, they end up making poor choices.

It is, however, possible to harness the power of inertia to help individuals start saving earlier and more. A growing body of evidence shows that simply

Figure 9-10. *Effects of Automatic Enrollment on 401(k) Participation*

Percent participating

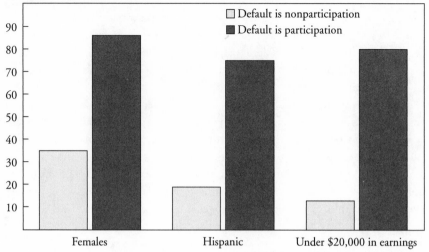

Females   Hispanic   Under $20,000 in earnings

Source: Brigitte C. Madrian and Dennis F. Shea, "The Power of Suggestion: Inertia in 401(k) Participation and Savings Behavior," *Quarterly Journal of Economics* 116 (November 2001): 1149–87.

changing the default option in 401(k) plans from an opt-in system to an opt-out system, where individuals are automatically enrolled in the plan, can significantly increase retirement saving.[37] Inertia and procrastination, which were obstacles to participation under an opt-in 401(k) system, actually help increase enrollment in an opt-out system because doing nothing means being enrolled in the plan.

Automatic 401(k)s are most effective when combined with other automatic features such as automatic escalation of contributions over time, automatic investment in a prudent and diversified portfolio, and automatic rollover of retirement assets. Increasing the amount saved over time, improving investment outcomes, and retaining assets in the retirement system when there is a job change ultimately lead to higher retirement balances and improved retirement security. A strategy of saving earlier and more in 401(k)s will benefit all workers, but it is particularly relevant for women whose employment patterns make them more likely to experience job disruptions.

AUTOMATIC ENROLLMENT. Automatic enrollment has been shown to raise 401(k) participation rates dramatically when applied to new hires, especially to new hires who are female, members of minority groups, low earners, or some combination of the three (figure 9-10).[38] Automatic enrollment often cuts nonparticipation rates from roughly 25 percent to as little as 5 or 10 percent of newly eligible employees. Workers will begin contributing to their 401(k) account at an earlier age than they would have in the absence of automatic enrollment and will earn investment returns over a longer period of time.

AUTOMATIC ESCALATION. Building in annual increases in 401(k) contribution rates (automatic escalation) could further improve women's retirement saving. The vast majority of plans with automatic enrollment have a default contribution rate of only 3 percent or less, which is less than half of the average pretax contribution rate of about 7 percent of pay.[39] In the absence of automatic escalation, the majority of participants who are automatically enrolled tend to remain at the automatic contribution level.[40] Automatic escalation helps ensure that inertia does not keep these employees at the low initial default contribution rate.[41]

AUTOMATIC INVESTMENT. When employees are confronted with an array of investment options, they may not have the time or the expertise to make prudent investment decisions, and many 401(k)-type accounts fail basic standards of diversification and sound asset allocation: millions of workers are overconcentrated in their employers' stock or overinvested in safe but low-yielding money market funds. Automatic investment can direct assets into balanced, prudently diversified, and low-cost vehicles and can help discourage overconcentration in employer stock and in low-yielding funds, such as money market or stable-value assets, unless the employee makes other choices.[42] This strategy could improve 401(k) asset allocation and investment choices while preserving employees' right to direct their accounts themselves if they so choose.

AUTOMATIC ROLLOVER. When an employee switches jobs, the funds in her retirement account would be automatically rolled over into an IRA, 401(k), or other plan offered by the new employer (automatic rollover), unless the worker actively chooses otherwise. Automatic rollover can help participants retain previously accumulated retirement savings in the tax-favored retirement system when they change jobs. Recent empirical evidence suggests that a simple reframing of the options for preretirement distributions could reduce the proportion of lump-sum distributions and the resulting leakage from retirement accounts.[43]

ADOPTION OF AUTOMATIC 401(K)S. The number of employers that offer automatic enrollment in a 401(k) has been increasing each year. The Pension Protection Act (PPA) of 2006 addressed several employer concerns regarding automatic 401(k)s and provided new incentives to encourage more employers to adopt them (see chapter 2). According to a 2007 Wells Fargo survey, 44 percent of surveyed employers reported using automatic enrollment in 2007, an increase from 26 percent in 2006. Among employers with automatic 401(k)s, 42 percent use 3 percent as the default contribution rate, while 20 percent use a higher default rate.[44] About one-fourth of employers who offer automatic enrollment also automatically escalate contributions.[45]

More remains to be done to expand and improve the automatic 401(k). Plans that use automatic features need further encouragement to evolve from first-generation to second-generation automatic features (see chapter 2). A first-generation automatic 401(k) might typically automatically enroll only new hires at a 3 percent contribution rate, without escalation. Investments would be in a stable-value or money market fund. A second-generation automatic 401(k) improves on each of these default choices. It would automatically enroll existing nonparticipating employees as well as new hires at a 5 or 6 percent automatic contribution, escalating automatically up to a significantly higher level. Assets would be invested automatically (that is, by default) in a low-cost professionally managed account or life-cycle fund.

Automatic IRAs

Automatic 401(k)s have succeeded in increasing retirement plan participation, but they apply only to workers with employer-sponsored retirement plans.[46] One of every two workers, an estimated 75 million workers, has no access to such plans.[47] These tend to be part-time workers or workers with short job tenure and, as noted earlier, workers with these characteristics tend to be women. A new proposal would create a system whereby workers without access to employer-sponsored retirement plans could contribute to a low-cost, diversified IRA through direct payroll deposits. IRAs are portable, and employees can continue to contribute to IRAs even when they switch jobs (see chapter 4).

Bipartisan legislation was proposed in 2007 to implement the Automatic IRA.[48] Under this proposal, workers would be enrolled in an IRA, and deposits to the IRA would be made automatically each pay period, unless the employee actively chose not to participate in the program. A firm that is not ready to adopt a 401(k) or other retirement plan would offer its employees the ability to save in an IRA every payday by payroll deposit, much as millions of employees have their paychecks deposited directly to their bank accounts. It is easier to save small amounts on a regular basis; and once payroll deposits begin, they continue automatically unless the worker later opts out. Employers above a certain size (ten employees, for example) that have been in business for at least two years but that still do not sponsor any plan for their employees would be required to offer employees this payroll-deduction saving opportunity.

The Automatic IRA would involve no contributions or other outlays by employers, who would merely offer their payroll system as a conduit that employees could use to save part of their own wages in an IRA. Participating employers would receive temporary tax credits, would be required to obtain a written waiver from any employee who does not participate, would be encouraged to use automatic enrollment, and would be able to protect themselves from fiduciary liability. Employees, or the employer, could designate the IRA that would receive the savings, including, as a fallback for those unable or unwilling to choose, a national platform IRA that could be based on the federal employees' Thrift Savings Plan accounts. The default investment would be a diversified, low-cost, life-cycle fund, with other choices available (see chapter 4). The self-employed would be encouraged to save by extending payroll deposit to independent contractors, facilitating direct deposit of income tax refunds, and expanding access to automatic debit arrangements linked to IRAs, including on-line and traditional means of access through professional and trade associations.

Additional Polices for Moderate- and Low-Income Families

As noted earlier, in recent years more women are choosing to remain unmarried and have children outside of marriage, particularly among women with lower educational attainment. While incentives to increase saving in 401(k)s and IRAs will be beneficial for all women, including women with lower and moderate income, the tax incentives to save are weaker for them than for higher-income households because the value of the tax benefit depends on the families' tax bracket, and they are in a lower tax bracket. In addition, eligibility rules for certain means-tested programs that would be beneficial for lower-income women, such as the food stamp program and Medicaid, actually penalize families for saving for retirement. Therefore, we propose tax incentives that are particularly beneficial for moderate- and lower-income households and policies that remove the penalty to saving and make saving easier.

SAVER'S CREDIT. The Saver's Credit was specifically designed to benefit moderate- and lower-income families.[49] Enacted in 2001, the Saver's Credit gives taxpayers earning less than $52,000 a tax credit for contributions to 401(k) plans, IRAs, and similar retirement savings vehicles. Depending on the taxpayer's income, households can receive a credit of either 10, 20, or 50 percent of their contributions to a retirement account. In its current form, however, the Saver's Credit is nonrefundable: it merely offsets a taxpayer's tax liability, providing no saving incentive for almost 50 million lower-income households that have no income tax liability. Making the Saver's Credit refundable would provide an important incentive to these households to save regularly and continually. It would also help secure the retirement of those with the lowest incomes, thus making them less dependent on Social Security income and means-tested government programs during their retirement years. There is also evidence that restructuring the credit as a matching contribution that is automatically deposited into an IRA could increase the incentive to save.[50]

Simplifying the Saver's Credit with a single 50 percent credit rate, phased out smoothly above the income eligibility limit, and expanding the eligibility limit to include households with income of up to $70,000 a year would increase the incentive to save and help middle-class Americans, including women, save for a secure retirement.

ASSET TESTS. Outdated asset tests in means-tested public assistance programs (such as food stamps, Supplemental Security Income, Temporary Assistance for Needy Families (TANF), and Medicaid) penalize lower- and moderate-income households that save.[51] Beneficiaries of many of these programs tend to be women. To be eligible, applicants generally must meet an asset test as well as an income test. While the asset tests usually do not count accrued benefits under a defined benefit plan as assets, too often they do count 401(k) or IRA balances or both. This has the effect of a steep implicit tax on 401(k) and IRA saving. As a result, families with incomes low enough to qualify for a means-tested program under the income test might respond by saving less.

Although some state programs have eliminated asset tests, or at least aligned the treatment of defined contribution plans with that of defined benefit plans, many have not. Asset tests treat retirement saving in a confusing and seemingly arbitrary manner, with different restrictions state by state and account by account. Congress and the states should therefore eliminate this implicit tax on retirement saving by mandating that retirement accounts such as 401(k)s and IRAs be disregarded for eligibility and benefit determinations in federal and state means-tested programs. Exempting retirement accounts from being considered in means-tested programs would treat retirement savings fairly and consistently and would send an important signal to families that rely or might need to rely on means-tested programs in the future: you will not be penalized for saving for retirement.

Eliminating asset rules for retirement savings will have some short-term costs because additional lower-income households will qualify for and use means-tested benefit programs. These costs should be modest, however; and if moderate- and low-income households can save for a more secure retirement, fewer people will have to rely on public benefits in old age.

SPLIT REFUNDS. In any given year, most American households receive an income tax refund. For many, the refund is the largest single payment they can expect to receive each year. In 2004 over 100 million individual income tax filers (out of a total of 131 million) were eligible for tax refunds averaging more than $2,000 each (resulting mainly from overpayment of withholding taxes). For many middle-income families, the refund presents a unique opportunity—a "savable moment"—to increase personal savings, whether for retirement or for shorter-term needs.[52] This is particularly true because evidence suggests that many people tend to view large, extraordinary payments (such as their tax refunds) as separate and different from their normal wages or other income.[53]

Until recently, however, tax filers could only designate one account at a financial institution to which their tax refund could be deposited. This all-or-nothing approach discourages many households from saving any of the refund. When some of the refund is needed for immediate expenses (as is often the case), depositing the entire amount in a saving account, such as an IRA, is not a feasible option. As a consequence, while more than 49 million tax filers in 2004 received their federal tax refunds by direct deposit, fewer than 3 percent of tax filers directed their refund into a savings account.

Allowing households to split their refunds makes saving simpler and, therefore, more likely. A middle- or lower-income household that wishes to save can do so by directing part of the refund into a saving account. Because federal income tax refunds total nearly $230 billion a year, even a modest increase in the proportion of refunds saved every year could bring about a significant increase in retirement saving.

Beginning in the 2007 tax filing season, the Internal Revenue Service (IRS) permitted tax filers to split the direct deposit of their refunds between two or three accounts. Although the new ruling was not widely publicized, almost 80,000 tax filers instructed the IRS to deposit their refund into two or more accounts. More should be done for subsequent tax filing seasons to inform tax filers and preparers about the ability to split refunds. Use of tax preparation software that is programmed to permit direct deposits to multiple accounts should also increase the proportion of tax filers who save during tax filing season.

Additional Areas for Consideration

In addition to the specific policy recommendations above, there are a number of key areas where further policy development could prove extremely helpful for women in retirement.

Annuitization

A critical component of retirement security for women would include a strategy to increase annuitization of retirement assets. Guaranteed lifetime-income products provide insurance against outliving one's retirement resources, which make them particularly valuable to women because they have longer life spans than men and must fund a longer retirement period.

Despite the benefits, the market for guaranteed lifetime-income products in the United States is very thin. In their current form, annuities lock in wealth that may be needed for medical expenses or bequests; they tend to be (or are widely perceived as being) priced too high for an individual with average life expectancy or too complex for ordinary consumers to understand and compare; the product and market structure exposes consumers and suppliers to considerable risks (such as interest rate risks or reinsurance risks); and regulation has limited the attractiveness of purchasing annuities through employer-sponsored retirement plans.

In addition to these financial barriers, behavioral biases may also inhibit the demand for guaranteed lifetime-income products. Individuals may be reluctant to convert a lump sum into a stream of payments because they perceive the exchange to be a bad deal or a loss—perhaps because they have a sense of ownership over the lump sum instead of a stream of payments or because they are overly concerned with the possibility that they may die soon after converting their lump sum to a stream of payments.

The market for guaranteed lifetime-income products needs to be restructured to accommodate the potential growth in demand as more workers retire with large DC balances. The reinsurance market for guaranteed lifetime-income products will likely require a "jump-start" through some form of government involvement. A more developed reinsurance market will likely reduce at least one component of suppliers' costs, which may make available a wider variety of guaranteed lifetime-income product features at lower prices. Consumers also need appropriate incentives to overcome financial, psychological, and emotional barriers to annuitization. Small, periodic contributions to a lifetime-income fund should mitigate the aversion to "giving up" a large lump sum; presenting information on retirement benefits as an income stream rather than as a lump sum may help attune workers to the notion of annuitization, and automating the accumulation and the annuitization stage will likely make the annuitization decision effortless and, therefore, less costly.

The vast store of wealth in 401(k) plans provides a potential launching point for a new lifetime-income product. An alternate delivery mechanism for such a product may also be necessary to reach the 75 million workers with no employer-sponsored retirement coverage. As the market for guaranteed lifetime income grows, the establishment of a federal "insurer of last resort" may be necessary to protect annuitants if suppliers face catastrophic losses. These and other issues relating to annuitization are developed more fully in chapters 6 and 7.

Housing Equity

The most important financial asset for most elderly households is housing equity; yet, the elderly do not appear to be consuming their housing wealth. The proportion of elderly persons who are income-poor but housing-equity-rich is sizable, and this group tends to be mostly widows.[54] Elderly women's consumption in retirement could be increased by tapping into their housing equity through reverse mortgages. This financial product allows the elderly person to withdraw equity from the home without having to sell or move out of the home. This latter feature appears to be particularly appealing to homeowners. Despite the possibility of increased consumption in retirement through reverse mortgages, the demand for this financial product is quite low. One possible explanation is that many homeowners want to leave a bequest to their children. Leaving the house to their children (instead of selling it before they die) allows them to benefit from the step-up in basis (a readjustment of the value of an appreciated property for tax purposes), which reduces their tax liability. To design incentives to encourage homeowners to tap into their housing equity, more work needs to be done to understand why the current market for reverse mortgages is thin.[55]

Medical and Long-Term Care Expenses

A significant proportion of elderly persons will face some out-of-pocket health expenses despite health insurance coverage through the Medicare program. On average, medical out-of pocket (MOOP) expenses in the mid- to late-1990s accounted for about 10 to 20 percent of elderly persons' income. For the elderly living under the poverty line, MOOP spending was as much as 30 percent of income.[56]

At each age, women are estimated to face higher expected health care costs for their remaining lifetime than men. This result is partly attributable to women's longer life span; however, even when differences in male-female survival probabilities are accounted for, expected spending remains higher for women than for men.[57] In 2003 MOOP expenses among Medicare beneficiaries averaged 24 percent of income for females compared with 19 percent for males.[58]

MOOP spending on institutional care, such as nursing home care, also tends to be higher for women than for men. Women's greater longevity makes them more likely to live to ages where the risk of needing long-term care is high.[59] Women are also more likely to outlive their husbands, which leaves them without a partner to care for them should they need long-term care. Not surprisingly, almost three-quarters of nursing home users are women, most of whom are unmarried.[60] Nursing home costs in 2006 averaged about $70,000 a year, and the average length of stay for current residents was 2.5 years.[61] The Medicaid program may cover some part of that cost, but MOOP spending for nursing home care would still be substantial.[62] One study estimates that over a ten-year period, entry into a nursing home leads to a drop in household wealth of $20,000 for unmarried women (equal to 60 percent of median wealth) and $40,000 for married women (equal to a third of median wealth). The study found that wealth changes for men were much smaller.[63]

As a consequence, the risk of incurring out-of-pocket nursing home expenses has been regarded as primarily a woman's risk. Although the Medicaid program provides coverage for long-term care costs, the conditions for eligibility can be restrictive.[64] Given burgeoning state budget pressures, the eligibility criteria for the Medicaid program could potentially tighten in the future, which would shift more of the risk of out-of-pocket nursing home expenses to nursing home recipients or their family members.

Given the high cost of nursing home care and limited public coverage, the potential benefit of having long-term care insurance coverage to protect against out-of-pocket nursing home costs should be high—particularly for women.[65] In practice, however, demand for this insurance is low. This may be because individuals underestimate their risk of needing long-term care, mistakenly believe Medicare (the health insurance program for the elderly) will cover the costs of long-term care, or, if they are aware of Medicare's limited coverage, they plan to rely on the Medicaid program as the insurer of last resort.[66]

Greater efforts to educate and inform individuals about their risk of incurring out-of-pocket nursing home costs are needed. Learning about the potential risk of needing long-term care, particularly among elderly, single women, and learning about the limited scope of the coverage under the Medicare and Medicaid programs will, over time, change individual perceptions about saving for long-term expenses.

The thin market for long-term care insurance may also result from current product and market limitations. Most elderly individuals prefer to "age in place," meaning they prefer to receive long-term-care services in their home rather than in an institution. The current emphasis in the United States, however, is on providing such services at the institutional level. In addition, the availability of skilled home-care workers is limited or priced too high for the average consumer. Financial incentives and structures need to be designed to enable the market to evolve and align with the long-term-care preferences of consumers.

Conclusion

Elderly women today have lower retirement resources than elderly men, and these gender differences are projected to persist for future cohorts of retirees, despite secular improvements in women's earning power. Yet, women will have greater need for retirement resources because they tend to outlive their husbands, face a decline in income at widowhood and incur out-of-pocket medical expenses from their husband's death or their own medical needs. These problems can be addressed through a series of policy reforms that will help women save more and secure access to sufficient resources to fund their retirement.

Notes

1. Recent contributions include Jonathan Skinner, "Are You Sure You're Saving Enough for Retirement?" *Journal of Economic Perspectives* 21 (Summer 2007), pp. 59–80; and Shlomo Benartzi and Richard Thaler, "Heuristics and Biases in Retirement Savings Behavior," *Journal of Economic Perspectives* 21 (Summer 2007), pp. 81–104.

2. Some of the major institutional changes over the first half of the twentieth century include increases in the demand for office workers and part-time workers, growth in postsecondary institutions and improvements in home technology that reduced the time spent on housework. See Claudia Goldin, "The Quiet Revolution That Transformed Women's Employment, Education and Family," Working Paper w11953 (Cambridge, Mass.: National Bureau of Economic Research, January 2006).

3. In a given year, women are more than twice as likely as men to work part-time (U.S. Bureau of Labor Statistics, *Charting the U.S. Labor Market in 2006* [2007], www.bls. gov/cps/labor2006/chart5-5.pdf). Among those in the baby-boom cohort (born between 1946 and 1960), half of women are projected to have six or more years with no earnings compared with a third of men; see Chad Newcomb, "Distribution of Zero-Earnings Years by Gender, Birth Cohort, and Level of Lifetime Earnings," Research and Statistics Note 2000-02 (Social Security Administration, 2000).

4. Francine D. Blau and Lawrence M. Kahn, "Gender Differences in Pay," Working Paper 7732 (Cambridge, Mass.: National Bureau of Economic Research, 2000).

5. Government Accountability Office, "Women's Earnings: Work Patterns Partially Explain Difference between Men's and Women's Earnings" (October 2003), www.gao.gov/new.items/d0435.pdf.

6. There is some evidence that the narrowing wage gap results partly from the selection of women with higher earnings potential entering the labor force in the 1980s. See Mark Doms and Ethan Lewis, "The Narrowing of the Male-Female Wage Gap," *FRBSF Economic Letters,* February 2008, for more discussion.

7. Authors' calculation using Federal Reserve Board, 2004 Survey of Consumer Finances.

8. Craig Copeland, "Employment-Based Retirement Plan Participation: Geographic Differences and Trends, 2004," Issue Brief 286 (Washington: Employment Benefit Research Institute, 2005).

9. Vickie L. Bajtelsmit and Nancy A. Jianakoplos, "Women and Pensions: A Decade of Progress?" Issue Brief 227 (Washington: Employee Benefit Research Institute, 2000); Peggy D. Dwyer, James H. Gilkenson, and John A. List, "Gender Differences in Revealed Risk Taking: Evidence from Mutual Fund Investors," *Economics Letters* 76 (July 2002), pp. 151–58; Annika E. Sunden, and Brian J. Surette, "Gender Differences in the Allocation of Assets in Retirement Savings Plans," *American Economic Review* 88, no. 2 (1998), pp. 207–11; Leslie E. Papke, "How Are participants Investing Their Accounts in Participant Directed Individual Account Pension Plans?" *American Economic Review* 88, no. 2 (1998), pp. 212–16; Leslie E. Papke, "Individual Financial Decision in Retirement Saving Plans: The Role of Participant-Direction," *Journal of Public Economics* 88 (2003), pp. 39–61.

10. When employee contributions are made to DB plans (which is far less common than employee contributions to 401(k)s), those are immediately vested as well. Employer contributions to DC plans must vest at least as fast as either 100 percent ("cliff vesting") after three years of service or ratably beginning at two years and reaching 100 percent vesting after six years of service. Employer contributions to DB plans must vest at least as fast as either 100

percent after five years of service or ratably beginning at three years and reaching 100 percent vesting after seven years of service. Internal Revenue Code Section 411(a)(2).

11. Hewitt Associates, "Survey Findings: Trends and Experiences in 401(k) Plans" (Lincolnshire, Ill.: 2005).

12. Life expectancy from birth is taken from Elizabeth Arias, "United States Life Tables, 2003" (Hyattsville, Md.: National Center for Health Statistics, 2006).

13. Women fare poorly relative to men if annuity rates are based on age and gender. Currently, not all private annuity contracts use gender in computing annuity rates. If, instead, gender-neutral annuity rates are used, women will fare better than men because of their longer life span. Gender-neutral pricing is required for computing annuity values for 401(k)plans, which may partly explain the higher annuitization rates among female TIAA-CREF participants than among male participants. See John Ameriks, "The Retirement Patterns and Annuitization Decisions of a Cohort of TIAA-CREF Participants," Research Dialogues 60 (New York: TIAA-CREF Institute, 1999).

14. 401(k) plans have rules that protect the spouse as a beneficiary. If the married worker chooses to take distributions as an annuity, the spouse is protected under Employment Retirement Security Income Act rules regarding spousal annuity. If the worker dies before receiving benefits, the assets automatically go to the surviving spouse. Spousal consent is also required if the married worker decides to select a beneficiary other than the spouse.

15. Karen Holden and Sean Nicholson, "Selection of a Joint-and-Survivor Pension," Discussion Paper 1175-98 (University of Wisconsin, Institute for Research on Poverty, 1998).

16. Divorce rates more than doubled between 1960 and 1980 and have been gradually declining since 1980. For additional discussion, see the National Marriage Project, *The State of Our Unions, 2007: Social Health of Marriage in America* (Rutgers University, July 2007).

17. As opposed to earlier decades, college-educated women have been marrying at higher rates than their peers since the 1980s.

18. Data for 1960 through 1994 from Office of the Assistant Secretary for Planning and Evaluation, "Trends in the Well-Being of America's Children & Youth," PF2.2: Percentage of All Births to Unmarried Mothers (Department of Health and Human Services, 1997), http://aspe.hhs.gov/hsp/97trends/PF2-2.htm. Data through 2005 from Federal Interagency Forum on Child and Family Statistics, "America's Children: Key National Indicators of Well-Being, 2007," table FAM2.B, www.childstats.gov/americaschildren.

19. B. E. Hamilton, J. A. Martin, and S. J. Ventura, "Births: Preliminary Data for 2005," *National Vital Statistics Reports, vol.* 55 (Hyattsville, Md.: National Center for Health Statistics 2006).

20. One reason is that unmarried women do not benefit from the economies of scale that make living as a married couple less expensive than living as two separate individuals.

21. Data from Census Bureau (www.census.gov/population/socdemo/hh-fam/fm1.xls).

22. Kathleen McGarry and Robert F. Schoeni, "Widow(er) Poverty and Out-of-Pocket Medical Expenditures at the End of Life," *Journals of Gerontology Series B: Psychological Sciences and Social Sciences* 60, no. 3 (2005), pp. S160–68.

23. Nadia Karamcheva and Alicia H. Munnell, "Why Are Widows So Poor?" (Boston College, Center for Retirement Research, 2007).

24. McGarry and Schoeni, "Widow(er) Poverty and Out-of-Pocket Medical Expenditures at the End of Life."

25. Karamcheva and Munnell, "Why Are Widows so Poor?" Similar results are found by Purvi Sevak, David R. Weir, and Robert J. Willis, "The Economics of a Husband's Death: Evidence from the HRS and AHEAD," *Social Security Bulletin* 65, no. 3 (2003); and

McGarry and Schoeni, "Widow(er) Poverty and Out-of-Pocket Medical Expenditures at the End of Life." Sevak, Weir, and Willis find that among nonpoor married couples age 70 or older, 12 percent of widows became poor after losing a husband. Similarly, Johnson, Mermin, and Uccello find that a husband's death increases a woman's risk of sliding into poverty by 36 percent; see Richard W. Johnson, Gordon B. T. Mermin, and Cori E. Uccello, "When the Nest Egg Cracks: Financial Consequences of Health Problems, Marital Status Changes, and Job Layoffs at Older Ages" (Washington: Urban Institute, 2006).

26. Figure from Karen Holden and Cathleen Zick, "Insuring against the Consequences of Widowhood in a Reformed Social Security System," in *Framing the Social Security Debate,* edited by R. Douglas Arnold, Michael Graetz, and Alicia Munnell (Brookings and the National Academy of Social Insurance, 1998), pp. 165–67.

27. Blau and Kahn, "Gender Differences in Pay."

28. Timothy M. Smeeding, "Social Security Reform: Improving Benefit Adequacy and Economic Security for Women," Aging Studies Program Policy Brief (Syracuse University, Maxwell School of Citizenship and Public Affairs, Center for Policy Research, 1999).

29. The normal retirement age is 65 for those born in 1937 and earlier. The retirement age gradually rises for cohorts born after 1937 but before 1960. For cohorts born in 1960 and later, the normal retirement age is 67.

30. A 65-year-old woman in 2004 could expect to live another twenty years, whereas a 65-year-old man could expect to live another seventeen years (www.cdc.gov/nchs).

31. Courtney Coile, "Retirement Incentives and Couples' Retirement Decisions," *Topics in Economic Analysis and Policy* 4, no. 1 (2004).

32. IRA earnings rules are based on household earnings. If the noncaregiving spouse continues to work, the caregiver may continue to be eligible to contribute.

33. The current IRA contribution limits are $4,000 ($5,000 if age 50 and older) for 2007 and $5,000 ($6,000 for age 50 and older) for 2008. After 2008, the contribution limit will be annually indexed in $500 increments, adjusted for the cost of living. See www.law.cornell.edu/uscode/html/uscode26/usc_sec_26_00000219—-000-.html#b_1_A and www.irs.gov/pub/irs-pdf/p590.pdf.

34. The United Kingdom provides a Carer's Allowance for caregivers who meet certain requirements.

35. Under current Medicaid rules, transfers made within sixty months of applying for Medicaid assistance delay or disqualify eligibility. The delay varies with the value of the transfer (assuming the applicant also meets the income and needs criteria).

36. See Pamela Herd, "Crediting Care of Marriage? Reforming Social Security Family Benefits," *Journal of Gerontology: Social Sciences* 61B, no. 1 (2000), pp. S24–34; and Howard Iams and Steven Sandell, "Changing Social Security Benefits to Reflect Child-Care Years: A Policy Proposal Whose Time Has Passed?" *Social Security Bulletin* 57, no. 4 (1994), pp. 10–24.

37. See J. Mark Iwry, William G. Gale, and Peter R. Orszag, "The Potential Effects of Retirement Security Project Proposals on Private and National Savings: Exploratory Calculations," Policy Brief 2006-2 (Washington: Retirement Security Project, November 2006). The study estimates that the automatic 401(k) could bring about a net increase of $44 billion a year in national saving.

38. Brigitte C. Madrian and Dennis F. Shea, "The Power of Suggestion: Inertia in 401(k) Participation and Savings Behavior," *Quarterly Journal of Economics* 116 (November 2001), pp. 1149–87; and James Choi and others, "Defined Contribution Pensions: Plan Rules, Participant Decisions, and the Path of Least Resistance," in *Tax Policy and the Economy,* vol. 16,

edited by James Poterba (MIT Press, 2002), pp. 67–113. Related approaches have also proven effective but generally are less powerful. One such approach is to require employees to make an explicit election so that inertia does not prevent them from participating or lead them to contribute less than they would if they were required to choose. Another approach presents employees with a presumptive contribution rate packaged together with an investment option—not as a default but as an easy choice employees can make by checking a single box.

39. Hewitt Associates, "Trends and Experiences in 401(k) Plans 2005 Survey (Lincolnshire, Ill.: 2005). In 2005 the proportion was 75 percent. More recent data are available from the 2007 Hewitt survey.

40. Between 65 and 87 percent of new plan participants save at the default contribution rate. This percentage declines slowly to 40–54 percent after two years and to about 45 percent after three years; see James Choi and others, "For Better or For Worse: Default Effects and 401(k) Savings Behavior," in *Perspectives on the Economics of Aging*, edited by D. Wise (University of Chicago Press, 2004), pp. 81–121.

41. Richard Thaler and Shlomo Benartzi, "Save More Tomorrow: Using Behavioral Economics to Increase Employee Saving," *Journal of Political Economy* 112, no. 1, pt. 2 (2004), pp. S164–87.

42. William G. Gale and J. Mark Iwry, "Automatic Investment: Improving 401(k) Portfolio Investment Choices," Policy Brief 2005-4 (Washington: Retirement Security Project, May 2005); William G. Gale and others, "Improving 401(k) Investment Performance," Issue Brief 2004-26 (Boston College, Center for Retirement Research, December 2004); and J. Mark Iwry, "Promoting 401(k) Security" (Washington: Tax Policy Center, September 2003).

43. William G. Gale and Michael Dworsky, "Effects of Public Policies on the Disposition of Lump-Sum Distributions: Rational and Behavioral Influences," Working Paper 2006-15 (Boston College, Center for Retirement Research, August 2006).

44. Wells Fargo, "Strategic Initiatives in Retirement Plans," 2007 Survey Analysis (Brentwood, Tenn.).

45. According to the 2007 Wells Fargo Survey, 21 percent of employers that offer automatic enrollment also automatically escalate contributions. According to the Hewitt Trends and Experience in 401(k) Plans 2007 Survey, 28 percent of employers that automatically enroll participants also automatically escalate contributions.

46. Among wage and salary workers ages 18 to 64, an estimated 60.5 million workers do not have access to employer-sponsored retirement plans. Authors' calculation using March 2006 Current Population Survey data.

47. Copeland, "Employment-Based Retirement Plan Participation," figure 1, p. 7. An additional 16 million workers either are not eligible for their employer's plan or are eligible but fail to participate. Quantitatively similar but updated figures for 2006 are available in the Employee Benefit Research Institute Issue Brief 311.

48. S. 1141 and H.R. 2167.

49. J. Mark Iwry, William G. Gale, and Peter R. Orszag, "The Saver's Credit," Policy Brief 2005-2 (Washington: Retirement Security Project, March 2005); and J. Mark Iwry, William G. Gale, and Peter R. Orszag, "The Saver's Credit: Issues and Options," Tax Notes (Washington: Tax Policy Center, May 3, 2004).

50. The explicit 50 percent credit is an implicit 100 percent match. For an example, consider a couple earning $30,000 who contributes $2,000 to a 401(k) plan. The Saver's Credit reduces that couple's federal income tax liability by $1,000 (50 percent of $2,000). The net result is a $2,000 account balance that costs the couple only $1,000 after taxes (the $2,000

contribution minus the $1,000 tax credit). This is the same result that would occur if the net after-tax contribution of $1,000 were matched at a 100 percent rate: the couple and the government each effectively contribute $1,000 to the account. While taxpayers should respond the same to equivalent implicit and explicit matches, empirical research provides evidence to the contrary. For a detailed discussion, see Esther Duflo and others, "Saving Incentives for Low- and Middle-Income Families: Evidence from a Field Experiment with H&R Block," *Quarterly Journal of Economics* 121, no. 4 (2006), pp. 1311–46.

51. For a detailed discussion of this issue, see Zoë Neuberger, Robert Greenstein, and Eileen P. Sweeney, "Protecting Low-Income Families' Retirement Savings: How Retirement Accounts Are Treated in Means-Tested Programs and Steps to Remove Barriers to Retirement Saving," Policy Brief 2005-6 (Washington: Retirement Security Project, June 2005)).

52. In fiscal year 2004 individual income tax refunds amounted to $228 billion and went to 106 million out of a total of 131 million individual income tax returns; see *IRS Databook FY 2004*, publication 55b, tables 1, 2, 8, 9.

53. Hersh M. Shefrin and Richard H. Thaler, "Mental Accounting, Saving, and Self-Control," in *Choice over Time*, edited by G. Lowenstein and J. Elster (New York: Sage Foundation, 1992).

54. Steven Venti and David Wise, "Aging and Housing Equity: Another Look," Working Paper 8606 (Cambridge, Mass.: National Bureau of Economic Research, November 2001).

55. Although the market for reverse mortgages has grown rapidly over the last few years, it still remains quite small. Davidoff and Welke estimate that less than 1 percent of eligible homeowners purchase reverse mortgages, even though a large number of older homeowners are housing-rich and income-poor; see Thomas Davidoff and Gerd Welke, "Selection and Moral Hazard in the Reverse Mortgage Market," Working Paper (University of California, Berkeley, Haas School of Business, October, 2005). The evidence of adverse selection and moral hazard in the market is mixed. Potentially, the presence of Medicaid may undermine demand. Andrew Caplin, "Turning Assets into Cash: Problems and Prospects in the Reverse Mortgage Industry," in *Innovations in Retirement Financing*, edited by Olivia S. Mitchell and others (University of Pennsylvania Press, 2000), ch. 11.

56. David S. Johnson and Timothy M. Smeeding, "Who Are the Poor Elderly? An Examination Using Alternative Poverty Measures," Working Paper 2000-14 (Boston College, Center for Retirement Research, 2000). The Census Bureau also calculates an adjusted poverty rate by age and finds that in 2005 overall elderly poverty would have risen from 10.2 percent to 16.4 percent if MOOP spending were deducted from family income (Census Bureau, Poverty Measurement Studies and Alternative Measures, 2007).

57. Berhanu Alemayehu and Kenneth E. Warner, "The Lifetime Distribution of Health Care Costs," *Health Services Research* 39, no. 3 (2004), pp. 627–42.

58. Craig Caplan and Normandy Brangan, "Out-of-Pocket Spending on Health Care by Medicare Beneficiaries Age 65 and Older in 2003," Research Report (Washington, AARP, 2004).

59. Peter Kemper and Christopher Murtaugh, "Lifetime Use of Nursing Home Care," *New England Journal of Medicine* 324 (1991), pp. 595–600.

60. Unmarried women include never married, divorced, and widows. William D. Spector and others, "The Characteristics of Long-Term Care Users," AHRQ Research Report 00-0049 (Agency for Healthcare Research and Quality, 2001).

61. The average cost for a private room was $75,000 annually, while an average semiprivate room cost $67,000; see "The Metlife Market Survey of Nursing Home & Home Care

Costs" (New York: MetLife Mature Market Institute, 2006). Length of stay data are from the 1997 National Nursing Home Survey (Hyattsville, Md.: National Center for Health Statistics, 1997).

62. Among full-year residents in 1996, Medicaid financed 58 percent of expenses, and 33 percent was paid out of pocket (total expenses for this group amounted to $36,368 per person). Medical Expenditure Panel Survey Research Findings 13: Expenses and Sources of Payment for Nursing Home Residents (Agency for Healthcare Research and Quality, 1996).

63. Individuals ages 70 and older are observed between 1993 and 2002, and median wealth for unmarried and married women is measured in 1993. During the same period, real median wealth increased by 19.7 percent for individuals who did not receive nursing home care. See Johnson, Mermin, and Uccello, "When the Nest Egg Cracks."

64. The statutory asset limits for eligibility are $2,000 for a single individual and $3,000 for a couple. At these levels, individuals must virtually deplete their resources before they can qualify for Medicaid nursing home assistance. Some states have exceptions that disregard certain assets (such as assets used to purchase an irrevocable Medicaid annuity), and these exceptions raise the effective asset limits. Although the effective asset limits are substantially higher in a small number of states, even with the exceptions, the effective asset limits are still relatively low for the majority of states.

65. Evidence suggests that individuals who are more risk averse or who are at greater risk of needing nursing home care are more likely to buy long-term care insurance. See Amy Finkelstein and Kathleen McGarry, "Multiple Dimensions of Private Information: Evidence from the Long-term Care Insurance Market," *American Economic Review* 96, no. 4 (2006), pp. 938–58.

66. Jeffrey Brown and Amy Finkelstein, "Why Is the Market for Long-Term Care Insurance so Small?" Working Paper (Massachusetts Institute of Technology, February 2007).

10

Strategies to Increase the Retirement Savings of African American Households

NGINA CHITEJI AND LINA WALKER

Concerns about whether African Americans are sufficiently prepared for retirement have been raised in academic circles, in the policy arena, and in the popular press.[1] The voices of African American citizens tell a story that suggests current levels of saving are a concern for this minority population. A quarter of African American survey respondents expressed reservations about having enough resources to simply take care of basic expenses during retirement, and about one-fifth reported that they expect to struggle during the first five years of retirement. By comparison, only one-tenth of all U.S. workers had this latter concern.[2]

In this chapter, we highlight differences in retirement resources between African Americans and other U.S. households, discuss their implications for retirement preparedness, and examine underlying reasons for these differences. Our goal is to move beyond simple comparisons of savings between groups to measures that provide a better assessment of whether African Americans are saving adequately for retirement and how they compare with other households. This analysis thus enables us to assess the extent to which the concerns voiced by African Americans are valid, evaluate the underlying reasons for racial differences in retirement preparedness, and identify policy options that would improve the retirement security of African American households.

We thank William G. Gale and anonymous referees for very helpful comments.

The primary finding is that African American households are less prepared for retirement than white households. They have saved smaller sums, largely because of differences in labor market experience and saving decisions. When one accounts for differences in income (which are driven by differences in labor market experience), the savings gap narrows but persists.

Retirement resources, however, also include claims to Social Security and defined benefit (DB) pensions, and when these are taken into account, African Americans on average have adequate resources for retirement. However, they continue to lag behind whites in that they have lower income-replacement rates than white retirees; a disproportionate fraction of African Americans have replacement rates that would be inadequate to support their retirement consumption. Part of the racial differences in retirement resources may stem from differences in family structure and networks but also from discrimination in labor and credit markets.

Given these differences in retirement preparedness, this chapter focuses on private market solutions that would differentially improve the retirement security of African American families. The policy proposals emphasize remedying information gaps, making it easier to save, and improving incentives to save, particularly for moderate- and low-income households. Specifically, the proposals recommend:

—Providing an ongoing financial mentoring program for children, starting at very young ages, to level the playing field for children who are not born into families with financial market expertise or who have limited opportunity to learn about financial management from related adults. A long-term financial mentoring program could be built upon existing financial education programs that target children but do not typically offer ongoing, sustained mentoring opportunities.

—Making it easier to save by increasing the adoption of automatic enrollment and other automatic features in 401(k) plans. This includes changing the default options in 401(k) plans so workers are automatically enrolled, and their contributions are automatically increased over time and invested in professionally managed, balanced funds, unless they actively chose not to participate. Additionally, when workers change jobs, assets in 401(k)-type plans should automatically be rolled over into an individual retirement account (IRA) or another retirement plan offered by the new employer to keep the funds in the retirement system.

—Helping millions of workers who currently do not have access to 401(k) plans save for retirement by creating a system whereby these workers can contribute automatically to a low-cost, diversified IRA through direct payroll deposits.

Table 10-1. *Savings of Pre-Retired and Retired Households*[a]
Dollars

Item	African American households	All U.S. households
Panel A. Pre-retired households (ages 51–64)		
Net worth[b]	123,400	399,800
	(27,500)	(142,300)
Net worth minus housing wealth	77,800	277,700
	(4,000)	(49,000)
Financial assets[c]	16,300	101,700
	(200)	(7,500)
DC/IRA	39,900	74,100
	(0)	(0)
Panel B. Retired households (ages 70 and older)		
Net worth	84,400	409,600
	(36,900)	(165,000)
Net worth minus housing equity	34,700	281,200
	(2,000)	(61,000)
Financial assets	14,000	145,300
	(300)	(20,000)

Source: Authors' calculations using data from the 2004 Health and Retirement Survey.
a. Mean values, with medians reported in parentheses.
b. "Net worth" includes financial assets, housing equity, value of transportation, value of business and real estate, other assets.
c. "Financial assets" includes stocks, bonds, certificates of deposit, and balance in checking and savings accounts.

—Expanding, simplifying, and making refundable the Saver's Credit so that incentives for saving are clearer and more rewarding and so those most in need of the credit could qualify even if they do not owe taxes.

—Reform the asset tests for federal means-tested programs so that lower-income families and those in need of public assistance are not penalized for accumulating retirement assets.

Before exploring these proposals in more detail, the chapter first compares the retirement resources of African American families to the average U.S. family and discusses some of the underlying reasons for the differences.

Differences in Retirement Resources

Many studies have documented that the average African American family has lower savings than the average U.S. family. Table 10-1 illustrates the extent of

Table 10-2. *Sources of Income among Retired Households (Ages 70 and Older)*[a]
Percent

Item	All U.S. households	African Americans
Retirement (pension) income	16.0	17.5
Social Security benefits[a]	34.9	33.1
Public assistance[b]	2.0	3.1
Assets and other income[c]	14.2	8.4
Earnings[d]	32.7	38.0

Source: Authors' calculations using data from the Current Population Survey.
a. "Social Security benefits" include workers', disability insurance, and survivor's benefits.
b. "Public assistance" includes SSI, unemployment and worker's compensation, veteran's payments, and welfare payments such as AFDC and TANF.
c. "Assets and other income" includes interest and rental income, income from dividends, educational assistance, financial assistance, alimony, and child support.
d. "Earnings" include wages and salary, self-employment, and farm income.

the racial savings gap, measured by net worth, among working-age households approaching retirement (ages 51–64).[3] The median net worth of African Americans is only around $28,000, compared with $140,000 for the median household nationwide.[4] The difference in savings between black households and all households is even larger if one excludes the value of housing equity.[5] The value of nonhousing assets for the median black family is one-twelfth that of the typical American family.[6]

Racial differences in retirement resources are also apparent among current retirees. The median African American family aged 70 and older has a net worth of $36,900, which is one-fourth of the net worth of the median U.S. household (see table 10-1). In addition, sources of income also differ between black and white retirees (table 10-2). Retired African American households are more likely than other retirees to rely on income from pension plans and earnings. Furthermore, income from assets as a share of total household income for African American households is about half as much as for other households.

To a large extent, these observed racial differences in retirement resources are attributable to racial differences in labor market experience, such as a higher unemployment rate and more part-time work.[7] These differences lead to lower average earnings for African Americans than for whites and to differential access to employer-sponsored retirement plans.[8] Some of the differences in retirement resources, however, are also attributable to racial differences in saving decisions. For instance, 401(k) participation and contribution rates are lower among black workers than among white workers, and investment choices are sometimes different.[9] In most (although not all) instances, these differences in labor market experience and saving choices adversely affect African Americans' retirement security.

Table 10-3. *Labor Market Outcomes, by Race and Gender*

Item	All men	White men	African American men	All women	White women	African American women
All workers						
Share of all workers (percent)[a]	53.2	44.5	5.3	46.8	37.5	6.2
Share working part-time[a]	12.3	12.3	13.2	27.1	28.5	20.1
Share working in public sector[b]	16.0		20.4	16.0		20.4
Job tenure: percentage with 20+ years (at current job)[c]	n.a.	10.8	8.9	n.a.	8.7	7.7
All workers						
Median hourly wage (dollars)[d]	15.04	16.82	12.23	12.18	12.94	11.14
Annual earnings[e]	42,210.00	47,814.00	34,480.00	32,649.00	34,133.00	30,398.00
All persons						
Employment rate (percent)[a]	73.3	74.7	63.6	60.7	60.7	61.6
Unemployment rate[f]	4.7	4.2	6.1	4.5	4.0	7.5
Labor force participation rate[g]	73.5	74.3	67.0	59.4	59.0	61.7

a. Authors' calculations based on data from the 2007 March Current Population Survey (now called the "Annual Social and Economic Supplement"), table PINC-05. Data are for 2006.

b. Figures listed are for workers regardless of gender, based on authors' calculations using data from 2007 Current Population Survey.

c. Census Bureau, *2007 Statistical Abstract of the United States,* table 593: "Distribution of Workers by Tenure at Current Employer." The national average is 9.4 percent (across both sexes and all races).

d. Median hourly wage data come from Lawrence Mishel, Jared Bernstein, and Sylvia Allegretto, *State of Working America 2004/2005* (Washington: Economic Policy Institute, 2005), pp. 166–67. The data are for 2003.

e. Data for median annual earnings for 2006 (in 2006 dollars) are from Census Bureau, *American Community Survey, Income, Earnings, and Poverty Data* (2006), table 7, p. 6.

f. Data are from www.bls.gov/cps/cpsaat3.pdf, "Employment Status of the Civilian Non-Institutionalized Population by Age, Sex and Race."

g. Data for 2006 are from Census Bureau, *2007 Statistical Abstract of the United States,* table 570.

n.a. Not available.

Differences in Labor Market Experience

African Americans are more likely to be unemployed than whites. Unemployment rates are 50 percent higher among African Americans and are apparent across all education groups, including college graduates who, as a group, tend to have the lowest unemployment rate among all workers (table 10-3).[10]

Even among those who are employed, labor market outcomes between African American and white workers differ. A larger fraction of black workers are employed in low-wage occupations than other workers: 15 percent of low-wage workers are African Americans, yet African Americans make up only 11 percent of the total workforce.[11] In addition, among men, African Americans are more likely to work part-time than whites: 13.2 percent of black men work part-time compared with 12.3 percent of white men.[12]

LOWER EARNINGS. As a result of these labor market differences, black families tend to have lower earnings than white families. As a group, black men earn about 72 percent of what white men earn and black women earn 86 percent of what white women earn (see table 10-3).

Low-earning households save less than high-earning households because they have a lower base from which to save. In addition, some empirical evidence suggests that households with low incomes tend to save a smaller fraction of their incomes than high-income households.[13] Thus, the combination of a lower base for saving and lower savings rate partly explains the racial gap in net worth.

Differences in earnings also have implications for retirement resources because retirement balances and pension payments often are tied to earnings. Under a defined contribution (DC) retirement plan, such as a 401(k) plan, the employer's contribution to the plan typically is a fixed percentage of the worker's earnings. Consequently, African American workers with lower earnings would receive lower levels of employer contributions than other workers with higher earnings.

Likewise, DB plans typically compute pension payments based on earnings and years on the job. Accordingly, workers with lower earnings accrue lower pension benefits than higher-earning workers, and workers with shorter tenure on the job accrue lower pension benefits than those with longer tenure. On average, African American workers have lower earnings and shorter job tenure than other workers (see table 10-2), which means they are more likely to accrue lower pension benefits in DB plans than other workers.

DIFFERENCES IN PRIVATE-SECTOR, EMPLOYER-SPONSORED RETIREMENT COVERAGE RATES. Racial differences in labor market experience also lead to differential access to employer-sponsored retirement coverage. In the private sector, black workers are less likely to be offered retirement coverage than other workers because they are more likely to work in part-time and lower-wage jobs, which typically do not offer coverage. The private sector coverage rate for African Americans is about three percentage points lower than the national average.[14] Compared with white workers, the gap is even greater: 50 percent of white workers in the private sector but only 42 percent of African American workers are covered by an employer-sponsored retirement plan.[15]

Furthermore, private-sector African American workers may become increasingly less likely to have coverage relative to other private sector workers. Between 1979 and 2004, coverage rates in private sector employment fell by about 10 percentage points among workers with a high school education (to about 40 percent) but stayed stable at about 60 percent for college-educated workers.[16] Because a higher proportion of African American workers have a high school education or less, to the extent that the trend continues, the gap in coverage rates between African American workers and white workers in the private sector may increase.[17]

DIFFERENCES IN PUBLIC-SECTOR EMPLOYMENT. Black workers, however, are more likely than other workers to be employed in the public sector.[18] This difference places black workers on a more favorable footing for retirement than other workers because most public-sector employers offer pension coverage, typically in the form of a defined benefit plan.[19] One of the advantages of DB plans over 401(k) and other DC plans is that workers generally are not responsible for making participation and contribution decisions: they are automatically enrolled in the plan if they are eligible, contribution rates are predetermined, and the assets are professionally managed. Generally, these features are beneficial to all workers (because inertia can prevent or delay a worker from participating), but they are particularly beneficial to low-income African Americans who, as a group, tend to have less financial market experience and lower financial literacy than other workers.

The other advantage of DB coverage over DC coverage is that benefits from a DB plan are payable for life (that is, as an annuity), whereas the majority of DC plans do not even offer the option to annuitize plan balances. Retirees in DC plans, therefore, must manage their assets to last their lifetime and face the possibility of outliving their resources should they live longer than expected. Thus, African American retirees who, on average, have greater access to DB pensions are better protected from the risk of outliving their resources than workers with DC-type retirement coverage.

Differences in Saving Decisions

While racial differences in earnings and access to employer-sponsored retirement plans lead to racial differences in retirement account balances, the choices that black workers make regarding retirement saving may further amplify these differences. Even when black workers are offered employer-sponsored retirement coverage through 401(k)-type plans, they make choices about participation, contribution levels, and investment that lead to lower relative savings in these retirement accounts.

For example, eligible black workers are less likely to participate in 401(k)-type plans than are eligible white workers. One study found that in 2004, 50 percent of eligible black private sector workers but 59 percent of white workers participated in their employer's retirement plan.[20] By not participating, workers are also losing any employer-matching contributions they might have received had they contributed to their 401(k) plan as well as the tax advantages that come with saving in these employer-sponsored retirement accounts.

There also is some evidence that contribution rates among African Americans with DC plans are smaller than those of other households.[21] Estimates suggest that the average contribution rate is 4.2 percent for African Americans, 5.5 percent for whites, and 5.4 percent across all DC plan participants regardless of race. This same study reveals that more than half of African Americans contribute 4 percent or less of their salary to their 401(k) account.[22]

Additionally, African Americans appear to be less likely than white workers to invest in and hold high-yielding assets, such as stocks.[23] To the extent that investment returns are lower as a result, the accumulated savings over time for a black worker would be lower than those of a white worker, on average. This difference in investment choices may partly explain the difference in accumulated assets between retired African Americans and other retired households. At the median, African American households age 70 or older hold about $300 in financial assets compared with $13,000 held by retired households nationwide.

Income-Adjusted Differences in Retirement Resources

The comparisons of net worth and other retirement resources discussed in the previous section are between groups with potentially very different income. As noted earlier, the earnings of black and white workers differ. Moreover, black families have lower income than other families, on average, and a disproportionately higher fraction of black families are in the nation's lowest income group. The median income for African American families nationwide ($32,000) is about two-thirds that of the typical U.S. household ($48,000).[24] In addition, 17 percent of African American families are poor, compared with 7 percent of white families and the national average of 8 percent.[25]

To assess the *relative* retirement preparedness of African American families, therefore, it is useful to examine whether African American households will have retirement resources comparable to other households with similar income. In this section we examine wealth levels of households, controlling for income. This income-adjusted comparison of wealth also can illuminate whether there are factors beyond income that differentially affect black and white households' retirement security. A cursory comparison of income ratios (two-thirds) to wealth ratios (ranging from one-twelfth to one-quarter) suggest that other factors may play a role.[26]

Table 10-4 presents data covering near-retired households that are in the lowest income group (living below the poverty line), those that are middle-income, and those that are among the richest 10 percent of U.S. households.[27]

As the table shows, the wealth gap persists when comparisons are restricted to households with similar income, a result consistent with findings from other studies.[28] The gap is narrower for households in the highest income group (at the median, the black-to-white wealth ratio is between one-half and two-thirds) but is wider for households in the lowest income group.

Table 10-4 also shows that the typical poor African American household has virtually no savings (zero IRA or DC balances, financial assets, or net worth); whereas the typical poor U.S. family has accumulated a small amount of wealth (primarily from home equity).[29] Among middle-income households, the typical African American household still has lower savings than other households. The net worth of a typical middle-class black family nearing retirement ($47,000) is only about half of the net worth of a typical similarly aged middle-class U.S. household ($95,000), indicating that middle-class blacks will be entering retirement with fewer resources than other Americans.

Similarly, black households in the top 10 percent of income have lower net worth than comparable households overall.[30] While the typical rich household in the United States has accumulated about $50,000 in retirement savings in IRA and DC accounts and about $90,000 in financial assets, the typical African American household in the nation's top income group has an IRA-DC balance of just $21,000 and financial asset holdings valued only at $13,000.[31] Blacks therefore have a resource deficit even when one considers the most well-to-do Americans.

Few black households, however, have incomes that place them in the top 10 percent of all Americans. In fact, black households that are in the top 10 percent of income among all black households have substantially lower income and lower net worth than all households in the top 10 percent of the U.S. population ($257,500 compared with $708,000). Comparing liquid wealth, such as financial assets, the typical black household at the top of the African American income distribution has no more than one-eighth the assets of the typical rich household (see table 10-4). Accordingly, African Americans who may very well consider themselves rich relative to their peers still lag far behind many other U.S. households when entering retirement.

Retirement Adequacy

The analysis to this point has focused primarily on household net worth, which includes the value of home equity, financial assets, and savings in tax-deferred retirement accounts, such as IRAs and 401(k)s. The measure of net worth, however, does not include expected claims to future benefits from Social Security and DB pensions. The importance of these two types of retirement income sources varies across households, and for some these benefits can account for a

Table 10-4. *Wealth and Asset Holdings of Pre-Retired Households, by Income Group*[a]
Dollars

Item	Below the poverty line		Median income groups		Top income decile group		Top African American income decile group
	African American	All households	African American	All households	African American	All households	
Total wealth (net worth)[b]	30,100	80,100	79,000	199,500	978,400	1,559,000	556,200
	(0)	(10,000)	(47,000)	(95,000)	(450,400)	(708,000)	(257,500)
Total wealth less housing equity (net worth less housing)	5,000	36,800	38,000	119,700	839,500	1,239,100	426,000
	(0)	(1,000)	(11,000)	(32,800)	(250,400)	(479,500)	(120,100)
Financial assets[c]	3,100	15,900	10,800	42,300	127,700	474,400	70,700
	(0)	(0)	(1,000)	(4,500)	(13,000)	(90,000)	(11,500)
IRA/DC	3,900	14,300	32,600	56,700	198,000[d]	169,300	152,500
	(0)	(0)	(0)	(0)	(21,000)	(50,000)	(15,000)
No. of obs.	257	800	256	1,457	30	484	88

Source: Authors' calculations using data from the 2004 Health and Retirement Survey.
a. Mean values, with medians reported in parentheses.
b. "Net worth" includes financial assets, housing equity, value of transportation, value of business and real estate, and other assets.
c. "Financial assets" includes stocks, bonds, certificates of deposit, and balance in checking and savings accounts.
d. Because of the small sample size, the mean value for IRA/DC balances is skewed upward by the presence of a single black household with a very sizable DC account balance.

substantial portion of retirement income. Because Social Security benefits are progressive, in that benefits replace a higher portion of earnings for low-income workers than for high-income workers, and because black households on average have lower incomes than other households do, the omission of Social Security benefits from a calculation of household resources would tend to overstate the differences in retirement preparedness between black and white households. Similarly, to the extent that black workers are more likely to receive DB benefits than white workers are, the omission of DB payments would overstate racial differences in retirement resources.

Income Replacement Rates

A more appropriate comparison of relative preparedness of those not yet retired therefore would account for these expected sources of funding, in addition to accumulated assets. One common approach is to evaluate whether and to what extent a household's expected retirement resources (including all saving, Social Security, and DB benefits) are sufficient to maintain its preretirement standard of living throughout retirement. That is to say, what percentage of the household's income before retirement can be replaced by accumulated savings and claims to benefits in retirement (the income replacement rate)? It is generally thought that an income replacement rate of 75 to 80 percent is needed to finance consumption during retirement and maintain preretirement standards of living.[32]

Estimates of expected mean retirement income of African American and white families counting all sources of income suggest that the replacement rate would be 73 percent for the average African American family and 83 percent for the average white family.[33] Thus, even after accounting for expected Social Security and DB benefits, a gap still exists in the degree to which African Americans and white families are prepared for retirement: African Americans lie near the lower end of the range deemed adequate to maintain their living standards while whites are slightly above the top of the range.[34]

Moreover, a recent study that examines families below the adequate range reveals that 40 percent of African Americans could expect to have a replacement rate that is lower than 50 percent; whereas only about one-quarter of white households had estimated replacement rates in that range.[35] Thus, a significant minority of households will not be financially prepared for retirement, and a disproportionate number of those households are expected to be African Americans.

Other Explanations for the Income-Adjusted Racial Wealth Gap

There are several possible reasons for the observed wealth gap between black and other families with comparable income. We focus on differences in family ties and networks, which result in differences in family risk-sharing, financial transfers, and financial literacy.

It is common to view household saving as a process governed solely by factors affecting the nuclear household; however, a growing body of evidence suggests that relationships with extended family members may affect the way that individuals prepare for retirement. Sharing resources, such as housing, may help older households meet some of their retirement needs and help some families accumulate wealth. At the same time, intrafamily transfers to support poorer kin members also may depress younger generations' ability to save for their own retirement. Furthermore, knowledge and skills about saving could be shared within the family, so young African Americans from lower-income families may not have the same learning opportunities as those from higher-income families.

Family Networks

Economists have argued that families can do almost as well as insurance markets in protecting against adverse events if family members pool risks and resources.[36] Choosing to pool risks and resources within the family can allow an individual to rely on other family members to help finance consumption when he or she experiences a loss in income and mitigate the need to save and shore up contingency reserves for the situation.

It is well documented that minority families, including African American families, are more likely to live in extended households than non-Hispanic white families.[37] Nearly one in four African Americans lives in an extended household compared with only one in ten non-Hispanic whites, and these racial differences remain even after we control for economic characteristics.[38] One study finds that black and Hispanic households are 14 percent more likely than non-Hispanic white households to be extended.[39]

To the extent that families that live together are more likely to help each other financially, the higher presence of extended households among African American families than non-Hispanic white families may explain part of the racial difference in wealth among those who are near retirement. Individuals may decide they do not need to save large sums independently because they believe they can rely on other family members for assistance. Evidence suggests that among single elderly women, co-residence with other family members appears to alleviate poverty for nearly one of every seven households, for example.[40] Similarly, single women benefit from living with other family members regardless of their racial background. However, because elderly African American women are one and a half times more likely than elderly non-Hispanic white women to be single and because a greater proportion of younger single mothers are African American than white, extended kin networks may represent a more important resource for both young and old black women than for white women.[41]

Even individuals or families that do not reside together may choose to share resources and to pool risks. Some studies suggest that African Americans are highly embedded in kin networks.[42] If individuals who are accustomed to turning to relatives in times of financial need can expect to rely on such family assistance during retirement, they would have less incentive to save independently for this life stage.

Financial Transfers between Family Members

While family structure and participation in kin networks can provide a barrier against poverty and act as a kind of retirement resource for the old, other studies suggest that African Americans' entrenchment in family networks may depress their ability to save while they are young. In particular, two studies find that middle-class African American adults are more likely to have poor relatives than other middle-class individuals and that the presence of poor relatives throughout the family tree is negatively correlated with an individual's wealth.[43] The authors argue that the total amount of savings that a middle-class African American household is able to accumulate during its working years is reduced because of the need to assist poor parents through financial transfers.

Financial transfers from older family members to younger members, on the other hand, can be beneficial for building wealth. In the empirical research that examines the effect of bequests and inter vivos transfers on wealth accumulation, there is general agreement that the receipt of financial transfers can positively affect the recipient's ability to accumulate wealth. Financial assistance to pay for schooling, for example, will improve an adult child's future earning opportunities; and the gift of a down payment to facilitate the purchase of a home will reduce the amount of debt that one's offspring have to take on to purchase a home. Thus, transfers can help younger generation family members build wealth earlier than they otherwise would. The literature has shown that African Americans are less likely to receive these types of transfers, even after we control for the economic resources of the adult child.[44] Most studies agree that this implies that young black families are at a disadvantage relative to other families that do receive financial assistance (at least in theory). There is less agreement, however, about the volume of transfers, whether they have large effects on children's saving behavior, and the exact extent to which they create a sizable gap between the wealth held by African American and that held by other households.[45]

Financial Literacy

Another possible consequence of African Americans' greater likelihood of having poor relatives throughout the family tree is that blacks are subsequently less likely than those with wealthier kin networks to acquire knowledge, skills, and opportunities related to saving and perhaps even a more basic understanding of financial matters. Research suggests that attitudes about saving, risk preferences, and investment choices may be learned or mimicked from parents.[46] These wealth-enhancing "traits" are more likely to be transferred to children by wealthy parents, who have greater understanding of, access to, and knowledge about financial markets than do low-wealth parents.[47] Increasing evidence also shows that financial illiteracy is not only widespread among the U.S. population but is particularly acute among specific demographic groups, such as those with low education, women, African-Americans, and Hispanics.[48]

Financial literacy can have a significant effect on retirement outcomes. Studies show that those with greater financial literacy are more likely to plan for retirement, and planners are more likely to approach retirement with higher wealth levels than nonplanners.[49] Evidence also suggests that those who have low financial literacy are significantly less likely to invest in stocks.[50] Thus, differences in financial literacy and financial market experience between African Americans and whites could explain part of the wealth gap.

What is less clear, however, is whether these differences in financial literacy and financial market experience remain after we control for income differences. In any event, because middle-class African Americans are more likely than white middle-class families to have poor parents and to the extent that poor parents are less likely to be financially literate, middle-class African Americans may be less financially literate than middle-class white families.

Policies

Our proposals to improve retirement security for African Americans focus on three areas in which African Americans differ from white households and for which there are demonstrable effective policy interventions. First, we focus on reducing information gaps and improving financial literacy of African Americans, which studies suggest would improve planning and investment choices by African Americans and ultimately could increase accumulated balances in retirement accounts. Second, we propose wider adoption of automatic features in 401(k) plans and IRAs, which would circumvent underlying reasons for the racial disparity in saving choices and improve participation and contribution rates, as well as investment outcomes, for African Americans. And, third, we propose improving saving incentives that specifically target lower- and moderate-income workers, who are disproportionately African Americans in part because of racial differences in labor market experience.

We do not present proposals to alter the family structure differences analyzed here, because these family networks offer both advantages and disadvantages.[51] Neither do we offer proposals aimed at correcting labor market differences between blacks and whites. We note, however, that the labor market differences discussed here undoubtedly are attributable to several causes: differences in levels of education, geographic proximity to "good" jobs, social networks, or employer discrimination, for example. Labor market discrimination, in particular, could lead to lower wages, jobs with lower benefits (such as lower or no retirement coverage), or even difficulty securing a job.[52] Some studies estimate that racial discrimination reduces the earnings of black workers by about 12–15 percent of the earnings of white workers, even after we control for other factors that affect wages.[53] However, there is still little consensus over the magnitude of racial discrimination that prevails in labor markets.[54]

In addition, discrimination outside the labor market can influence households' total wealth by creating barriers to fair and reasonable rates of interest on loans and by reducing homeownership. Because homeownership is one of the primary mechanisms through which individuals build wealth, discrimination against African Americans in housing markets or lending practices could lead to sizable racial differences in wealth. Studies have found evidence of racial discrimination in housing markets, both in seeking a home and in securing a mortgage.[55] Other research also suggests that when African Americans do succeed in purchasing homes, residential segregation in housing markets may mean that homes acquired by blacks tend to appreciate less than those of other families.[56] While all these issues are pertinent to African American retirement security, addressing discriminatory access to labor, housing, and credit markets is outside the scope of this paper.

Financial Mentoring

The research discussed here suggests that children from moderate- and low-income African American families lack access to information about saving and investment choices. Thus one possible strategy to increase retirement saving and investment outcomes among African American families would be to design policies that remedy these information gaps. Then individuals who are born into homes with limited information would be able to save as effectively as those born into families with financial market expertise.

Attitudes about saving are likely formed from an early age. Habits learned when one is young tend to carry into adulthood. If children are encouraged at a young age to start saving and if notions of budgeting are integrated into their daily lives, they may carry a positive attitude toward saving into their adult years. Furthermore, children who are introduced to financial institutions and financial terminology and given an opportunity to make financial decisions may overcome barriers (either informational or psychological) that might otherwise have inhibited participation in financial markets.

One approach, therefore, might be to develop a mentoring program targeted at very young children. The approach might couple young children with a financial institution that provides ongoing mentoring to the child over a period of time. The mentoring would begin at a very young age—as early as age 6— and continue until the child reaches age 18. At very early ages, children would be given simple financial goals, such as opening a savings account. As they get older and become more familiar and comfortable with money management, the mentoring would include discussions about saving with a target or for a particular outcome, long-term versus short-term saving goals, access to credit and paying down debt, and, if account balances are large enough (for older children), diversifying funds. It also could include discussion of realistic expectations about retirement and sources of retirement income.[57]

Such a mentoring program might be operated with a partnership between a financial institution and the public schools. Mentors from financial institutions would make regular and periodic visits to schools, where they would talk about financial matters in the way that families might talk about their finances. The mentor would discuss saving goals (such as preparing for college expenses, saving for Christmas), how an economic up- or downturn might affect a personal saving goal (such as working through the effect of a gas price increase or an increase in public transportation costs on a personal budget), or how changes in interest rates or equity returns might affect saving goals. The type of discussion and the frequency of these visits would vary with the age of the audience.

When such a proposal is designed, it may be important to create a sense of ownership over the account and the funds in it. Children would be encouraged to open and contribute to a saving account. One possibility might be to have the financial institution issue a passbook for the savings account, in which all transactions and remaining balance would be logged. Even if the amounts were small, the passbook could generate a strong sense of ownership and achievement because it is owned and maintained by the child and is a tangible reminder of the child's savings. The passbook would likely have a more meaningful effect at younger ages or among those with less access to or facility with online banking options, and its appeal may diminish with age or access. However, it may still serve to inculcate a prosaving attitude among very young children, and its benefits might be expected to survive beyond the functional usefulness.

A number of existing programs provide financial education and literacy training to children and adults.[58] Many of the programs that target children tend to focus on high-school-age children.[59] A small number of programs focus on younger children, but these tend to be short-term education programs and they do not offer long-term financial mentoring.[60] Children from families with financial market experience, however, learn from multiple and ongoing interactions regarding money management from their parents. Financial goals and needs change with age and circumstance, and the skills to adjust with these changes can only be acquired through a gradual but sustained mentoring program, yet none of the existing programs currently offers an ongoing and sustained mentoring opportunity.

Some of the existing programs may offer opportunities or platforms for providing long-term financial mentoring from a very young age, however. These include the Personal Economics Program offered by the American Bankers Association, which puts banks together with educators to teach people, including children, about banking services and financial management.[61] Additionally, many of the twelve Federal Reserve District banks work with local organizations to provide "teach the teacher" or "train the teacher" programs in an attempt to ensure that educators have the knowledge and resources they need to teach financial and economic topics effectively. Finally, Banking on Our Future, sponsored by Operation Hope, is a program that links volunteer banker-teachers with neighborhood schools, community groups, and beacon programs in school-based community centers. The youth are taught the basics of checking and savings accounts and the impact that credit and investment can have on their lives.

Automatic Saving

Financial mentoring alone, however, would be insufficient to ensure retirement security for many Americans. Many individuals, even those who are financially savvy, are at times too busy to take the time or the effort to sort through complicated financial decisions. As a result, they either postpone making these decisions or rely on simple rules of thumb that sometimes do not result in prudent investment choices.

For instance, many workers are offered the opportunity to save through their employer's 401(k) plan, yet many do not participate in the plan. In many 401(k) plans, workers must make an active decision to participate in the plan, deciding how much to contribute and which investment option provided by their employer to select. These decisions are complicated and can make the 401(k) enrollment decision daunting, particularly for workers who have limited investment experience. As such, many workers postpone or avoid making the enrollment decision.

Nonparticipation is particularly high among lower-income and minority workers.[62] It is also higher for African Americans than white workers. By not

Figure 10-1. *Effects of Automatic Enrollment on 401(k) Participation*

Percent participating

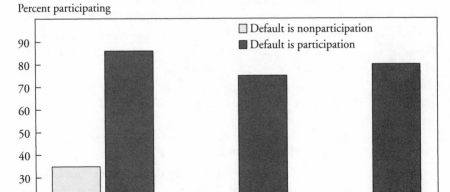

Source: Brigitte C. Madrian and Dennis F. Shea, "The Power of Suggestion: Inertia in 401(k) Participation and Savings Behavior," *Quarterly Journal of Economics* 116 (November 2001): 1149–87.

participating in a 401(k) plan, African American workers not only miss benefiting from any employer matching contributions and from the tax savings associated with such plans but also lose the opportunity of letting compounding returns grow their assets over time.

AUTOMATIC ENROLLMENT. A strategy that has proven successful at getting workers to participate in their 401(k) plan is to change the default option from an opt-in system to an opt-out system. Under an opt-out system, workers are automatically enrolled in their company's 401(k) plan unless the worker affirmatively chooses not to participate. With automatic enrollment, the employer selects a default contribution level, and at each pay period that portion of the worker's paycheck is directed into a default investment fund.

Automatic enrollment in 401(k) plans has been shown to increase participation significantly: in firms that implemented automatic enrollment, participation rates increased from 75 percent to as high as 95 percent among new hires.[63] The effect was even more dramatic among women, minority and low-income workers, increasing participation rates from 35 percent to 86 percent for women and from 13 percent to 80 percent for workers earning under $20,000 a year (figure 10-1).

With automatic enrollment in 401(k)s, workers who are unable or unwilling to make decisions about their 401(k) participation would still be able to participate in the plan. Automatic enrollment harnesses the power of inertia so that individuals save even if they make no effort. For African Americans who are eligible but do not participate in their 401(k) plan, automatic enrollment may "turn the tide" for them, helping them save earlier than they otherwise would have and earning investment returns over a longer period of time.

Automatic enrollment in 401(k) plans is most effective when it is combined with other automatic features. These include automatic enrollment with automatic increases in contribution rates over time, automatic investment in prudent and diversified funds, and automatic rollover of 401(k) assets when the worker leaves a job. Plans with these enhanced automatic features (second-generation plans) would help workers gradually save more over time, improve investment returns in their portfolios, and retain assets in the retirement system when they change jobs.

AUTOMATIC ESCALATION. Many first-generation plans typically enroll only new workers at a 3 percent contribution rate and do not increase contribution rates over time. The default 3 percent rate, however, is less than half the average pretax contribution rate of 7 percent of pay among participants in nonautomatic 401(k) plans.[64] Furthermore, the majority of participants who are enrolled under automatic enrollment tend to remain at the initial contribution rate if the company does not automatically increase their contribution rate over time.[65] Inertia keeps workers from saving more over time.

Building in automatic annual increases in contribution rates would help workers gradually save more over time with virtually no effort. Contribution rates could be increased by 1 percent per year, unless the participant opted out of those increases. Additionally, a second-generation plan might enroll new and current nonparticipating workers at a higher initial contribution rate, such as 5 or 6 percent.

These enhancements would help workers save more and take advantage of any additional employer matching contributions that they may have previously missed. Currently, about one-quarter of employers that offer automatic enrollment also automatically escalate contributions.[66] Wider adoption of automatic escalation would, over time, improve the financial position of many lower-income families, particularly African American families, who tend to have lower saving rates than higher-income households.

AUTOMATIC INVESTMENT. Research shows that many 401(k) participants tend to make poor investment choices: they overinvest in company stock, are too conservative in their investment choices, and seldom rebalance their portfolios as they age. These choices either expose them to too much risk or to low investment returns over time. As noted earlier, African Americans, on average, are less likely to hold stocks than white households. The result of this differential investment choice is that investment returns for African American households, on average, are lower than those for white households.

Many first-generation automatic 401(k) plans typically default contributions into a stable-value or money market fund. These tend to have lower investment returns than more diversified equity funds, such as life-cycle funds. However, recently promulgated regulations provide employers and plan sponsors with some degree of fiduciary relief if they offer qualified default investment alternatives that are professionally managed or balanced (such as life-cycle funds). These investment alternatives not only provide higher investment returns than stable-value funds, the portfolio is rebalanced over time to reflect changing retirement expectations and risk exposure. The default investment options would benefit all workers with 401(k)-type coverage, but they would be particularly valuable to African American participants by offering the potential for higher investment returns over time than might be achieved otherwise.

ADOPTION OF AUTOMATIC 401(K)S. The 2006 Pension Protection Act (PPA) addressed several employer concerns regarding automatic 401(k)s and provided new incentives to encourage more employers to adopt such plans (see chapter 2). In 2007, the first year after the law's enactment, the share of employers offering automatic 401(k)s increased to 44 percent, from 26 percent in 2006. The number offering automatic 401(k)s is expected to increase further over time as other incentives offered by the PPA become effective.

AUTOMATIC ROLLOVER. Under automatic rollover, when an employee changes jobs, the funds in her 401(k)-type account would be automatically rolled over into an IRA or another retirement plan offered by the new employer. The worker, however, can affirmatively choose not to roll over her funds. Many workers, particularly those with small account balances, tend to cash out their accounts when they leave a job, thereby losing the value of the tax-preferred saving and leaving them with less retirement saving. Recent empirical evidence suggests that simply making rollovers the default option can change the frame within which workers evaluate their options for preretirement distributions, leading them to leave their assets in a tax-preferred retirement account and preventing "leakage" from the retirement system.[67]

These strategies will benefit all workers with access to employer-sponsored retirement plans. However, they will be particularly beneficial for African American workers who, on average, have lower earnings, tend to invest in lower-return assets, and face higher risk of job disruptions than white workers.

AUTOMATIC IRAS. A significant minority of African American persons, however, do not have access to employer-sponsored retirement plans because they are employed in low-wage or part-time jobs. However, a new proposal would create a system whereby workers without access to employer-sponsored retirement plans could contribute automatically to a low-cost, diversified individual retirement account through direct payroll deposits. Because IRAs are portable from one employer to the next, employees would be able to continue contributing to the IRAs even when they switch jobs (see chapter 4).

Under this proposal, workers would be automatically enrolled in an IRA, and deposits to the IRA would be made automatically at each pay period, unless the employee actively chose not to participate in the program. A firm that is not ready to adopt a 401(k) or other retirement plan could offer its employees the ability to save in an IRA every payday by payroll deposit, a mechanism currently already available to millions of employees. Once payroll deposits begin, they continue automatically unless the worker later opts out. Employers above a certain size (say, ten or more employees) that have been in business for at least two years and do not sponsor any retirement plan for their employees could be required to offer employees this payroll-deduction saving opportunity.

The Automatic IRA would involve no contributions or other outlays by employers. Employers would merely offer their payroll system as a conduit that employees could use to save part of their own wages in an IRA. Participating employers would receive temporary tax credits, would be required to obtain a written waiver from any employee who does not participate, would be encouraged to use automatic enrollment, and would be able to protect themselves from fiduciary liability. Employees, or the employer, could designate the IRA to receive the savings, including, as a fallback for those unable or unwilling to choose, a national platform IRA that could be based on the federal employees' Thrift Savings Plan accounts. The default investment for the Automatic IRA would be a diversified, low-cost, life-cycle fund, with other choices available (see chapter 4). The self-employed would be encouraged to save by extending payroll deposit to independent contractors, facilitating direct deposit of income tax refunds, and expanding access to automatic debit arrangements linked to IRAs, including on-line and traditional means of access through professional and trade associations.

Thus, for many workers without access to 401(k)-type plans through their employer, including African American workers, the Automatic IRA would make it easier for them to save in a tax-preferred environment. Additionally for African Americans, the Automatic IRA with a default investment fund, such as a life-cycle fund, might provide higher returns than they otherwise would earn.

Saver's Credit

While 401(k)s and IRAs represent effective instruments for saving for retirement because of their tax-preferred status, for many low-income families, including some African American families, the incentives to save in a tax-preferred retirement account may be small. Contributions to tax-preferred retirement accounts reduce the saver's taxable income; thus, they generally benefit those with higher marginal tax rates more than those with lower marginal tax rates. Low-income families tend to face low marginal tax rates or to pay no taxes at all. They therefore stand to benefit less than other workers, or not at all, from tax incentives that reduce taxable income.

Tax credits, however, can be used to create strong incentives for low- and moderate-income households. For example, the Saver's Credit, which specifically targets moderate- and lower-income families, was enacted in 2001 to give taxpayers earning less than $52,000 a tax credit for contributions to 401(k) plans, IRAs, and similar retirement saving vehicles.[68] Depending on the taxpayer's income, households can receive a credit of 10, 20, or 50 percent of their contributions to a retirement account. Because African American families tend to have lower income than the average American family, they would disproportionately benefit from the Saver's Credit.

The Saver's Credit, however, is currently nonrefundable: it merely offsets a taxpayer's tax liability. Therefore, it provides no saving incentive for almost 50 million lower-income households that have no income tax liability. Making the Saver's Credit refundable would provide an important incentive to these households to save, which would improve retirement security for those families with the lowest incomes. This might have the added benefit of making them less dependent on Social Security income and means-tested government programs during their retirement years. There is also some evidence that restructuring the credit as a matching contribution that is automatically deposited into an IRA could further increase the incentive to save.[69]

The Saver's Credit also could be simplified with a single 50 percent credit rate, phased out smoothly above the income eligibility limit. It could be improved to reach a larger group of families by expanding the eligibility limit to include households with income of up to $70,000 per year. This would increase the incentive to save and help moderate and lower-income Americans, which includes many African American families, save for a secure retirement.

Updating Asset Test Rules

One final way that policymakers could improve the incentive to save is by modifying the rules for eligibility for public assistance program. Outdated asset tests in means-tested public assistance programs, such as Supplemental Security Income (SSI), Temporary Assistance for Needy Families (TANF), and Medicaid, penalize lower- and moderate-income households that save.[70] These programs help individuals in times of unexpected hardships or illness, or who may not have had a full working history and rely on these sources of public assistance to supplement their retirement needs. Beneficiaries of many of these programs are disproportionately African Americans.[71]

To be eligible for these programs, applicants generally must meet an asset test as well as an income test. While accrued benefits under a defined benefit plan are usually not counted as assets, many states often count 401(k) or IRA balances or both. This has the effect of a steep implicit tax on 401(k) and IRA saving. As a result, preretired families with incomes low enough to qualify for a means-tested program under the income test might respond by saving less. Similarly, families that suddenly experience a temporary disruption in employment would be required to nearly deplete their retirement savings before becoming eligible for the public assistance.

Although some state programs have eliminated asset tests, or at least aligned the treatment of defined contribution plans with that of defined benefit plans, many have not. The farm bill adopted in 2008 addresses the inconsistent treatment of assets in tax-preferred retirement accounts in the food stamp program by excluding those assets from the asset tests. However, asset tests in other public programs, such as SSI and Medicaid, continue to treat retirement saving in a confusing and seemingly arbitrary manner, with different restrictions state-by-state and account-by-account.

Congress and the states should therefore eliminate the implicit tax on retirement saving in these programs by mandating that retirement accounts such as 401(k)s and IRAs be disregarded for eligibility and benefit determinations in federal and state means-tested programs.[72] Changing the law to exempt retirement accounts from being considered in means-tested programs would treat retirement savings fairly and consistently and would send an important signal to families that rely or might need to rely on means-tested programs in the future: you will not be penalized for saving for retirement.

Eliminating asset rules for retirement savings will have some short-term costs as additional lower-income households will qualify for and use means-tested benefit programs. However, these costs should be modest, and if moderate- and low-income households can save for a more secure retirement, fewer people will have to rely on public benefits in old age.

Conclusion

Many African Americans have low absolute levels of retirement savings, and blacks' savings are low relative to the overall population. Because private savings and employer-sponsored pensions are key components of the retirement system in the United States, the observation that personal savings, pension coverage rates, and pension balances are all low present cause for concern, raising questions about how African Americans will fare in retirement and whether anything can be done to enhance their preparedness for this life course event. Several policy options are promising. Policies to boost retirement savings by remedying information gaps, by making it easier to save, by expanding access to opportunities to save on the job, and by raising the return to saving are likely to affect blacks positively, helping to ensure that African Americans are financially secure during the twilight years.

Notes

1. Jonathan Skinner, "Are You Saving Enough for Retirement?" *Journal of Economic Perspectives* 21, no. 3 (2007), pp. 59–80, provides a summary of the savings adequacy debate. Several recent studies argue that many U.S. households do save enough for retirement; these include John Karl Scholz, Ananth Sheshadri, and Surachai Khitatrakun, "Are Households Saving Optimally for Retirement?" *Journal of Political Economy* 114, no. 14 (2006), pp. 607–43; and Mark Aguiar and Erik Hurst, "Consumption versus Expenditure," *Journal of Political Economy* 113 (October, 2005), pp. 919–48. Eric Engen, William Gale, and Cori Uccello, "Lifetime Earnings, Social Security Benefits, and the Adequacy of Retirement Wealth Accumulation," *Social Security Bulletin* 66, no. 1 (2005), find that racial minority status is associated with less than adequate retirement wealth.

2. Employee Benefit Research Institute (EBRI), "2007 Minority Retirement Confidence Survey," EBRI Issue Brief (Washington: June 2007).

3. Net worth includes housing equity, financial, and nonfinancial assets less debts. Net worth does not include claims from expected Social Security and DB pensions, but it does include 401(k)s and IRAs.

4. Another way to think of this difference is to think of it in annuity terms. If a newly retired person were to purchase a single-life annuity with $28,000, it would yield only about $220 in income each month; whereas, an identical person with $140,000 would receive $1,100 in income each month (www.annuity.com for 5 percent and fifteen years).

5. It is sometimes assumed that housing equity is not used to support consumption because many elderly households are house-rich but income-poor, yet few tap into their housing equity (by selling and renting or downsizing, or through a reverse mortgage) to increase their nonmedical consumption; see Steven F. Venti and David A. Wise, "Aging and Housing Equity: Another Look," Working Paper W8608 (Cambridge, Mass.: National Bureau of Economic Research, November 2001). However, there is some evidence that housing equity may be used to finance late-life out-of-pocket medical expenses. Also, there has been recent growth in the market for reverse mortgages (which is a means of drawing down housing equity without having to move); however, demand remains very low for this product. See Thomas Davidoff and Gerd Welke, "Selection and Moral Hazard in the Reverse Mortgage Market," Working Paper (University of California–Berkeley, Haas School of Business, October 2005).

6. There is also a difference in the amount of financial assets held. Generally, holdings of financial assets, such as stocks and bonds, for the typical U.S. household are low but they are much lower for African American households ($7,500 versus $200). Authors' calculation using data from the University of Michigan 2004 Health and Retirement Survey.

7. Joseph Altonji and Rebecca Blank, "Race and Gender in the Labor Market," in *Handbook of Labor Economics,* vol. 3, edited by Orley Ashenfelter and David Card (Amsterdam: Elsevier Press, 1999), discuss differences in labor market outcomes extensively.

8. Because most of the literature on racial differences in labor market outcomes compares blacks with whites, much of our subsequent discussion will use whites as the reference point, even though the earlier sections of this paper compared blacks with the population at large.

9. Blacks also have a lower life expectancy than whites, which would affect the amount of saving for retirement. However, although racial difference in life expectancy at birth is large for those born in 1950 and are close to retirement today (around 8.3 years), the difference narrows significantly with age (among 65-year-olds, the difference is only 1.6 years, and by age 75, the difference is only 0.5 years) and with time (difference in life expectancy among those born in 2004 is 5.2 years. National Center for Health Statistics, United States 2006 (Hyattsville, Md.: 2006), table 27 (www.cdc.gov/nchs/data/hus/hus06.pdf#027).

10. Lawrence Mishel, Jared Bernstein, and Sylvia Allegretto, *State of Working America 2004/2005* (Washington: Economic Policy Institute, 2005).

11. Lawrence Mishel, Jared Bernstein, and Syvia Allegretto, *State of Working America 2006/2007* (Washington: Economic Policy Institute, 2007).

12. Some fraction of part-time workers may be those who were unable to find full-time employment.

13. Karen E. Dynan, Jonathan Skinner, and Stephen P. Zeldes, "Do the Rich Save More?" *Journal of Political Economy* 112 (April 2004), pp. 397–444.

14. Mishel, Bernstein, and Allegretto, *State of Working America 2004/2005.*

15. The difference between how blacks fare relative to the national average and how they look when compared with white workers emerges largely because the population average includes the coverage rates for Latinos, which are very low. See chapter 8.

16. Economic Policy Institute Datazone, "Change in Private Sector Employer-Provided Pension Insurance Coverage, 1979–2004" (Washington); Mishel, Bernstein, and Allegretto, *State of Working America 2004/2005,* table 3.15.

17. Kurt J. Bauman and Nikki L. Graf, "Education Attainment 2000: Census 2000 Brief" (U.S. Census Bureau, August 2003).

18. One fifth (20.4) percent of black workers are employed in the public sector; whereas only 16 percent of all workers are employed by the public sector (authors' calculations using U.S. Bureau of Labor Statistics, Current Population Survey data, March 2005.

19. Some state and local governments are offering DC plans, either wholly or partially; however the majority of state and local governments continue to offer DB coverage. See Alicia Munnell and others, "Why Have Some States Introduced Defined Benefit Contribution Plans?" Brief 3 (Boston College, Center for Retirement Research, January 2008), for changes at the state and local level; and Alicia Munnell, Kelly Haverstick, and Jean-Pierre Aubry, "Why Does Funding Status Vary among State and Local Plans?" Brief 6 (Boston College, Center for Retirement Research, May 2008), for the health of these pension funds.

20. Patrick Purcell, "Pension Sponsorship and Participation: Summary of Recent Trends" (Congressional Research Service, September 6, 2007).

21. Karen Smith, Richard Johnson, and Leslie Muller, "Deferring Income in Employer-Sponsored Retirement Plans: The Dynamics of Participant Contributions," Working Paper 20 (Boston College, Center for Retirement Research, August 2004). Because the average African American has lower lifetime income, this result is consistent with earlier studies that show lower saving rates among lower-income households.

22. The lower contribution rate may reflect, in part, lower savings rates among workers with lower earnings, as noted earlier.

23. Kerwin Charles and Erik Hurst, "The Correlation in Wealth across Generations," *Journal of Political Economy* 111 (2003), pp. 1155–82; Ariel Mutual Funds and Charles Schwab, "The Ariel-Schwab Black Paper: A Decade of Research on African American Wealth Building and Retirement Planning" (Chicago: Ariel Mutual Funds, October 2007).

24. U.S. Census Bureau, *2008 Statistical Abstract of the United States*, table 674.

25. Data from U.S. Bureau of Labor Statistics, Current Population Survey, March 2007, for ages 51–64 only using single race or two race categories.

26. The income ratio compares the median black income to the median U.S. income, and the wealth ratio compares the median black net worth (or net worth less housing equity) to the median U.S. net worth (or net worth less housing equity).

27. Household income is sorted into ten income groups (deciles). Highest-income households are those whose incomes are in the top decile group. Middle-income is defined as being in the fourth, fifth, or sixth decile of the national distribution of income.

28. See, for instance, Robert Barsky and others, "Accounting for the Black-White Wealth Gap: A Nonparametric Approach," Working Paper 8466 (Cambridge, Mass.: National Bureau of Economic Research, 2001), who find that only two-thirds of the wealth differential between whites and blacks is explained by differences in earnings.

29. The group averages are higher. On average, poor African American households hold about $4,000 in an IRA or DC account, about $3,100 in financial assets, and about $30,000 in total wealth. However, because mean values are strongly influenced by the highest and lowest values, the median values present a more reliable portrait of a typical household's situation.

30. The sample size for blacks is small enough to require the results to be interpreted with caution.

31. Authors' calculation using the 2004 University of Michigan Health and Retirement Study database.

32. Because families are no longer working and incurring work-related expenses, the amount they need in retirement to maintain their standard of living is lower, according to the replacement rate perspective.

33. These estimates include personal savings, savings in tax-preferred retirement accounts, expected pension benefits, and expected Social Security benefits. Mean retirement *income* derived from these three sources of savings is estimated at $28,100 for African Americans and $80,800 for whites (in 2001 dollars). The data are from Christian Weller and Edward Wolff, "Retirement Income" (Washington: Economic Policy Institute 2005). The study examines households ages 47–64, using data from 2001. The results reported above are computed using data from tables 2, 13, 18, and 20.

34. Although the range provides only an estimate of what a family would need, it nevertheless demonstrates racial differences in saving adequacy.

35. Weller and Wolff, "Retirement Income."

36. Laurence Kotlikoff and Avia Spivak, "The Family as an Incomplete Annuities Market," *Journal of Political Economy* 89 (April 1981), pp. 372–91.

37. Extended households can include grandparents, grandchildren, siblings, and other related family members. Racial differences in family living arrangements were apparent even in the first half of the twentieth century; see Steve Ruggles, "The Origins of African-American Family Structure," *American Sociological Review* 59 (February 1994), pp. 136–51. The difference between black and white living arrangements is larger today than it was fifty

years ago; see table 2 in Yoshinori Kamo, "Racial and Ethnic Differences in Extended Family Households," *Sociological Perspectives* 43 (Summer 2000), pp. 211–29).

38. Kamo, "Racial and Ethnic Differences in Extended Family Households." Data used in this source are from the 1990 Census.

39. Ronald Angel and Marta Tienda, "Determinants of Extended Household Structure: Cultural Pattern or Economic Need?" *American Journal of Sociology* 87 (1982): 1360–83. The authors control for income-poverty ratio, education, foreign birth, employment, and female headship.

40. Chenoa Flippen and Marta Tienda, "Family Structure and Economic Well-Being of Black, Hispanic, and White Pre-Retirement Adults" (University of Chicago, Center on Demography and Economics of Aging, September 1998).

41. Not all co-residence arrangements are beneficial to elderly family members, however. There is evidence to suggest that some family members, particularly single elderly men from black or Hispanic households, are worse off when other kin members co-reside with them because the new residents contribute very little financially to the household. Nearly 11 percent of single black and single Hispanic elderly men fall into poverty as family size increases; see Flippen and Tienda "Family Structure and Economic Well-Being."

42. Examples include Carol Stack, *All Our Kin* (New York: Basic Books, 1997); and Robert Taylor, Linda Chatters, and Vickie Mays, "Parents, Children, Siblings, In-Laws, and Non-Kin as Sources of Emergency Assistance to Black Americans" *Family Relations* 37 (1988), pp. 298–304.

43. Ngina Chiteji and Darrick Hamilton, "Kin Networks and Asset Accumulation," in *Inclusion in the American Dream: Assets, Poverty, and Public Policy,* edited by Michael Sherraden (Oxford University Press, 2005); and Mary Pattillo and Colleen Heflin, "Poverty in the Family: Race, Siblings and Socioeconomic Heterogeneity," *Social Science Research* 35, no. 4 (2006), pp. 804–22.

44. Paul Menchik and Nancy Jianakoplos, "Black-White Wealth Inequality: Is Inheritance the Reason?" *Economic Inquiry* 35, no. 2 (April 1997), pp. 428–42, control for incomes and other factors that contribute to racial wealth differences and find that inheritances could account for between 10 and 20 percent of the average difference in black-white household wealth. Kerwin Charles and Erik Hurst, "The Transition to Homeownership and the Black-White Wealth Gap," *Review of Economic Statistics* 84 (May 2002), pp. 281–97, find suggestive evidence that black homeownership rates may be lower than white homeownership rates (even controlling for similar income and wealth levels), because whites are more likely to receive financial assistance with the down payment than blacks.

45. This macroeconomic debate is discussed in Laurence Kotlikoff and Lawrence H. Summers, "The Role of Intergenerational Transfers in Aggregate Capital Accumulation," *Journal of Political Economy* 99 (August 1981), pp. 706–32; Laurence Kotlikoff, "Intergenerational Transfers and Savings," *Journal of Economic Perspectives* 2 (Spring 1988), pp. 41–58; and William G. Gale and John Karl Scholz, "Intergenerational Transfers and the Accumulation of Wealth," *Journal of Economic Perspectives* 8 (Autumn 1994), pp. 145–60.

46. Research on ways that parents model behavior for their children abounds in the psychology literature; see, for example, Walter Mischel, Yuichi Shoda, and Monica Rodriguez, "Delay of Gratification in Children," *Science* 244 (May 1989), pp. 933–38. Within the economics discipline, empirical studies of intergenerational correlation in behavior include John Knowles and Andrew Postelwaite, "Do Children Learn to Save from Their Parents" (University of Pennsylvania, 2005), (www.econ.upenn.edu/~jknowles/Research/KP.htm); Thomas

Dohmen and others, "The Intergenerational Transmission of Risk and Trust Attitudes," IZA Discussion Paper 2380 (Germany: Institute for the Study of Labor, 2006); Kerwin Charles and Erik Hurst, "The Correlation of Wealth across Generations," *Journal of Political Economy* 111 (December 2003): 1155–82; and Mark Wilhelm and others, "Tracking Giving across Generations," *New Directions for Philanthropic Fundraising* 42 (Summer 2004), pp. 71–82.

47. Melvin Oliver and Thomas Shapiro, *Black Wealth/White Wealth: A New Perspective on Racial Inequality* (New York: Routledge, 2006); Ngina Chiteji and Frank Stafford, "Portfolio Choices of Parents and Their Children as Young Adults," *American Economic Review* 89 (May 1999), pp. 377–80; and Charles and Hurst, "The Correlation of Wealth across Generations."

48. Annamaria Lusardi, "Household Saving Behavior: The Role of Financial Literacy, Information, and Financial Education Programs," Working Paper 13824 (Boston: National Bureau of Economic Research, February 2008).

49. Annamaria Lusardi and Olivia S. Mitchell, "Baby Boomer Retirement Security: The Roles of Planning, Financial Literacy, and Housing Wealth," *Journal of Monetary Economics* 54 (January 2007), pp. 205–24.

50. Maarten van Rooij, Annamaria Lusardi, and Rob Alessi, "Financial Literacy and Stock Market Participation," DNB Working Papers 146 (Amsterdam: Netherlands Central Bank, Research Department, 2007).

51. Furthermore, doing so would require one to make normative judgments about ways that relatives choose to interact with one another. Instead, we remind readers interested in policy that families are structured differently and the choices of one generation often can affect the choices of its offspring and their fortunes.

52. For a detailed discussion of racial discrimination in labor markets, see Altonji and Blank, "Race and Gender in the Labor Market."

53. William Darity and Patrick Mason, "Evidence on Discrimination in Employment," *Journal of Economic Perspectives* 12 (Spring 1998), pp. 63–90; and James Heckman, "Detecting Discrimination," *Journal of Economic Perspectives* 12 (Spring 1998), pp. 101–16.

54. The controversy that exists in the empirical literature stems largely from the fact that assessing the effect of race, by itself, requires researchers to account for and net out differences in productivity-related characteristics that may vary by race. However, some researchers argue that productivity-related characteristics cannot be fully controlled for and that wage differences may thus reflect these observed productivity differences. See, for instance, S. G. Sanders and others, "Why Do Minority Men Earn Less? A Study of Wage Differentials among the Highly Educated," *Review of Economics and Statistics* 88 (May 2006), pp. 300–13.

55. For example, black applicants faced a higher probability of having an application for a home loan rejected, even when their income and other risk characteristics were comparable to other applicants. See Alicia Munnell and others, "Mortgage Lending in Boston: Interpreting HMDA data," *American Economic Review* 86 (March 1996), pp. 25–53, for more details. See also Margery Austin Turner and others, "Discrimination in Metropolitan Housing Markets: National Results from Phase I of HDS2000" (Washington: Urban Institute, November 2002).

56. Oliver and Shapiro, *Black Wealth/White Wealth,* estimate that the "cost" to black households is lower average appreciation of housing value of about $28,000. This estimate does not control for income; however, many researchers argue that blacks face residential segregation regardless of their income level. Accordingly, if one were to control for income, it is likely that this cost would not vanish.

57. Survey evidence suggests that some individuals may have potentially unrealistic retirement expectations. Ariel Mutual Funds and Charles Schwab, "The Ariel-Schwab Black Investor Survey: Saving and Investing among Higher Income African Americans and White

Americans" (October 11, 2007), found that about half of African American households say they expect to live off rental income during retirement and that 12 percent of African Americans expected to rely *primarily* on this type of income when financing consumption during retirement. Yet, a survey of current retirees indicates that fewer than 20 percent of African American retired households had any rental income.

58. Those targeted at adults tend to help with navigating complicated financial transactions, such as applying for a mortgage, or offer retirement planning tools, such as helping workers understand the time frame over which they must fund their retirement and what resources are available to them in retirement, including public programs, private saving, and financial products.

59. Among these programs are Financial Literacy 2010, a national campaign to increase the financial savvy of the average high school student.

60. In the United States, Banking on a Future targets children ages 9–18. Internationally, Aflatoun targets children ages 6–14.

61. American Bankers Association Education Foundation, "Our National Programs," www.aba.com/consumer+connection/CNC-aboutef.htm.

62. For additional details, see Brigitte C. Madrian and Dennis F. Shea, "The Power of Suggestion: Inertia in 401(k) Participation and Savings Behavior," *Quarterly Journal of Economics* 116 (2001), pp. 1149–87.

63. Madrian and Shea, "The Power of Suggestion."

64. Among automatic plans, 42 percent have a 3 percent default rate and 20 percent have a higher default rate; Hewitt Associates, "Trends and Experiences in 401(k) Plans, 2005 Survey" (Lincolnshire, Ill.: 2005).

65. James Choi and others, "For Better or For Worse: Default Effects and 401(k) Savings Behavior," in *Perspectives on the Economics of Aging,* edited by David Wise, pp. 81–121 (University of Chicago Press, 2004).

66. According to a 2007 Wells Fargo Survey, 21 percent of employers that offer automatic enrollment also automatically escalate contributions. According to the Hewitt Associates survey for 2007, 28 percent of employers that automatically enroll participants also automatically escalate contributions.

67. William G. Gale and Michael Dworsky, "Effects of Public Policies on the Disposition of Lump-Sum Distributions: Rational and Behavioral Influences," Working Paper 2006-15 (Boston College, Center for Retirement Research, August 2006).

68. J. Mark Iwry, William G. Gale, and Peter R. Orszag, "The Saver's Credit," Policy Brief 2005-2 (Washington, Retirement Security Project, March 2005); J. Mark Iwry, William G. Gale, and Peter R. Orszag, "The Saver's Credit: Issues and Options," *Tax Notes* (Washington, Tax Policy Center, May 3, 2004.

69. The explicit 50 percent credit is an implicit 100 percent match. For example, consider a couple earning $30,000 who contributes $2,000 to a 401(k) plan. The Saver's Credit reduces that couple's federal income tax liability by $1,000 (50 percent of $2,000). The net result is a $2,000 account balance that costs the couple only $1,000 after taxes (the $2,000 contribution minus the $1,000 tax credit). This is the same result that would occur if the net after-tax contribution of $1,000 were matched at a 100 percent rate: the couple and the government each effectively contribute $1,000 to the account. While taxpayers should respond the same to equivalent implicit and explicit matches, empirical research provides evidence to the contrary. For a detailed discussion, see Esther Duflo and others, "Saving Incentives for Low- and Middle-Income Families: Evidence from a Field Experiment with H&R Block," *Quarterly Journal of Economics* 121, no. 4 (2006), pp. 1311–46.

70. For a detailed discussion of this issue, see Zoë Neuberger, Robert Greenstein, and Eileen P. Sweeney, "Protecting Low-Income Families' Retirement Savings: How Retirement Accounts Are Treated in Means-Tested Programs and Steps to Remove Barriers to Retirement Saving," Policy Brief 2005-6 (Washington: Retirement Security Project, June 2005.

71. For instance, nearly 30 percent of TANF and SSI recipients are black. For characteristics of TANF recipients by race, see www.urban.org/publications/411553.html; for characteristics of SSI recipients by race, see www.socialsecurity.gov/policy/docs/ssb/v65n2/v65n2p1.html.

72. See proposals by Robert Greenstein and Zoë Neuberger in "Removing Barriers to Retirement Saving in Medicaid and Supplemental Security Income," Policy Brief 2008-3 (Washington: Retirement Security Project, 2008).

About the Contributors

NGINA CHITEJI is associate professor of economics at Skidmore College and former research fellow at the Institute for Race and Wealth at Howard University.

MICHAEL DWORSKY is a graduate student at Stanford University and was formerly a senior research assistant at the Brookings Institution.

WILLIAM G. GALE holds the Arjay and Frances Miller Chair in Federal Economic Policy at the Brookings Institution and is also director of the Retirement Security Project.

CHRISTOPHER GEISSLER is a graduate student at Duke University and was formerly a senior research assistant with the Brookings Institution.

BENJAMIN H. HARRIS is a senior research associate with the Brookings Institution. He is also an affiliated researcher with the Urban-Brookings Tax Policy Center.

J. MARK IWRY is senior adviser to the secretary and deputy assistant secretary for retirement and health policy at the U.S. Department of the Treasury. He was formerly a nonresident senior fellow at the Brookings Institution, a principal of the Retirement Security Project, research professor at Georgetown University, and counsel to the law firm of Sullivan & Cromwell LLP.

DAVID C. JOHN is principal to the Retirement Security Project and a senior research fellow at the Heritage Foundation. He was also a vice president at the Chase Manhattan Bank and held senior positions with a credit union trade association and a Washington law firm.

RUTH LEVINE is a research assistant at the Brookings Institution.

PETER R. ORSZAG is the director of the Office of Management and Budget and was formerly the director of the Retirement Security Project.

LESLIE E. PAPKE is professor of economics at Michigan State University.

ERIC RODRIGUEZ is the vice president of the Office of Research, Advocacy, and Legislation at the National Council of La Raza.

JOHN A. TURNER is director of the Pension Policy Center. He has a PhD in economics from the University of Chicago.

LINA WALKER recently joined AARP's Public Policy Institute and previously was the research director for the Retirement Security Project, as well as a research assistant professor at Georgetown Public Policy Institute. She also has worked at the Congressional Budget Office and the Office of Policy Analysis of the Maryland General Assembly.

SPENCER WALTERS is a student at the University of Michigan Law School and was formerly a research analyst with the Retirement Security Project.

Index